The Cross of Nails

OLIVER SCHUEGRAF

The Cross of Nails

Joining in God's Mission of Reconciliation

Community of the Cross of Nails

Translated by
Gren Hatton

CANTERBURY
PRESS
Norwich

© Oliver Schuegraf 2012

This edition published in 2012 by the Canterbury Press Norwich
Editorial office
3rd Floor, Invicta House,
108–114 Golden Lane,
London EC1Y 0TG

Canterbury Press is an imprint of Hymns Ancient & Modern Ltd
(a registered charity)
13A Hellesdon Park Road, Norwich,
Norfolk, NR6 5DR, UK

Published in Germany 2008 by Verlag Otto Lembeck, Frankfurt

www.canterburypress.co.uk

British Library Cataloguing in Publication data

A catalogue record for this book is available
from the British Library

978 1 84825 239 4

Typeset by Regent Typesetting, London
Printed and bound in Great Britain by
CPI Group Ltd, Croydon

Contents

Dean Emeritus James Diamond passed away on 21 July 2011.

He was a reconciler, a formative figure in our Cross of Nails network for many years and a dear friend of mine.

This English edition of the book is dedicated to his memory.

Foreword

I tell you, a prophet is not taken seriously in his homeland.

(Luke 4.24)

Oliver Schuegraf came to join us at Coventry Cathedral as a guest from the Lutheran Church in Bavaria. He returned to his German home four years later as a valued friend and colleague, so much 'one of us' that he had become an ambassador of our Cathedral in places as far off as North America and South Africa. Such integration into the life of an Anglican Cathedral was one of the fruits of the Meissen Accords, making it possible for the clergy of the Church of England and of the Protestant Church in Germany to be fully accepted by each other.

On returning home, Oliver determined to share the remarkable story of Coventry's worldwide ministry of reconciliation with his own people. It was the forgiveness that was offered to the German people at Christmas 1940, six weeks after the bombing of Coventry and the destruction of its Cathedral, that led to the formation of the Community of the Cross of Nails, a worldwide network of Christian centres of peacemaking. Hence this book, the fruit of Oliver's first-hand experience, first published in German in 2008.

Nor was this volume the first in German to tell of the consequences of the death and rebirth of Coventry Cathedral. As I have discovered on many visits, the very name of Coventry resonates remarkably with large numbers of German people in a way that it does not, yet deserves to, in Britain. May this translation help to put that right. That it should be so is not really surprising. Long before most British people thought it right, only two years after the War's end, with a great deal of bitterness still in the air, Coventry held out the hand of friendship to the heavily bombed seaport of Kiel, leading to the first Anglo-German city twinning. There followed, even more controversially, the twinning with what was then Communist-ruled Dresden where Allied bombers had killed some twenty-five thousand people shortly before the War's end. The Coventry–Dresden story is just one of many in this tale of imaginative peacemaking, a tale that spans the globe, from Cape Town to Ground Zero in New York City.

This pioneering book does more than simply tell a story. In a hitherto unprecedented way, Oliver Schuegraf reflects as a theologian on the deeper meaning of reconciliation in this contemporary situation. In any good library, this book needs to be classified not only as religious history but as contextual theology. His doctorate in divinity is a deserved consequence of Oliver's experience, research and reflection.

As Sir Basil Spence's iconic Cathedral marks its golden jubilee in 2012, this volume constitutes a valuable contribution to the celebration of its achievements on the world stage.

Paul Oestreicher
Canon Emeritus of Coventry Cathedral

Introduction

I shall remember the city I love.
Her tall spires gleaming, gold tipped above.
Godiva processions, the ancient fair,
And where the centuries met in Broadgate Square.

With glittering windows of bright modern shops,
And above on the skyline old messy roof tops.
Peeping Tom staring at all who passed by,
The great Market Clock ne'er telling a lie.

I shall remember the beauty of dawn,
That shone on the wreck that November morn.
Gone the old buildings the pride of the City,
And homes of the poor, O! Lord have pity.

Yet brave were the smiles that shone through the tears
Though night must come with Horror and Fears
And still the proud spires looked up to the sky,
Godiva's fair city could never die.

I shall remember the dear friends I knew
Who gave up their lives 'True Coventry Blue'.
And the sirens that screamed as they laid them to rest,
In one long grave forever blessed.

Our great Cathedral, dim and all holy,
With quiet sanctuary and care for the lowly.
Where the spirits of those from the ages passed,
Did join in our prayers until the last.

I must remember 'ere Christ was dead,
In pain and anguish still He said,
'Forgive them for they know not what they do';
And so, on the days when our dreams come true,

When the last 'All clear' has died away,
Let me remember Lord that I may pray.
My life forever more shall worthier be,
Of those who died for Coventry.
　　　　　('Godiva's Coventry', Miriam Garratt)

On 14 November 1940, Coventry was destroyed by German bombs. Since that time, Coventry's name has been linked with the horrors of the Second World War, but also at the same time with the desire for reconciliation of both British and German people. The bombing of Coventry is, as it has always been, the reference point for the world-wide Community of the Cross of Nails and its work of reconciliation. This book is about both of these aspects.

But, why should thoughts of the destruction of Coventry still have a role to play sixty years after the end of the war, and why should it still be a motivating force in striving for reconciliation in the world? Shouldn't we be laying this old story to rest in the archives, isn't it far more important to be forward-looking? An example may serve to present an alternative viewpoint: on 30 October 2004, I was sitting in my office in Coventry, listening spellbound to the John Gaunt Show on BBC West Midlands radio. Queen Elizabeth II was on her way to pay a state visit to Germany, and the British press was full of discussions over the question whether as head of state she should apologize for the bombing of Dresden. John Gaunt invited his listeners to call in and give their opinions on the air. During the three-hour programme, a wide variety of opinions was expressed and one contribution in particular affected me profoundly:

Caller:　　　Are you trying to send my blood pressure through the roof?

John Gaunt:　No, why? What have I done to upset you?

Caller:　　　Blinking Dresden! So what? Who started the damned war? It's all right for you, you didn't go in it, you were lucky enough not to be involved in it. And it's thanks to the boys who blasted Germany and desecrated the whole perishing country, that you haven't had to go into another war.

John Gaunt:　So, do you ... do you think ... then ...?

Caller:　　　Apologize? No!

John Gaunt:　Do you think, then, it was just ordinary German people, and they all deserved to lose their lives through carpet-bombing? Do you really believe that the ordinary people of Coventry [*Gaunt meant to say Dresden*] deserved to die in that way?

I'm just saying, that it's more than fifty years on, and time to think about reconciliation. Why shouldn't we apologize? Those tactics were filthy, and yes, the Germans were using them as well. But we're big enough now, aren't we, to look at this and say: perhaps we were wrong?

Caller: No, we shouldn't apologize. The people in Germany voted for that swine. I'm glad that we ...

John Gaunt: They didn't vote for him in that way, though, did they? Come on.

Caller: I'm not interested in what they did.

John Gaunt: You can't put the blame on them ... Are you honestly saying you're blaming ordinary Germans for Adolf Hitler?

Caller: Well, they didn't sort of stand up against him at that time, when they could have done right at the beginning. In any case, what about all the others ... it wasn't just Coventry. There are other cities over here that they bombed. Cardiff, Swansea ... you name it, they got it.

John Gaunt: Of course ...

Caller: Even villages.

John Gaunt: But both sides killed innocent people. My point is, now, fifty years on ...

Caller: Of course.

John Gaunt: ... you talk as if you still hate Germans.

Caller: I'm not very fond of them, I must say.

John Gaunt: Why? What's wrong with German people?

Caller: Because my father was in the First World War, he put his age on. He was taken by these Germans, put into ... he was wounded, put into ... a camp. And because a crowd of them in November decided they'd cook the potatoes given to them by Belgian women – what did they do? They pulled him out, then took all his teeth out, without anaesthetic.

John Gaunt: I agree ...

Caller: The Second World War ...

John Gaunt: Slow down, slow down. My uncle Arthur was torpedoed by the Germans ...

Caller:	Yes, in the Second World War ...
John Gaunt:	He spent eighteen days in a life-raft. He then went and built the bridge over the River Kwai. However, fifty years on we have to learn forgiveness. I'm sorry, I disagree with you. You're still bitter, and I think you're being racist towards the Germans.
Caller:	Why not?
John Gaunt:	And though I respect the fact that you were there and I wasn't, and I understand what you said about your father, we mustn't be racist. We must move on, in a spirit of reconciliation.
Caller:	Well all right, then. Let them reconcile themselves with us, come over on their bended knees and say: I'm sorry for starting two world wars. You tell that to the other people they killed in Europe and elsewhere. I've got no sympathy for them whatsoever. And that's an end to it.
John Gaunt:	Thank you. I disagree with you completely, but thank you.[1]

The destruction of Coventry can still unleash drastic emotions – even so long after the end of the war. That caller was even stirred up by memories of the First World War, which is often referred to as the Great War. Healing and reconciliation still have not come to some people, and perhaps they never will.

On the other hand, the striking reconciliation between British and Germans, to which Coventry has contributed, continues to shine out to mankind today and to influence them to make their own efforts for peace. And so, to set against the above example, I offer another one: every Friday, the Litany of Reconciliation is prayed in the ruins of Coventry Cathedral, and – weather permitting – afterwards there is a simple service of Eucharist. Just how much has been accomplished between the British and the Germans is illustrated by the fact that, for many years, a German pastor has served in the cathedral, and has even presided over this Friday midday service. On Friday 25 February 2005, we were visited in Coventry by Stuart Hoke, Anglican priest at St Paul's Church in New York.[2] Later on, he recorded his impressions of Coventry in an online video to his church community. I was amazed

---

1 BBC West Midlands, 2005.

2 The little church of St Paul's stands surrounded by skyscrapers directly opposite Ground Zero, where until September 11 2001 the towers of the World Trade Center soared up. For more about this Cross of Nails Centre, see Chapter 10.2 pp. 105–12.

by the powerful emotions that were evoked in him by my rather modest utterances, which I had made on so many similar Fridays. My original words seemed to gain more significance in his memory than they had actually possessed in reality:

> 'There he was, standing in the ruins of Coventry Cathedral, celebrating the Eucharist. It was a Eucharist of Reconciliation, and there was a large group of people there – pilgrims, tourists, curiosity seekers ...
>
> And he said to them after the service: 'Look at me! I am a young German Lutheran minister. I am offering the sacrament of unity in this place. Unity and reconciliation and forgiveness.' And he said: 'Do you understand the symbolism of this?' And they all said: 'Oh yes.'
>
> Well, I was standing in the back, and I just ... ah ... teared up immediately, because it was just immediately for me resonant of what we are about at St Paul's.'[3]

During my time in Coventry, I was constantly amazed by the power of the ruins of Coventry Cathedral to move people and to bring alive the message of reconciliation. More than once I was able to experience that for people from the most crisis-torn regions of the world the encounter with this place became an incentive to fight unceasingly for justice and reconciliation. The link back to Coventry's ruined cathedral and its history of reconciliation is more than a mere nostalgic reminiscence of times gone by; and the special starting-point of the Community of the Cross of Nails has been in no way overtaken or superseded by the many-voiced choir of all those organizations and people who are working in the world with all kinds of different templates for reconciliation.

This book will look more closely at the history of the Community of the Cross of Nails, and at the work that it is doing. The first part of the book explores the historical roots of the Community of the Cross of Nails and the astonishing developments that took place in the wake of 14 November 1940. In the second part, the reconciliation work of several Cross of Nails Centres is described, with emphasis on some current projects in centres. Many of the earlier Cross of Nails Centres have been described in detail elsewhere – in Helmut Gröpler's *The Angels Held their Breath*, published in 1992. This book may be seen as a continuation of Gröpler's book, and will refer to it more than once. Finally, in its last section, the book attempts to formulate a kind of 'theology of reconciliation' out of the examples that have been given.

---

3 Trinity Television and New Media 2005.

This book does not aim to provide a comprehensive history of the Community of the Cross of Nails, and neither can it hope to describe *all* the Cross of Nails Centres worldwide. Indeed, the choice and the emphasis of the following chapters is a very personal one, based on my experiences during my time in Coventry, where I served from September 2002 until January 2006 as co-ordinator of the worldwide Community of the Cross of Nails at the International Centre for Reconciliation in Coventry Cathedral. As already mentioned, there is a tradition that a pastor from the Evangelical[4] Lutheran church in Bavaria would be sent to Coventry, to work there as a chaplain in Coventry University, and also to spend part of his/her week on duty at the cathedral. During this time I had the good fortune to get to know many centres, and the people who support them. I often think with pleasure of the many enriching discussions and experiences, and I am grateful for all the theological studies for which these meetings provided the stimulus. So, this book is also a little account of my years in Coventry.

First of all, though, I would like to thank all my former travelling-companions in Coventry and in the worldwide Community of the Cross of Nails, who accompanied me between 2002 and 2006. Special thanks to all those 'Cross-of-Nailers' who have supplied me over the last year with material and current information for this book. My added thanks to all those who have taken the trouble to proof-read it and minimize the number of typographical errors. Particular thanks to my wife Martina, PD Dr Achim Budde and Frau Helga Wagner. I thank Dr Wolfgang Neumann of Lembeck Publishing Co., for his good support and advice during the printing. The Community of the Cross of Nails in Germany has made it possible to print the German edition of this book, with a very generous grant – and special thanks are due to them for this.

Oliver Schuegraf
Feuchtwangen/Hanover, February 2008

---

4 Some caution is required with this word, since two German words with quite different meanings are both translated by the English word 'Evangelical'. In English the word 'Evangelical' is generally used to refer to a specific type of theology and churchmanship, and the German word for this is 'evangelikal'. The German word 'evangelisch', however, simply refers to a church that has its origin in the Reformation period; therefore most German churches include the word 'evangelisch' in their name, even though they are not evangelical in theology or churchmanship. However in English this purely historical meaning is also translated as 'evangelical'. In this book the English word 'Evangelical' always refers to the German word 'evangelisch', with one exception in footnote 149 on p. 120, where it does indeed refer to the German word 'evangelikal'.

Foreword to the English Edition

GROWING TOGETHER IN HOPE

In this book Oliver serves us well in telling the story of how a provincial English Cathedral destroyed in war became the inspiration of a unique network committed to work and pray for peace, justice and reconciliation.

The Community of the Cross of Nails is about people of faith reaching out in obedience to Christ's command to love our enemies and forgive those who harm us. In a world of depressingly familiar challenges, Christian reconciliation so defined is the source of healing and hope.

Since Oliver's book was first published in German the future of the network has been under review. Today we now speak of CCN Partners rather than Centres. ICONS (International Cross of Nails Schools) are growing in number. Renewed recognition of Coventry Cathedral as a place of inspiration and pilgrimage is increasing interest in belonging to the CCN. The desire to support each other and share resources of wisdom and skills across the network has created a new energy in our relationships. All of this has a new focus in St Michael's House, one of our Jubilee projects, as a space for learning and spiritual renewal for those involved in the hard work of reconciliation.

CCN Partners share a common commitment to grow together as they each engage with at least one of three main themes.

Healing the wounds of history

This has always been at the core of the Community of the Cross of Nails. Wounds from the legacy of war and violent conflict, if not tended carefully with forgiveness and justice, breed the contamination of vengeance and hate. Wounds from the exploitation of others result in poverty and disempowerment. Wounds are left on the earth as a result of human environmental pollution in an industrial age.

These wounds of history continue to dominate the global agenda. Nearly every contemporary conflict has deep roots in *past* wrongs. Global poverty shames us in our failure to ensure a basic quality of life for all God's children. Ecological disaster feeds the growing poverty gap and threatens new wars for scarce resources.

By addressing such concerns many of our CCN Partners nurture real hope among hurting and wounded people and communities.

Learning to live with difference and celebrate diversity

In every country and region where CCN Partners are found, questions of identity, belonging and the nature of a genuinely plural, just and inclusive society are crucial for stability and peace. Christian churches themselves continue to struggle to address genuine disagreements on a range of profound issues of belief and practice.

Our *present* requires new patterns of community where we learn how to live together with deep differences. Equity, diversity and interdependence are critical themes for discussion and prophetic and imaginative acts of hope.

The CCN must be a place where we find grace to appropriately celebrate the rich diversity that God has created in human beings. So it is important for our ministry of reconciliation that we do not run away from debates over gender, sexuality, race and ethnicity. Nor should we stand aloof from the ongoing political questions on what it means to share public and civic space with those of different faiths and cultures.

Building a culture of peace

The most fundamental threat to the *future* of us all is the collective failure of moral imagination to find ways to resolve our differences and disputes without recourse to violence.

Our world lives in, and perversely thrives on, a constant state of war. Economies depend on the billions spent on war. Yet war results in the catastrophic failure of governments and societies to support the life and health of their people. The targeting of civilian populations through the terror of bombing and the horror of sexual violence has become a tactic of choice for those set on the eradication of those who, being different, are seen as less than human.

Responsibility for re-imagining an alternative rests with us all. We need to commit the same energy and resources as those who wage war into making and building peace. We need to teach our young people the things that make for peace and the skills to seek peace and pursue it in their relationships. CCN, as a network of ordinary people in a world still seduced by violence, needs to find a new voice to challenge and change the prevalent culture of our time.

The God who gives us the ministry of reconciliation does not leave us without hope. God simply asks us to be a reconciling and reconciled people, who in the ordinariness of our lives bear witness to the extraordinary gift of hope we are given in Christ.

The story of this book does not stop within its covers. It continues in the worship, prayers, life and service of our CCN Partners and ICONS around the world. Be part of it. Visit **www.crossofnails.org** or **www. stmichaelshouse.org.uk**.

Canon David W. Porter
Coventry Cathedral
June 2012

Introduction to the
English edition

I am very excited and grateful that an English edition of this book is now available. Some words of thanks are due from me to all those who have made this possible:

First of all, regarding the printing and publishing of the book, I must once more thank the German Community of the Cross of Nails, without whose generous financial support this edition would not have been possible. The German Community regards its support for this book as a contribution to the golden jubilee of Coventry Cathedral in 2012, showing its commitment to the international Community of the Cross of Nails and its deep and lasting friendship with Coventry Cathedral. Thanks are also due to Canterbury Press for including this book in their portfolio.

Secondly, I would like to thank Gren Hatton for his meticulous work of translating the book into English. It was a joyful experience to discuss various text passages with him thoroughly, in search of the most appropriate and comprehensible translation.

Finally, I would like to express my gratitude to Canon David Porter, Canon Director for Reconciliation Ministry at Coventry Cathedral. By contributing a second foreword to the English edition he helped to resolve a dilemma: The Community of the Cross of Nails is a living and developing network. Therefore things have moved on, both in Coventry and in the Cross of Nails Centres described in the following pages, since this book was first published in German in 2008. An attempt to update and rework the text seemed fraught with difficulties – where to begin, and how much to add? In the end it would probably have been a completely different book. Therefore we decided that the English version of the book would strictly follow the original text, and Canon David Porter kindly agreed to provide the reader with some details of the most recent work of the Community of the Cross of Nails. The book thus still provides an up-to-date picture of a worldwide project that continues to adapt to the ever-changing needs of a world in which it seeks with God's help to enable reconciliation.

Oliver Schuegraf
Hanover

PART ONE

Coventry's Mission of Reconciliation

All have sinned and fallen short of the glory of God.
(Romans 3.23)

The hatred that divides nation from nation, race from race, class from class:
FATHER, FORGIVE!

The covetous desires of people and nations to possess that which is not their own:
FATHER, FORGIVE!

The greed which exploits the work of human hands and lays waste the earth:
FATHER, FORGIVE!

Our envy of the welfare and happiness of others:
FATHER, FORGIVE!

Our indifference to the plight of the imprisoned, the homeless, the refugee:
FATHER, FORGIVE!

The lust which dishonours the bodies of men, women and children:
FATHER, FORGIVE!

The pride which leads us to trust in ourselves and not in God:
FATHER, FORGIVE!

Be kind one to another, tender-hearted, forgiving one another, as God in Christ forgave you.
(Ephesians 4.32)

(Coventry Litany of Reconciliation)

I

'Father, forgive'

'Father, forgive': chancel of the ruined cathedral of Coventry.

On the wall of the chancel in the cathedral of St Michael in Coventry, destroyed in 1940 by German bombs, two words are carved:

'Father, forgive.'

In the year 1948, Provost Richard (Dick) Thomas Howard had these words 'Father, forgive' engraved. At the time, this inscription did not go undisputed. Many of Coventry's inhabitants, if they were ready to forgive at all, would have preferred a different version: Father, forgive *them* – the Germans. This attitude is understandable. On 14 November 1940, Coventry was attacked by German bombers. 'Operation Moonlight Sonata' ('Operation Mondscheinsonate') was the cynical code name given to this military operation, whose objective was to destroy the city both physically and psychologically. The attack was part of the airborne offensive over Great Britain, in which the German Luftwaffe

aimed to gain domination of the British airspace by a massive programme of surface bombing, paving the way for a planned invasion.
The German enemy intelligence service had recommended the Midland
city of Coventry because its world-famous aircraft industry and many
other factories were spread out all around the inner city, and hence
it was anticipated that the effect of fire-bombing both factories *and*
homes would be particularly dramatic.

At about 7.20pm, the first of the German bombers appeared over
Coventry. For eleven long hours, a total of four hundred and forty-
nine aircraft bombarded the city. Before long the cathedral, the symbol
of the city, was a victim of the flames – firebombs had hit its roof.
Because of the flatness of the roof, the bombs could not roll off before
they ignited, but released their full effect directly on the spot. The four
volunteers of the cathedral night-watch who were on duty that night
(among them Provost Howard) had no chance of quenching the flames,
and neither did the fire-fighters who came hurrying along shortly afterwards. When the sirens sounded the all-clear next morning, only the
tower and the outer walls of the medieval building were left standing,
and within the walls there was just a great mound of rubble:

'By early morning the destruction was complete. Every roof was
gone, and the whole Cathedral lay open to the sky. The matchless
pillars, arcades, and clerestories of the nave, chancel, and aisles were
lying on the ground in long piles of broken masonry.'

So wrote Howard, the eyewitness; and he added a theological interpretation of the horrors of that night:

'All night long the city burned, and her cathedral burned with her –
emblem of the eternal truth that, when men suffer, God suffers with
them. Yet the tower still stood, with its spire soaring to the sky –
emblem of God's overruling majesty and love.'[5]

Indeed, a large part of the medieval inner city lay in ashes and rubble,
through which the main streets could barely be discerned. Supplies had
broken down. Five hundred and fifty people lost their lives that night;
for the first time in Great Britain, it was necessary to bury the victims
in mass graves.[6]

---

5 Howard, 1962, pp. 14–15.
6 However, the factories escaped to a large extent undamaged, so that most of them
were soon able to resume their operations.

Coventry's mediaeval cathedral in ashes and ruins after 14 November 1940.

Joseph Goebbels, the German Reich's minister for public information and propaganda, noted in his diary that Coventry was now just a ruin: 'The reports on Coventry are horrifying. The city has been totally obliterated by a blast of bombs. The British cannot disguise the fact, they can only cry over it. And they got what they deserved.'[7] It was particularly ghoulish that Goebbels was able to remark casually in the very next sentence, referring to the new Viennese film 'Dear Augustin', that it was 'no great work of art, but very appealing and heart-warming, and a bit of bomb-propaganda for Vienna. That's something the Viennese are good at'.[8]

Meanwhile, the Nazi regime was fomenting another kind of bomb-propaganda. The 'successful' destruction of Coventry was used to promote internal warmongering, and the German newspapers praised

---

7 *Die Tagebücher von Joseph Goebbels* (The Diaries of Joseph Goebbels): c.f. Fröhlich, 1987, p. 402.

8 Fröhlich, 1987, p. 402.

the attack as a stroke of revenge for Munich.[9] Via the Nazi press, a disturbing new word found its way into the devil's dictionary: 'coventrieren', i.e. to 'coventrate'. The daily paper in Coventry's neighbouring city Birmingham, on the other hand, ran the headline on 16 November: 'Coventry – our Guernica'. Coventry had become a symbol of further escalation and a new level in bomb warfare.

In the face of this act of violence, hate and a desire for revenge would have been an understandable reaction. But Provost Howard sought for a different way. A mere six weeks after the destruction of Coventry and its cathedral by German bombers, in a radio broadcast transmitted worldwide by the BBC at Christmas 1940 from the cathedral ruins, Provost Howard addressed his audience:

> 'What we want to tell the world is this: that with Christ born again in our hearts today, we are trying, hard as it may be, to banish all thoughts of revenge; we are bracing ourselves to finish the tremendous job of saving the world from tyranny and cruelty; we are going to try to make a kinder, simpler – a more Christ-Child-like sort of world in the days beyond this strife.'[10]

Seldom had any victim reached out a hand to his oppressor in such a courageous and visionary manner as the British priest. These words are amazing, but they are not completely without precedent. Remembrance Day 1940, as in every year, had commenced with a service in the cathedral, and in the midst of war, thoughts turned to those who had fallen. Few people today remember that Provost Howard also incorporated into the liturgy the following amazing prayer:

> Let us pray for our enemies:
> Lord of boundless love, who in thine hour of agony didst pray for those who nailed thee to the Cross, we beseech thee for our enemies that thou wouldest turn their hearts and incline them to mercy.
> So that when this hour of conflict is passed / they and we may be united in the bonds of Christian love / and work together as friends / for the advancement of thy kingdom by the power of thy Son / Jesus Christ our Lord.[11]

---

9 In November 1940, Hitler had returned to Munich, as he had done the previous years, to commemorate his attempted coup of 1923. However, the celebrations on 8 November had been interrupted by a British air raid.

10 Howard, 1962, p. 22.

11 Coventry Cathedral, 1940, p. 9.

The ruins of Coventry's old cathedral.

Four days later saw the destruction of the cathedral in which that prayer was uttered. The Provost's intercession indicates just how intensely he had been thinking about reconciliation between the two nations, even before 14 November. The message of his Christmas sermon was certainly not prompted by any sunny skies, but the magnitude and the significance of his words were all the greater for that: out of the visible evidence of senseless destruction, a place of renewal and of reconciliation was to come into being. And for Provost Howard, this new beginning signified renewal for *everyone*. That is why, in 1948, his instruction was to carve only the words 'Father, forgive' on the chancel wall, and not 'Father, forgive *them*'; for so might only Jesus have spoken on the cross. We mere mortals, on the other hand, are all in need of forgiveness, without exception. Without that, there can be no new beginning, no renewal.

From this spirit, in the course of time, the Litany of Reconciliation also came into being (1959), which since that time has been prayed at noon on every Friday, in the open air in the chancel of the ruined cathedral. Come rain or shine, people meet in the ruins to pray the Litany together. With a glance at the words 'Father, forgive', they gather around the altar that was erected in January 1941, on the site of the old ruined altar, built of stones and memorial slabs from the old cathedral.

The first line of the prayer reminds those gathered together of one of the basic insights of the Epistle to the Romans (Romans 3.23):

All have sinned, and fallen short of the glory of God.

At the heart of the Litany is the recurring call 'Father, forgive': this cry of repentance is the congregation's response to the seven verses of the Litany. Seven times we are reminded of Mankind's sinful behaviour. The structure is closely mirrored upon the seven deadly sins.

Finally the prayer ends with the call for reconciliation from the Epistle to the Ephesians:

Be kind one to another, tender-hearted, forgiving one another, as God in Christ forgave you.

(Ephesians 4.32)

Suggestions for further reading

More detailed information about the destruction of the old cathedral and Howard's vision may be found in Howard, 1962; and Thomas, 1987, p. 68ff. See also Gröpler, 1994, pp. 11–30.

2

The Reconciliation Message of the double cathedral

It was already made clear that Provost Howard had the most profound theological understanding of the tragic events of 14 November 1940. From very early on, he interpreted the story of Coventry Cathedral by analogy with the Passion of Jesus Christ. In his book *Ruined and Rebuilt*, Howard wrote:

'As I watched the Cathedral burning, it seemed to me as though I were watching the crucifixion of Jesus upon His Cross ... That such a glorious and beautiful building, which had been the place where Christian people had worshipped God for five hundred years, should now be destroyed in one night by the wickedness of man, was surely a monstrous evil that nothing could measure. It was in some mysterious way a participation in the infinite sacrifice of the crucifixion of Christ.

As I went with this thought in my mind into the ruined Cathedral on the morning after the destruction, there flashed into my mind the deep certainty that as the Cathedral had been crucified with Christ, so it would rise again with Him. How or when, we could not tell; nor did it matter. The Cathedral would rise again.'[12]

In the fate of the cathedral, Howard recognized the central core of the Christian message – namely, that death and destruction will never have the final word. God is greater than Evil, and His love will overcome it. This was Howard's conviction, and it is precisely this message that is symbolized by the new cathedral that has stood since 1962 alongside the ruins of the old one.

---

12 Howard, 1962, p. 16.

Coventry's ruined cathedral with its bell-tower.

The laying of the foundation stone by Queen Elizabeth II in May 1956 was preceded by a long phase of thinking and sounding out. There was particularly heated discussion over the question of whether the ruined cathedral really should be rebuilt, and if so, in what style. In the end, an invitation was issued for competitive tenders, and by July 1951 more than two hundred designs had been submitted. Rather unexpectedly, the competition was won by Basil Spence, with a modernistic design whose layout is nevertheless rooted firmly in the style of a mediaeval cathedral. Spence's book *Phoenix over Coventry. The Building of a Cathedral* is a gripping tale, and highly recommended reading for anyone who wants to learn more about the building of the cathedral: of the basis of the architect's conception, and of his collaboration with the UK's most outstanding and well-known artists of the time such as Sir Jacob Epstein (the statue of St Michael and the Devil on the cathedral's outer wall), John Piper (the Baptistry window, 24m high and 15m wide), Graham Sutherland (the wall-tapestry in the apse) and John Hutton (the glazed south wall with engravings).

Glazed south wall of the new cathedral with engravings by John Hutton.

What interests us here, however, is the seeds of the design's internal concept, in which a theological and religious dimension is also embodied in the architecture. Even during his first visit to Coventry in October 1950, Basil Spence had already arrived at the decisive insight: 'I saw the old cathedral as standing clearly for the Sacrifice, one side of the Christian faith, and I knew my task was to design a new one which should stand for the Triumph of the Resurrection.'[13] And thus he later declared, when submitting his design proposal to the competition:

> Through the ordeal of bombing, Coventry was given a beautiful ruin … As the Cathedral stands now, it is an eloquent memorial to the courage of the people of Coventry. It is felt that the ruin should be preserved as a garden of rest … and the new Cathedral should grow from the old and be incomplete without it.
>
> The author of this design does not see this building as a planning problem, but the opportunity to create a Shrine to the Glory of God.[14]

'Self-sacrifice and resurrection', respectively 'memorial to a night of bombing and a shrine to God's glory' – this twin conception in the design, whose motif had already struck Provost Howard on the very day after the destruction, became the all-defining concept for the newly emerging double church. The old and the new cathedrals form a single unit, as do the Cross and the Resurrection. Only by looking at them both together, as a whole, is it possible to understand fully the mission of Coventry: the one as a monument that preserves the memory of suffering, death and the Cross; the other as an architectural sign of faith that releases the resurrected to a life in reconciliation. An open canopy links the two parts of the double church.

The old cathedral remains a deliberate ruin, an open wound that reminds us ever and again of Christ's suffering and of the suffering of Coventry. The visitor can look out from the ruins into the new cathedral through a glass 'wall' that stretches over the whole height and breadth of the entrance façade. The tapestry in the apse, dominating everything else in the building, is visible even from the ruins – and especially so at night.

The whole metaphor of the new church, with that majestic tapestry in the apse, proclaims the second part of the double message – Jesus Christ is risen from the dead and he will come again in glory. However, this woven Christ still bears the wounds of his crucifixion – caused by the nails that were driven into the Cross. They remain as visible testimony to his vulnerability and to the unjust suffering that he had to bear; yet it was precisely through this suffering that he broke free

---

13 Spence, 1962, p. 6.
14 Spence, 1962, pp. 117, 120.

from the spiral of violence and counter-violence. Alongside the tapestry, the visitor's gaze is immediately drawn to the slight yet massive altar, reminding us that we are called to new life and that we receive this call anew in every Eucharist. As the visitor finally turns and looks back, this memorial to death and the Crucifixion remains visible from all points of the new nave, through the glass façade.

Graham Sutherland's tapestry.

On Friday 25 May 1962, the cathedral was formally consecrated by Bishop Cuthbert Bardsley. In the ornately designed order of service for this occasion, the introductory words contained yet another explicit reference to the character of a double church. To explain why the old custom had been set aside (in which the bishop knocks on the door of the new church, it is opened to him, and he then enters the building for the first time with the priests and the congregation, and takes possession of it), the order of service reads as follows:

We speak of the consecration of the new Cathedral; we should more accurately speak of the consecration of the new wing of the Cathedral. The new church is the old church enlarged; the old and the new are, architecturally and ecclesiastically, one thing. A Christian congregation has been in possession of the Church of St Michael in Coventry for many hundreds of years ... This situation is vividly attested by the lettering in the floor of the nave of the new building:

TO THE GLORY OF GOD,
THIS CATHEDRAL BURNT
NOVEMBER 14 AD 1940.
IT IS NOW REBUILT, 1962.[15]

The theological double motif of the cathedral was then taken up again, in a psalm setting by John Austin (1613–69), with which the actual consecration ceremony commenced. The choir and congregation sang:

Antiphon: Why seek ye the living among the dead? He is risen, he is not here: he is gloriously ascended, and the heavens have received him. Alleluia, alleluia.

PSALM

Raise thy head, O my soul, and look up : and behold the glory of your crucified Saviour.

He that was dead, and laid in the grave : low enough to prove himself Man,

Is risen and ascended into heaven : high enough to prove himself God.

Enter, bright King, attended with thy beauteous angels : and the glad train of thy new delivered captives;

Enter, and repossess thy ancient throne : and reign eternally at the right hand of thy Father.

Glory be to the Father, and to the Son : and to the Holy Ghost;

As it was in the beginning, is now, and ever shall be : world without end. Amen.

---

15 Coventry Cathedral, 1962, p. 2.

Antiphon: Why seek ye the living among the dead? He is risen, he is not here : he is gloriously ascended, and the heavens have received him. Alleluia, alleluia.[16]

Death and resurrection, grave and ascension, Man and God – the twin poles of Austin's poem are reflected in the architecture that encircles the community attending the consecration ceremony: the eye is drawn to Sutherland's tapestry, whilst to the rear the ruins of the old cathedral can be seen through the glass façade.

Her Majesty Queen Elizabeth II was present once again among the guests of honour, as she had previously been for the laying of the foundation stone. However, on this occasion it was a new provost who accompanied the British queen into the church: in 1958 Dick Howard had resigned and handed over his office to a younger man. On 27 September, Harold (Bill) Claude Noel Williams had been installed as the cathedral's new provost.[17]

However, even before the royal and episcopal processions entered the church, a clear ecumenical sign had already been given. The great assembly of the Church's representatives that entered the cathedral included not only bishops of the worldwide Anglican community, but also invited guests from the British free churches and envoys of the European Reformed, Lutheran and Orthodox churches: among those who had travelled from Germany were Kurt Scharf, Bishop of Berlin, and Adolf Wischmann, president of the offices for Foreign Affairs of the German Evangelical Church (Evangelische Kirche in Deutschland, EKD). The Swedish Church was represented by the Archbishop of Uppsala. London-based Bishop Anthony Bloom was present on behalf of the Russian Orthodox Church. However, no Roman Catholic envoy accepted the invitation; although it was the eve of the Second Vatican Council, this was still a bridge too far.

But ecumenism, the reconciliation between the confessions, should not be restricted to a single instance of celebration – and this is the role of the Chapel of Unity. The idea had already been proposed back in 1944, that a Chapel of Unity should be attached to the new cathedral, a chapel dedicated to Christian unity, which should belong to the Anglican and the free churches together as a building and as a place of

---

16 Coventry Cathedral, 1962, p. 17.

17 One reason for his appointment may have been that, as a native of South Africa, he understood the need to exert himself in the cause of reconciliation. His father was British, his mother had Dutch roots. Throughout his life, he kept in mind what his mother had taught him: 'Christians heal the wounds of history' (Williams, c.1989, p. 2).

The old cathedral, viewed through the glass wall of the new cathedral.

prayer. In the West Crypt under the ruins of the old cathedral, a first provisional Chapel of Unity was set up in 1945, to serve until a corresponding place came into being in the new cathedral.[18] A year before the consecration of the new cathedral, Provost Williams described the concept in one of the many lectures that he gave during a visit to Germany, in the following terms:

'We at Coventry have made a great and necessary acknowledgement. That the Church has no right to speak a word of reconciliation to a divided world, until it has shown the will to be reconciled in itself. The Church – in the face of the world challenge of atheistic materialism – cannot afford the luxury of fighting within itself. So in Coventry Cathedral we have built a Chapel of Unity which in a year's time will be handed over as the common possession of all Christian denominations which wish to share in it. It is the sacramental expression in stone of all our ecumenical hopes. It will serve as the base for a long operation of discovery leading us in the end to a Christian Unity that is real.'[19]

It is significant that, when looking out from the Chapel into the nave of the cathedral, the gaze falls upon the baptismal font and not upon the Anglican altar – it was a conscious decision to place this symbol of Christian unity at the focus, rather than the place of that sacrament which, sadly, is still a ground for divisions between the various confessions.

Today, this chapel is still administered by an ecumenical committee, which decides on how it will be used. Several ecumenical groups meet here regularly for prayer, and the expatriate German Evangelical community celebrates its Sunday afternoon service in this place. During the week of prayer for Christian Unity, Christians of all denominations come together day by day to pray. For many years the Catholic chaplain of nearby Coventry University celebrated his weekly Mass here. In short, the Chapel of Unity makes it clear that from the very beginning Coventry set itself the task not only of reconciling nations, but also of reconciling the Christian Church.

---

18 See Howard, 1962, pp. 30–7.

19 Williams, 1961, p. 11. At the same time, we should not conceal the difficulties and the ecumenical and inter-Anglican differences of opinion that accompanied the building and administration of the Chapel. See Williams, c.1989, pp. 49–54.

Suggestions for further reading

More detailed information on the building of the cathedral and its architectural and theological concept may be found in Basil Spence's own very entertaining description (which includes many illustrations): Spence 1962; and also in Howard 1962 and Thomas 1987 pp. 68–117. The guidebook by Thomas is more accessible reading than the other two works. On pp. 161–80, Thomas gives his own personal assessment of the controversial discussion as to how far, in hindsight, Spence's design may be considered as architecturally successful and liturgically useful. For German readers, Gröpler, 1994 pp. 31–66, also gives an insight into the building of the church.

3

The Cross of Nails

We now turn our attention back once again to the day when Coventry Cathedral was destroyed, and to the piles of wreckage left behind after the church had burned down. Among the debris and rubble in the ruins of the nave lay hand-forged nails of various sizes; they were the mediaeval nails that had held together the wooden roof of the cathedral. On 15 November an event occurred that was to have important consequences for the future of the cathedral. Provost Howard records the details:

'On the morning after the destruction of the Cathedral the Revd A. P. Wales, the Vicar of a Coventry church which had suffered grievous damage, picked up from the Cathedral ruins three large sharp nails, and, binding them with wire into a cross, took it to show to the Bishop. That was the first cross to be made from Cathedral nails.

Three months later I took a young friend of mine, Stephen Verney, a student at Balliol College, Oxford, round the Cathedral. I noticed that he had picked up two small nails and bound them with a bit of wire into a cross. He said: "I have never felt the meaning of the Cross so powerfully as here in these ruins."'[20]

The Cross of Nails – put together from one vertical and two horizontal nails – quickly became the most powerfully impressive and well-known symbol of the cathedral and its work of reconciliation. The Cross of Nails has undergone a shift of meaning in the course of time, or to be more precise it has gained additional significance. Gröpler summarizes this as follows:

In the beginning it was more than anything else a symbol of remembrance of Coventry, a kind of 'souvenir', a reminder of the cathedral destroyed by bombs, and of the hope that this Crucifixion would be

---

20 Howard, 1962, p. 24.

followed by a Resurrection. Later on it became primarily a sign to express the community of churches, a sign of brotherhood in mutual care and of solidarity. Finally it became a symbol of forgiveness, of reconciliation and of a new beginning.[21]

Thus, at first the Cross of Nails was understood as a kind of 'souvenir': very soon it was being presented to representatives of Christian Churches and to public figures who had been affected by the story of Coventry, and had become fellow campaigners in the struggle for reconciliation and peace. In this Cross, the Provost found a gift that said more than words could say, a gift that created a profound association between Coventry and those to whom it was given. It is a fact that these crosses were initially sent out based on no grand plan or particular criteria,[22] for instance to Winston Churchill, other prime ministers and ambassadors, and also to foreign bishops and professors. In this way, more than a hundred crosses were presented in the early years.[23]

Within the diocese of Coventry itself, the Cross of Nails gained a special significance in the days immediately preceding the consecration of the new cathedral. Spiritual preparations for the consecration had already been under way for three years; it was not only the mother church of the diocese that was to be consecrated, but also a consecrated people living around it – that was the idea. This emotionally moving path of inner renewal was vividly portrayed by Stephen Verney, at that time the *Diocesan Missionary*, in the booklet 'Fire in Coventry'.[24] At first the bishop's clergy began to meet regularly in small groups. In the next stage, groups of clergy and laity from three parishes each came together to joint discussions and working-groups on the future of the church; then a parish assembly took place in each parish of the diocese, culminating in forty days and nights of prayer of the whole diocese as the final phase of the programme of renewal.

The Cross of Nails played a central role in those forty days and nights before the 25 and 26 May 1962. On Palm Sunday 1962, it left the ruins of the old cathedral and was carried in a great procession from parish

---

21 Gröpler, 1994, p. 86f.

22 Provost Williams commented on the practice of his predecessors: 'In 1957 Richard Howard and Basil Spence had made a fund-raising tour of Canada. It was on that tour that Provost Howard distributed crosses of nails fairly liberally here and there in Canada. They were to cause confusion in later years, when the crosses were distributed only within the network of centres linked with Coventry Cathedral in a specific ministry of reconciliation' (Williams, c.1989, p. 25). With regard to the Community of the Cross of Nails, see Chapter 5, pp. 36–41.

23 Further examples may be found in Gröpler, 1994, pp. 82–4.

24 See Verney, 1988.

to parish through the whole diocese. In Kenilworth, for example, the Cross was passed on at three o'clock in the morning from one parish to the next:

> In the distance we could discern the approach of the vicar of St John's, carrying the Cross of Nails, and followed by his contingent with torches, and with three banners bearing the words 'A Diocese Prays', 'A Consecrated Cathedral demands a Consecrated People' and 'Father Forgive'. There was a sense of oneness and brotherhood in the hearts of every one of us as we saw them approach. Here was the Church of England passing on its message from parish to parish through the diocese. High Church or Low Church didn't enter into it; this remarkable feature of unity in diversity that is characteristic of our church was being demonstrated.
>
> The two groups met, and the ceremony of 'handing over' was begun: 'Receive this Cross of Nails, brought to you with love and the prayers of your fellows from the ruined sanctuary of our Cathedral of St Michael. Cherish this cross, as a token of the merciful forgiveness of God, declared to us in the Passion of our Saviour Jesus Christ. Watch about this cross, in prayer for one another and for us, for Cuthbert our Bishop, and for all in this Diocese of Coventry who love and serve the Lord Jesus.'
>
> Such were the words accompanying the handing over. Then, as the cross was delivered into the hand of the priest of the receiving company, the first priest said in a loud voice, 'Christ reigns.'
>
> Then followed the prayer 'Almighty God ... grant that we walking in the way of the cross, may find it none other than the way of life and peace.'
>
> This was followed by silence. The Cross was raised aloft. St John's returned to their church, and we took the cross further on its pilgrimage.[25]

The last stage of the forty-day procession was undertaken by Bishop Cuthbert himself. From St John's in Coventry he carried the Cross all the way through the densely crowded inner city and back into the ruins. There it was received by the Provost, who brought it into the new building. And so, on the eve of the consecration, the Cross of Nails arrived at last in the new cathedral, and took up its final resting place within the great altar cross that had been fashioned by Geoffrey Clarke. In the words of Verney: 'There it would stand with all its old significance, and

---

25 Verney, 1988, pp. 32–3, quoting a report in a parish newsletter.

in addition now as the symbol in the mother church of the love and prayer and unity of the diocese.'[26]

In addition to the original symbolism of the Cross of Nails – a sign of death and destruction, and of hope in resurrection and a new beginning – a second level of significance can be seen here. In its forty days of journeying, the Cross of Nails had become a sign of the unity of the community of the diocese of Coventry, to its mother church and above all to each other. It drew together people of the most diverse theological convictions, of different generations and social status, and directed them towards a single common goal: towards the God who sent renewal through the Holy Spirit in Jesus Christ. An inter-Anglican ecumenical dimension had become tangible here in the Cross of Nails.

However, as we have seen, Gröpler finds yet a third symbol contained in the Coventry Cross: that of forgiveness and reconciliation. Just how the Cross of Nails could become a symbol of reconciliation will now be described in the following pages.

---

26 Verney, 1988, p. 32.

4

Reconciliation with Germany

As we have already seen, Provost Howard was driven by the vision that out of the suffering of Coventry would grow a service of healing and reconciliation – starting with those places that had suffered as much in the war as had Coventry and its cathedral. He wanted to reach out a hand to the enemy in the hope that British and German people might one day come together without bitterness and hate. One obvious sign of this duty of reconciliation was the Cross fashioned out of three nails taken from Coventry's ruined cathedral. Provost Howard reports that, as early as 1946, the first contacts were made with the Germans: in that year, as in 1940, the Christmas radio message was broadcast to the British Empire from Coventry. A Catholic priest from Hamburg, with his choir of children, took part in the Christmas service in the provisional Chapel of Unity. Howard greeted the German priest, and took up his twin theme that is now so familiar to us: 'Reconciliation and Rebirth'.

'You know what happened to us here in Coventry, and you can easily picture what it was like. We know what happened to you in Hamburg, and I can partly imagine it. ...

I think I see between us at our feet, the Christ Child lying in His crib. Across the Child I stretch out my hand and put it into yours, my brother ... Looking down into the face of the infant Jesus – God in human flesh – two words spring to my lips to say to you. The first word is "Forgiveness" ... The second word is this – "New Birth". Here in Coventry we have 20,000 new homes to build, a whole new city centre and a Cathedral to restore. Your task is even greater. But more important still, there is a new spirit to be born – new courage, new faith, new unselfishness, new pity for each other's sufferings, new family love and purity.'[27]

---

27 Howard, 1962, p. 87.

The answer from the Hamburg priest was just as forgiving as it was trail-blazing: '"Forgive us our trespasses, as we forgive those who trespass against us." If only these words could be echoed in all our hearts! If only we could cast out bitterness and hatred and begin again, then I believe that our children – yours and ours – may live together in peace and brotherhood.'[28] Thus spoke the German priest in 1946.

Shortly afterwards there were to be other opportunities in which the longed-for reconciliation between British and Germans could be realized both symbolically and in personal testimony. This is not the place in which to describe all these meetings and new beginnings, but two examples – representative of the many others – will give some idea of the impetus with which reconciliation under Coventry's Cross of Nails developed during the post-war years. Firstly, the story of the first Cross of Nails given to a German church, St Nikolai in Kiel. And secondly, a reminder of Coventry's most well-known gesture of reconciliation, the collaboration in the rebuilding of the Diakonissenkrankenhaus (Deaconesses' Hospital) in Dresden in 1965.

---

28 Howard, 1962, p. 87.

4.1 Kiel

Kiel was one of the German towns that suffered great destruction. The town was a target for enemy action on account of its naval base and shipyards – although, during the later stages of the war, there was also bombing of residential districts and the inner city. 'In a total of about ninety attacks, 2,293 citizens were killed. ... Not a trace was left of the historic architecture; the destruction and damage extended to 78% of the built-up area. Five million cubic metres of rubble lay on the ground, the equivalent of twenty-three cubic metres per inhabitant.'[29] These bare figures, collected by J. Friedrich in his much-discussed book *Der Brand (The Fire)*, are sufficient on their own to illustrate the scale of the destruction and suffering. However, there was in Kiel – as in Coventry – a visionary figure who dared to hope that a peaceful conclusion might be formed from out of the horrors of war. In January 1947 Kiel's newspaper published an appeal from the mayor, Andreas Gayk. In his address, Gayk first recounted the story of a British officer named Williams, a native of Coventry who had been stationed in Kiel:

'This man, whose home town has been ruthlessly demolished by the German Luftwaffe, came to Kiel as part of Marshal Montgomery's victorious armies, to Kiel which is one of the worst-hit towns of northern Germany. Yet this man did not feel any satisfaction in seeing that the Royal Air Force had given like for like, but from the first moment did everything in his power to help a town which had shared the fate of his own native town, and to alleviate the distress which he had known from his own experience.'[30]

Out of his meeting with this British soldier, Kiel's Mayor Gayk formed the desire to make contact with Coventry. His appeal in the Kiel newspaper continued in these words:

'The time has come when the chasm that has been torn open between the peoples of Europe must be bridged over and ways of mutual understanding between man and man sought that will lead us out of the bottomless pit of misunderstanding into which we were plunged in the recent past! ... What do you think to the idea, that we should combine to form a 'Society of Friend of Coventry' – and that the

---

29 Friedrich, 2002, p. 192.
30 *Kieler Nachrichten*, 1947, p. 1.

names of the devastated cities of Kiel and Coventry should become the symbol of our spiritual and moral awakening?'[31]

Coventry also responded to the appeal. On 14 September 1947, a little delegation set off for Kiel, including the Mayor, a trade union representative, and Provost Howard, bearing with them a Cross of Nails. It was the first official Anglo-German inter-city exchange.

Howard recorded the week's events in a diary, which is preserved in the cathedral archives. In a little notebook, he jotted down his impressions and meetings. Several of Howard's entries describe the state of the town; at one point he says, very briefly but succinctly; 'The desolation everywhere is tremendous, the destruction complete.'[32] In another place he writes: 'The town is frightfully devastated – like a centre of Coventry, extended everywhere.'[33] Also poignant are his assessments, contained in jottings, on how the inhabitants of Kiel viewed their own situation:

'They evidently dislike the British occupation + want to be free. ... They are all anti-Nazis. ... There seems to be no 'war guilt' – They identify themselves with opposition to the Hitler regime – They seem to expect us to treat them as though they had always been opposed to it + were victims of it – They cannot understand why they should have to be 'controlled' + go on suffering.

Among ourselves [the members of the Coventry delegation] there was much discussion about all this. On the one hand, while the war was on these Germans did fight on the Nazi side – Their sons killed ours – Can they throw off the responsibility for their deeds – Must they not go on suffering for the corporate deeds of their nation – Could they be trusted to be a new kind of German people who would never rise to militarism again, as they profess.

On the other hand, did they know of the evil deeds of their leaders, the concentration camps etc – Were they not compelled to fight by circumstances beyond their choice – Once the war began, can they be blamed for fighting for their country – And, here is a great point, between 1935–36 + even right up to 1939 did we British give the anti-Nazi element in Germany any help at all in their fight against Nazidom.'[34]

---

31 *Kieler Nachrichten*, 1947, p. 1.
32 Howard, 1947 (Notes), p. 21.
33 Howard, 1947 (Notes) p. 37.
34 Howard, 1947 (Notes), pp. 39–41.

These are questions that tackle the theme of 'guilt and forgiveness' head-on; a weighing up of the pros and cons, which show that Provost Howard sought to avoid any kind of black-and-white distinction; insights that enabled him to take the step towards reconciliation. He knew about guilt and about guilty involvement, in which ultimately the British side had also been involved. Both sides had been tragically bound together during the war, and now it should be 'friendship' that would form a new bond between the two nations. This motto was to be the recurrent theme of his time in Kiel, for the hope of 'friendship' is so much easier to understand, and its demands are more modest, than the complex theological word 'reconciliation'.

On the afternoon of 15 September, Howard spoke to a group of Protestants and Catholics, including Provost Lorenzen, whose church of St Nikolai in Kiel had suffered heavy damage just like Coventry Cathedral. In his diary entry, Howard recalled that he had bidden the assembled group to recognize in his face the face of Christ as it was shown forth in the life of Christ in Coventry, just as he saw now in their faces the face of Christ in Kiel. 'The unity between us in [Christ] was real + so we were already friends in Him', he continued reflectively in his diary.[35] Then he held aloft a Coventry Cross of Nails, and explained where it came from and what it was made of, and that he now wished to give it to Provost Lorenzen for his church. Howard then spelled out the theological significance of the Cross. He was handing over the Cross as a symbol of God's forgiveness, as a symbol of our own mutual forgiveness, and as a symbol of the power of God, who forgives all our sins through the death and resurrection of Christ, and brings goodness out of suffering.[36]

These three aspects were to become the defining and constantly recurring elements of Coventry's message of Reconciliation. Thus it is apparent that, as early as 1947, there was a theological basis for awarding the Cross of Nails, even if the idea of a unifying *Community* of the Cross of Nails was only developed over the course of time (see Chapter 5).

A few days later, Howard visited the ruins of St Nikolai, and was given in return a stone from the ruined church, which was initially displayed in the provisional Chapel of Unity and is now on view in the cathedral's treasury.

On 18 September Provost Howard gave his final address to the company of the Friends of Coventry, which had come into being in

35 Howard, 1947 (notes), p. 43.
36 Howard, 1947 (notes), p. 43.

response to Mayor Gayk's appeal and had by now grown to include eight hundred members. 'We in Coventry and Kiel are longing for material and cultural reconstruction', so runs the draft of his speech for this occasion. However, in the final analysis this rebuilding would depend upon the *spiritual* resources that both sides were able to bring to it. Howard mentioned, by way of example, the need for genuine remorse, for a vision of true goodness, and for active participation in one another's suffering. In the end, all these qualities would come from God, the source of all goodness; without God, the rebuilding would be foredestined to failure. But unfortunately, both churches had shown themselves to be very inadequate as tools through which the power of the gospel might be instilled into the lives of mankind.

'So I want to put it to you today that one of the great tasks before this Society of the Friends of Coventry and Kiel is this: that by our friendship for each other ... we shall help each other to find our way onwards towards a new experience of faith in and obedience to Jesus Christ, the inspirer + energy of our reconstruction, so that on the one hand the Churches may demonstrate a more practical form of Christianity without losing their spirituality, and also that the common people may gladly find their home once again in the Churches. Without such a new discovery on the part of the Church and of the people I see no hope whatever for a healthy and permanent reconstruction. With such a new light + new power of Christ in our midst, there is every hope of ultimate peace and happiness for your beloved Kiel and our beloved Coventry.'[37]

Finally the Provost focused upon the stone from the church of St Nikolai, which was destined to take its place in Coventry's chapel dedicated to unity. In this part of his talk, he returned again to the theme of friendship, and assured his audience that this chapel would belong to them just as much as to the inhabitants of Coventry, and that therefore it would be a chapel of the Friends of Kiel in Coventry.

37 Howard, 1947, Address.

4.2 Dresden

Provost Williams involved himself seamlessly in the visionary reconciliation work of his predecessors. At Easter 1959, six months after taking up his position in Coventry, he embarked on his first visit to Germany, the first of many. In a television interview, holding a Cross of Nails in his hands, he summed up his hopes: 'As you Germans helped to make Coventry a symbol of hatred and destruction, so now under the sign of the Cross of Nails, join hands with us to make it a symbol of reconciliation.'[38] Later on, during a lecture in Berlin, Williams was confronted for the first time by a question from one of his audience: 'And what about Dresden?'

'I must have looked as foolish as I felt, because I simply did not know what he meant. I soon did. When I returned to England I found out a great deal more, and the seed was sown which would grow right into one of the most important projects Coventry was ever to undertake.'[39]

And indeed, this simple question led on to the rebuilding work in Dresden and the awarding of a Cross of Nails to the Diakonissen-krankenhaus (Deaconesses' Hospital), which was to become one of the most famous Cross of Nails Centres in Germany.

By the 1960s, sixteen German volunteers from Aktion Sühnezeichen had already helped to restore the sacristy of the ruined cathedral as a meeting-place.[40] This led to close contacts between Germans and British, which created lasting impressions and friendships. Whenever I think of these friendships, thoughts of Jill Garner always come to my mind; Jill passed away only recently, but right up to the last she was always involved with the group of ladies who take care of the flowers in the cathedral – and she also regularly attended the ecumenical services in the Chapel of Unity. Many of those German volunteers back in the 1960s stayed with Jill; when she spoke about them, it was as though she was talking about her own children. She treasured all the letters

---

38 Williams, c.1989, p. 36.

39 Williams, c.1989, p. 38.

40 See Gröpler, 1994, pp. 133–6. In 1958 the synod of the EKD (German Evangelical Church) had founded the Reconciliation Service (later to become the Aktion Sühnezeichen Friedensdienste, or 'Action Reconciliation Service for Peace', ARSP), on the initiative of Dr Lothar Kreyssig. The goal of this organization was to send out young Germans into countries that had suffered under the Nazi regime, in order to seek atonement there through rebuilding projects.

that they sent from Germany over the years, and whenever she heard again from one of them she would come scurrying over to me, to say 'Guten Tag' and read out her latest letter.

In 1965 some young folk from the UK were dispatched to help with rebuilding work in Dresden. In the Sunday service on 14 March 1965, these British volunteers were formally sent off to their work of rebuilding – and the special liturgy that was composed for the occasion made it crystal clear that this initiative was all about reconciliation between the British and German peoples, and that it was motivated by a deep-seated Christian faith. First of all, the volunteers were called forward by Provost Williams in order to be introduced to the congregation, and the following liturgical exchange took place:

The Provost addresses them again:

> Do you believe that peace between men and nations is the fruit of humility and penitence?
>
> *Response:* We do.
>
> *Provost:* Do you believe that loving and humble service to our enemies has power to heal the hurts and sorrows of war?
>
> *Response:* We do.
>
> *Provost:* Do you believe yourselves called to a ministry of reconciliation in Dresden?
>
> *Response:* We do.
>
> *Provost:* Will you so discipline yourselves there as to meet every circumstance with love and patience and good humour?
>
> *Response:* We will.
>
> *Provost:* Will you remember that the reputation of Christ and his church is in your hands?
>
> *Response:* We will.
>
> *Provost:* Then I will commission you for your task.

They kneel down. The Provost extends his right arm over them, and says:

> In the name of God, who has created all men for friendship with himself;
> In the name of Jesus Christ, who bade us love our enemies;

> In the name of our Lord the Spirit, who rescues and
> restores us;
> we send you to Dresden.
> Receive our commission
> to serve Christ there in your fellow men.[41]

In his brief speech, Williams ventured the following comparison: 'This work is the restoration of a Christian hospital for the healing of sick persons. But it is an analogy of a greater act of healing than that – the healing of a deep wound of history, in the name and under the authority of Jesus Christ.'[42]

A review by Deaconess Elisabeth Becker, preserved in the archives of the Lutheran Diakonissenanstalt (Deaconesses' Institute) in Dresden, commences with the words: 'The first task of the young team that came together in Dresden was to set up a symbol of reconciliation. As a result, the place attracted a certain amount of public interest, despite the fact that it was immured within the walls of the deaconesses' house.'[43] For seven months, from March to September 1963, the young men and women from England worked alongside German helpers from Aktion Sühnezeichen, clearing away rubble from a wing of the Diakonissenkrankenhaus that had been destroyed by British bombers. A short passage from the memoirs of Sister Elisabeth illustrates clearly the mutual quirks and idiosyncrasies that the Germans and the British saw in one another:

> In the matter of rules and regulations for the camp, the difference between German love of ground-rules and British individuality was particularly evident. The Germans mourned the lack of firm or precisely documented instructions, whilst the British resisted anything that even remotely resembled a "forbidden" notice. Neither side would allow the other to see how much they suffered under the conflicting arrangements in which they lived together – indeed, they made a point of it – it was a great triumph of individual self-control. These differences were continually smoothed over by friendly good-humoured jesting.[44]

---

41 Coventry Cathedral, 1965, p. 2.
42 Williams, 1965, p. 2.
43 Becker, no date, p. 3.
44 Becker, no date, p. 13.

The male volunteers had to get up at 5.30am, in order to walk the mile or more from their quarters in the tower of the Drei-Königs-Kirche (Church of the Three Kings) to the Diakonissenkrankenhaus, where breakfast was served for everyone at 6.00am. After their work was done, the volunteers organized their free time together, held daily prayers (the intercessions were translated by an interpreter on each occasion) and full-length services. The Coventry Litany of Reconciliation was recited together every Friday on the stroke of noon, with everyone standing in a circle on the work-site. A report in the *Coventry Evening Telegraph* in 1965 also noted that, after they had walked back to the Drei-Königs-Kirche in the evenings, the men also had to climb up seventy-five steps before they could drop gratefully onto their beds in the church tower.[45] Thanks to special visas granting them free right of passage in all territory of the German Democratic Republic (GDR), the British were able to take up invitations at the weekends from German families in all parts of the country, or go sightseeing in Weimar and elsewhere.

Provost Williams visited Dresden again at the end of the work-programme. On 9 September 1965, he held an evening service in the chapel of the Diakonissenkrankenhaus, together with Pastor von Brück, who held administrative office in the Lutheran Church of Saxony. In his speech of thanks, the German pastor focused upon the fifth request in the Lord's Prayer, which is such a central motif for Coventry: 'Our prayers for forgiveness would be sheer hypocrisy, if we could not bring ourselves to stretch out our hand to our brother and say: brother, sister, forgive! We say it now, at this very moment, to the British, and we are certain that the British will also say the same to us in return.'[46] As a final gesture, Williams handed the Rector of the hospital a Cross of Nails, which the Rector fastened to the lectern of the chapel. In Williams' speech, another facet of the Cross of Nails became evident. The Provost spoke of the two-fold symbolic significance of the Cross of Nails, in directing thoughts back to the war and the destruction. Hope itself would be crucified, on a daily basis, wherever people, families or states were divided. 'In receiving this Cross,' said Williams, 'you join with us in the commitment, that we will never allow divisions to grow up between us, that we will work and pray that divisions between mankind may be abolished.' Thus the Cross of Nails also points to the future, reminding Christians that they are able to serve in practical ways, all around the world; and the reconstruction camp for the Diakonissenkrankenhaus hospital was just such a practical service of

---

45 *Coventry Evening Telegraph*, 1965, p. 9. Details also in Gröpler, 1994, pp. 136–42.
46 Quoted from *Der Sonntag*, 1965.

reconciliation.[47] Two years later, on 3 September 1967, the first rebuilt section of the Diakonissenkrankenhaus was officially opened amid celebrations, and once again Provost Williams was present, to preach an inaugural sermon on this occasion.

I have spoken of Dresden in this manner many times in the course of my work with the Community of the Cross of Nails. And yet, the true facts of the matter are far more complex and complicated, as Merrilyn Thomas makes clear in her recent book *Communing with the Enemy*. Using data from Stasi archives and other sources, together with material from interviews, the author shows that, behind this reconciliation project which changed the lives of many of its participants, there were other quite different political currents and motivations at work. On both sides of the Iron Curtain, religion was also used during the Cold War as an instrument of psychological warfare. Thus Walter Ulbricht hoped that via this project, the fundamental opposition of many of Germany's Christian groups (such as that under the bishop of Saxony, Gottfried Noth) would be alleviated. 'Overt oppressive measures against Noth would have risked widening the gulf between the regime and its Christian citizens. A less blunt instrument was necessary. The Coventry–Dresden project presented Ulbricht with just such an instrument.'[48] For the implementation of the hoped-for project required discussion and co-operation between the Church and the East German authorities, and thus strengthened the government regime. Aktion Sühnezeichen, on the other hand, the project's German partner, was part of the West's advance guard in its rapprochement with the East (according to Thomas), used by Berlin's ruling mayor of the day, Willy Brandt, to prepare the way for his subsequent Eastern European policy ('Ostpolitik'). Moreover, on the British side there were Christians who were in favour of a Christian/Marxist dialogue in order to reduce the tensions of the Cold War – notably Paul Oestreicher, who at this time was active on behalf of the British Council of Churches and the BBC, and would later become the leader of Coventry Cathedral's *International Centre of Reconciliation*. Provost Williams too, and Martin Turner who led the Dresden group, were also open to such an initiative. And finally the British government, which had no official contact with the GDR and did not recognize it (as a consequence of the Hallstein Doctrine (1955–70)), was interested in unofficial channels of information, and hoped that their sanctioning of projects such as that between Coventry

---

47 Quoted from *Der Sonntag*, 1965.
48 Thomas, 2005, p. 154.

and Dresden would lead to orderly and peaceful change in the country, according to the author of *Communing with the Enemy*.[49]

Even though one sometimes gets the impression when reading Merrilyn Thomas's book that she is rather too ready to see conspiracies everywhere, her investigation contributes significantly to illustrating the complexity of the undertaking. There is certainly no disputing the fact that the work camp in Dresden did much for reconciliation and rapprochement between British and Germans. Interest from the media brought these German/British encounters to the attention of the general public. And in addition, the cumulative influence of those who took part should not be underestimated; right up to the present day they are still talking about their experiences, moving the mission of reconciliation forward, as for example Sister Edith Haufe. Sister Edith has been for many years the point of contact for the Community of the Cross of Nails in the Diakonissenkrankenhaus in Dresden, and is always ready to bear witness to the 'Spirit of Coventry', as she calls it, to folk in congregations and communities, institutions, convents, adult education centres or other forums. Looking back, she recalls:

The news of the rebuilding of the Diakonissenkrankenhaus was not received with universal acclaim, either in Great Britain or in what at that time was the German Federal Republic (BRD). By that time, the East/West conflict had become deeply engraved in many hearts. It was all the more hopeful, then, to see the young British folk who were sent out to Dresden in March 1965 ... It is good that Christ has reconciled us with the Father. That is unique, and unrepeatable – it is valid for all times and all places; and because it is so, therefore reconciliation is possible, between men and between nations. Moreover, it is a process in which we will always be learners – and that is why the process of reconciliation will continue. Even after Coventry's work

---

49 If one follows the memoirs of Williams, all such political considerations were far from his mind: 'I always insisted on holding Coventry Cathedral aloof from partisan politics or ideologies, either local or national or international. The Cathedral has, I believe, always had influence when it has remained faithful to its single, simple vocation to work for the healing of division through bringing both sides of the conflict to stand before the judgement of God's forgiveness. I have consistently believed that the Cathedral will have no influence in the name of Jesus Christ if it takes political sides. It sounds heroic to "take a stand", but it inevitably implies immobility and inflexibility. The image of both sides to the conflict 'joining hands' in a patient and positive dialogue and 'taking a stand' together before the Shrine of Reconciliation in the Ruins of Coventry Cathedral, is the Christian way' (Williams, c.1989, p. 43). Thomas, on the other hand, suggests that Williams definitely had contacts in the British Foreign Office, and also implies that Williams' memoirs contain inaccuracies because they were written a long time after the events of 1965 (Thomas, 2005, p. 221f).

of reconciliation, we have not reached the end-point. I am happy that we have a lasting link with Coventry Cathedral, and that many friends from those days still visit us today, and we sometimes visit them too.[50]

However, based on the account by Merrilyn Thomas, it is important to stress the point that there were also political interests in the background supporting the project, and that some of these were in direct opposition to the central theme of reconciliation. The sincere efforts for reconciliation with former wartime enemies, and the imposition of political interests by those who renewed hostilities during the Cold War, are inseparably interwoven. It is evident that, even in the midst of reconciliation work, new guilt and entanglement may arise – and this is an idea that will be examined more closely in the third section of this book.[51]

---

50 Haufe, 2007.
51 See Chapter 16, pp. 173–8.

5

The beginnings of the Community of the Cross of Nails

Provost Williams ended the prologue to his unpublished memoirs with the following words: 'Richard Howard, in the heat of the fire which had destroyed his church, had seen a vision, and had set up symbols to convey it. My work was, with my colleagues, to give that vision a programme.'[52] The vision and the symbol were already in place: the *symbol* of the Cross of Nails was given to places where there was a wish to remain in close contact with Coventry and to join in building the vision of reconciliation across the trenches of old enmities. The first Cross of Nails to be presented in this sense was that handed over by Provost Howard in Kiel; others followed, presented in other places, which soon came to be known as Cross of Nails 'centres'.

It is time now to turn our attention to the *programme*, i.e. the creation of the Community of the Cross of Nails. Here too, Williams' memoirs provide useful references. On the occasion of his first visit to Germany in 1959, which we have already mentioned, Williams remarked on the award of a Cross of Nails to the parish of Neu Tempelhof:

> 'That was not only the first Cross of Nails to be presented to Berlin, but it was the first to go anywhere in the programme of creating a network of Christian centres held together by a common determination to "heal the wounds of history", a programme which a few years later led to the establishing of the Community of the Cross of Nails.' [53]

At first the Community of the Cross of Nails recruited individuals who had shown an interest, people who had taken the decision to adopt the rules of Coventry's so-called *Common Discipline* themselves. About two hundred people in the cathedral congregation were following

---

52 Williams, c.1989, p. 3.
53 Williams, c.1989, p. 37.

these rules, along with many people in the USA. The rules are based on Benedictine principles. Provost Williams had always been fascinated by the Benedictine way of life; and when he took up his position in Coventry he was delighted to learn that the original medieval cathedral of Coventry had been a Benedictine foundation. Another significant stimulus to Coventry to develop a set of 'guidelines for living' came as a result of close contact with the German Benedictine abbey of Otto-beuren. The first draft versions of the rules for living date back to the mid-1960s, and they were subsequently realized in various ways. In no case does the *Common Discipline* impose additional burdens on the members of the Community of the Cross of Nails; rather, it is a simple set of instructions for putting Christian values into a well-balanced and fruitful relationship. It rests upon five pillars: 1) Silence, 2) Study, 3) Family life, 4) Community, and 5) Service.[54]

In a little book published in 1982, Williams described these five principles of the rules for living: the regular '*being still* before God' allows the individual to find the inner harmony that enables unity with God and with others. Only by regular *study* (of the Bible) is right and proper judgement possible, which leads to intellectual integrity instead of prejudice. The *family* into which we were born is the first place in which we develop a sense of community; and since all the tensions and conflicts of the world can be reflected within a family, so here too must reconciliation and forgiveness be practised. Moreover, we are called upon to practice the Christian virtues in the network of relationships that we choose for ourselves. The Church, in particular, should be a model of a reconciled *community* in a divided world. And finally, we must turn outward to face the world and work for reconciliation in it, and by *serving* in this way, fulfil the task that was envisioned for the Church.[55]

In time, the term 'Community of the Cross of Nails' came to be applied to the alliance of all those centres that felt themselves to be bound together by the Coventry Cathedral's Cross of Nails, its vision of reconciliation and its rules for living. Soon the network extended over every continent. From the foregoing text, it is evident that the time would come when a provost would no longer be able to handle the cathedral's work of reconciliation without assistance. And so from 1974 onward, the cathedral's international work was directed by one of the cathedral's resident canons; by Canon Kenyon Wright (1974–81) as the first Director of the *International Centre for Reconciliation* (ICR), by his successor Canon Peter Berry (1981–86), then of course by a

---

54 For more details, see Williams, c.1989, p. 95f.
55 See Williams, 1982, pp. 3–12.

priest very well known in Germany, Canon Paul Oestreicher (1986–98). After him came Canon Andrew White (1998–2004), then Canon Justin Welby (2002–06, initially working together in tandem with Andrew White), and Martin Hayward as managing director (2006–08). Finally, since September 2008 David Porter serves as Canon Director of Reconciliation. Each of these people brought their own very special gifts and previous experiences. Provost Bill Williams focused particularly upon the USA, whilst at the same time Kenyon Wright had a special interest in India due to his own personal background. Under Paul Oestreicher the focus extended to Eastern Europe and South Africa; and Andrew White brought with him to Coventry a profound knowledge of the Near East, so that the focus extended yet again. Justin Welby intensified the work in Nigeria. Finally, David Porter can draw on his experience as former director of the Centre for Contemporary Christianity in Ireland. He was also an appointed member of the Northern Ireland Civic Forum.

In addition to the reconciliation projects that come directly managed by Coventry and which are the responsibility of the respective Director of the ICR and his team,[56] the ICR also looks after the needs of the worldwide Community of the Cross of Nails and its numerous centres. In recent years both of these duties – Coventry's own reconciliation work and its service on behalf of the Community of the Cross of Nails – have often been carried out with very variable intensity and resources, due not least to a very insecure financial position. Thus, for example, Canon Berry did his work without any assured income. At times the Reconciliation Centre consisted of no more than the appointed cathedral canon and one or two volunteer workers. At other times, however, the ICR had up to twelve people on its paid staff.

Over the years, the Community of the Cross of Nails has also included national levels with their own separate structures. First of all, a national parent organization was created in the USA; individual members and Cross of Nails Centres may enter the Community of the Cross of Nails in the USA.[57] A similar development in Germany took substantially longer – only with the collapse of the Wall and Germany's reunification did it become possible in February 1991 for representatives of German Cross of Nails Centres from the old and the new federal states to meet in a joint conference. More than sixty people from about twenty East- and West-German church parishes, Evangelical academies and

---

56 For more details of the work of the ICR, see Chapter 14, pp. 150–65.

57 This has now been extended to become the Community of the Cross of Nails in Northern America. A current snapshot of this national alliance is given in their current handbook: 'Community of the Cross of Nails in Northern America 2006'.

diaconal institutions to whom a Cross of Nails had been presented, came together in the deaconesses' house in Dresden. Out of this meeting, one year later, emerged the German Community of the Cross of Nails, as a registered society with a steering committee (*Leitungskreis*) and board (*Vorstand*) as its governing bodies.

The steering committee drew up its short-term aims for Cross of Nails work in Germany:

1. To explore the possibilities for collaboration between all of the twenty-two Cross of Nails Centres in Germany, i.e. exchange experiences on each centre's own individual work, and motivate towards common projects, but without in any way limiting each centre's independent work on reconciliation projects.
2. We want to walk together on the road to just peace, looking upon the Cross of Nails as a commitment to behave to one another, despite our divided past and the tensions of our present, just as plain ordinary Germans in the spirit of truthfulness and reconciliation.
3. As a further target, we have resolved to intensify the work for reconciliation between East and West Germany, and also between Eastern and Western Europe, and to seek contacts to enable us to recommend additional sites to the Provost of Coventry Cathedral for the foundation of further Cross of Nails Centres.[58]

Lastly, at a meeting in Halle in 1993, the steering committee of the German Community of the Cross of Nails adopted their own form of the rules for living. Key spiritual elements of the German Community's rules included the Reconciliation Prayer and the intercession for one another, together with joint work for reconciliation in theatres of conflict all around the world. It is worthwhile to quote two of these rules for living, for they give a good insight into the motivations, the hopes and the goals of the Community of the Cross of Nails. Under the heading 'Community of the Reconciled' is written:

We long for a community in which trust is tangible and friendship can grow. Isolation and loneliness are on the increase in our society, and this affects families, married couples, single folk and children alike. We want to overcome feelings of alienation, bear with tension and conflict, share our joy and our grief, and learn to talk about our own weaknesses and our own strengths. As members of the Community of the Cross of Nails, we will therefore:

58 Leitungskreis der Deutschen Nagelkreuzgemeinschaft, 1991.

- foster relationships and links
- work together with existing Christian communities, congregations and other organizations ...

Our Community will work for consolidation in a united Germany. We will play our part in allowing a culture of hospitality to develop among us. We will share in the beliefs and lives of others and work to ensure that enemies do not remain enemies. We feel ourselves to be a part of the worldwide Community of the Cross of Nails, which offers us the opportunity to experience the Community of the Reconciled outside our own national borders and beyond the bounds of our own spiritual confession. This will enrich our lives. We are grateful for the spiritual and social initiative of ecumenical and international understanding that comes from Coventry. We will try in our own way to embody and continue this initiative. In so doing, we will maintain and preserve our spiritual fellowship with Coventry Cathedral.[59]

Shortly afterwards came the 'Service of Reconciliation':

We want to play our part in abolishing enmity, misunderstanding and alienation between people and races. We are searching for peaceful ways to reach understanding ...

We want to help in overcoming images of hatred, mistrust and envy. Our movement is based on following the path that leads towards good and honest peace. To the best of our ability, we will share in the discussion and creation of a worldwide economic order in which labour, goods and money are fairly apportioned.

We will work to abolish divisions and schisms between Christians.

We will help to resolve disagreement between people of different cultures and religions.

And we will start with our homeland. Our ability is limited; so we will tackle our local situation, where the duty of reconciliation within our territory is appropriate for us and within our capability.[60]

In their policy document, the German Community of the Cross of Nails referred to the rules for living as 'guidance in personal spirituality'. At the same time, it must be said that the *Common Discipline* has not been at the forefront in recent years; especially at Coventry Cathedral it was no longer seen as the focal point for the formation of community, as it

---

59 Leitungskreis, 1993, Article 4.
60 Leitungskreis, 1993, Article 6.

was in the early years. Also, during my time in Coventry, adoption of the *Common Discipline* was not a formal obligation as a precedent to the presentation of a new Cross of Nails. Both Coventry and the German Community of the Cross of Nails leave it to the discretion of the individual centre to decide what role the rules for living will play in the life of that centre. This implies that, at the present time, it is merely an option for those who want to commit themselves to the ideals of Coventry Cathedral.

Suggestions for further reading

Two of the early centres have already been described in Chapter 4. Gröpler, 1994, pp. 91–112 describes some other centres from the early years.

PART TWO

The Worldwide Community of the Cross of Nails

Presenting person:
Receive this Cross of Nails, brought to you with the love and the prayers of your brothers and sisters from the ruined sanctuary of our Cathedral Church of St Michael.

Cherish this Cross, as a token of the merciful forgiveness of God, declared to us in the Passion of our Saviour Jesus Christ.

Watch about this Cross, in prayer for one another and for us, for all in this Diocese of Coventry and for those involved in reconciliation work at our Cross of Nails Centres around the world, who love and serve the Lord Jesus.

Everyone:
Almighty God, grant that we walking in the way of the Cross may find it none other than the way of life and of peace.

Presenting person:
Eternal God, you have come among us in Christ to reconcile the world to yourself, and have entrusted us with the ministry of reconciliation.

Strengthen all who work for the healing of conflict and pain amongst your human family.

Bless all those in many places who, inspired by the Cross of Nails, bear witness to the grace and truth of your crucified and risen Son, our Saviour Jesus Christ.

Amen.

(Extract from the liturgy for the presentation of a Cross of Nails)

6

The Community of the
Cross of Nails today

The words on the preceding page are those used when a Cross of Nails is presented and a new centre is welcomed into the Community of the Cross of Nails. But who is eligible for such a cross? What pre-conditions must be satisfied, and what is expected of a Centre of the Cross of Nails?

In the early years following the destruction of the cathedral, the Cross of Nails was presented without any specific overall concept and with no consistent set of criteria. And even later on, the procedure for accepting a new centre into the Community of the Cross of Nails was subject to variation. Sometimes there were explicit criteria for the presentation of the symbol of reconciliation from Coventry, at other times the criteria were somewhat more implicit. During the years when I was working in Coventry, the rules for the process of acceptance were as follows: The Cross of Nails may be presented to a church community or other institution which – following the example of Coventry – campaigns for reconciliation and expresses the wish to become part of the worldwide Community of the Cross of Nails. When accepted into the Community of the Cross of Nails, the new centre pledges to stay in close contact with Coventry and with the existing centres in their own country, and to make an appropriate place for the Litany of Reconciliation within their spiritual life.[61]

The German Community of the Cross of Nails, which checks any new application from within Germany before forwarding it to Coventry, also has a similar procedure. An award can be made if:

- it is a group of people/individuals and/or a community/group that is prepared to 'honour' the Cross, in the words of the presentation ceremony, and to serve the cause of worldwide reconciliation that is inherent in this,

---

61 See International Centre for Reconciliation, 2003.

- the activities of the community/group, both in the past and in the present, clearly support action for reconciliation 'in the spirit of Coventry',
- they are prepared to practise spiritual solidarity, in mutual intercession with each other, and to make a place in the spiritual life of this community/group for the Coventry Litany of Reconciliation.[62]

Today there are about one hundred and sixty Centres of the Community of the Cross of Nails around the world. This network includes church communities, schools, diaconal establishments, non-governmental organizations (NGOs), and also a young offenders' penal institution. At the same time it is a community of different denominations, and one that spans the whole world. Anglicans, Roman Catholics, Lutherans, Baptists, all are members of the same community; and there are Crosses of Nails in Europe, North America, Cuba, Burundi, Hong Kong, India and Australia, to name just a few of the centres.

It is not easy to estimate the exact size of the Community of the Cross of Nails at any given time, for changes in personnel or other reasons may cause a centre to lose contact with the Community or change the focus of its work. Thus, some centres are very active whilst the members of other centres may not be involved in any specific action at a given moment, though they continue to be on the prayer-lists of the Community in the hope that some day they will find new life and new purpose.

The following pages will focus in more detail on some of these Cross of Nails Centres. This can be no more than a few examples – centres from very different regions of the world and with very varied kinds of reconciliation work – to give an impression of the diversity within the Community of the Cross of Nails. It creates a kaleidoscope of many coloured pieces, showing clearly that reconciliation today takes many and varied forms. Each centre is doing its best, in its own little corner of the world and with such materials as it has at hand, 'to make a kinder, simpler – a more Christ-Child-like sort of world', to quote Dick Howard once again.[63] We will see that this really can happen in very many different ways – from large funded projects requiring significant manpower and financial resources, to local initiatives which, though small, make no less valuable a contribution to healing and reconciliation in the world.

---

62 Leitungskreis, 2003, Article 1.2.4.
63 See Chapter 1, p. 6.

Out of all the centres that found a place in my heart during my time in Coventry, and whose staff and work I came to know at first hand, I have tried to make a selection that is as representative as possible. Of course, there are many other centres whose work is equally deserving to be included, and I hope they will forgive me limiting myself to just fifteen examples.

I should add one further note about my methodology: I invited representatives from all the centres described in the following pages to send me information about their work – and I also asked them to describe their personal relationship with the Coventry Cross of Nails and their own experiences in their work for reconciliation. Their first-hand reports appear time and again in the following text – and thus, in addition to my own 'external' viewpoint, you will also have the views of those who are directly responsible in the centres. In order to identify these 'internal insights' clearly to the reader, such passages are set in shaded boxes to distinguish them from the main text.[64]

---

64 In some cases, the people I asked for help referred me to contributions already published in books, newsletters etc., in which they had recorded their own experiences or thoughts. Quotations from these documents that were sent to me are set in the same way as those that were written specifically for this book.

6.1 Wurzburg Cross of Nails Ecumenical Initiative

I am the enemy you killed, my friend.
I knew you in this dark; for so you frowned
yesterday, through me as you jabbed and killed.
I parried;
but my hands were loath and cold.
Let us sleep now …

On 16 March 2005, these disturbing words rang out from the gallery of Wurzburg's crowded Kiliansdom (Cathedral of St Kilian). It was a performance of Benjamin Britten's War Requiem, in the presence of the Bishop of Coventry, and including the choirboys of Coventry Cathedral; that same work had been heard for the first time on 25 May 1962, as the composition commissioned to mark the rededication of Coventry Cathedral, in which the composer had linked the traditional text of the requiem mass with verses by the poet Wilfred Owen, who was himself killed in the First World War. In what is probably his best known poem 'Strange Meeting', a German and a British soldier come face to face; however, these wartime foes no longer feel any hatred for each other. 'Strange friend, here is no cause to mourn' begins the tenor in the above dialogue – and the bass ends it with the words 'Let us sleep now'. These one-time enemies have become friends, they have made peace. Finally the chorus of boys' voices begins to sing the *Requiem aeternam*: 'Grant them eternal rest, O Lord, and may light perpetual shine upon them'.

On 16 March Wurzburg was destroyed,[65] and the date is graven deep in the collective memory of the residents of Wurzburg. At the end of the concert to mark the sixtieth anniversary of the attack, the audience spread out onto the Domstraße, the road leading from the cathedral, to commemorate the flaming inferno of 1945, along with a total of seventeen thousand of Wurzburg's inhabitants. In keeping with the annual custom, at 9.20pm all the bells in the town pealed out together.

---

65 At 9.25pm, the centre of the town was silhouetted in green by 2000 light-bomb blind-markers; they were followed by flares, which provided the required brightness. The town was exposed in the glare of a total of 20,000 coloured lights. Within less than twenty minutes, 90% of Wurzburg lay in ruins; 256 high-explosive bombs and 397,650 firebombs had been dropped. The logbook of 5th Bomber Group, which carried out the raid, comments tersely: 'good fires'. Five thousand of the town's 107,000 inhabitants died in that attack, which created an estimated 2.25 million cubic metres of rubble, corresponding to a cube covering the same surface area as the city's Residenz palace but five times as high. And this inferno enveloped the Lower Franconian metropolis within mere weeks of the end of the war – American forces were already at the edge of the town, and twenty days later it was conquered. See Friedrich, 2002, pp. 312–16; and Oppelt, 1947, pp. 9–77.

'Remembrance and commemoration' – this is also the basic raison d'être of the Wurzburg Cross of Nails Ecumenical Initiative, at whose invitation the Bishop of Coventry and the Cathedral Choirboys were in Wurzburg on March 16 2005. However, the movement also looks to the future – Wurzburg's 'Cross of Nails group' has taken on the task of using what happened in the past to develop lessons for the future. Thus the theme of the Wurzburg Centre is 'preserve the memory, and practise reconciliation'. However, it took a long time before it was possible to incorporate this motto into the preamble of the constitution of the Wurzburg Cross of Nails Ecumenical Initiative and the initiative was presented with a Cross of Nails. Exemplary for many other centres, Wurzburg shows that it takes people with vision, and most of all people who are prepared to be patient, people who are deeply affected either by meeting with Coventry or by some other Cross of Nails Centre, and who go on tirelessly to seek out partners who can help them to create a reconciliation initiative 'in the spirit of Coventry'. Johanna Falk, one of the co-founders of the Wurzburg Centre, shares her memories:[66]

'My work for the Cross of Nails began in 1996, when our BRÜCKE Editorial Circle [a local ecumenical newsletter] paid a visit to England and met Paul Oestreicher. Unfortunately I was not able to go along on the trip. However, after the group came back home they organized an information evening in the Ecumenical Centre, and it made a big impression on me.

In 1997 I took part in the Ecumenical Study Course in Josefstal on the Schliersee, Germany's southernmost Cross of Nails Centre. There were over fifty of us, Christians from all over Europe, and we were preparing for the Second European Ecumenical Assembly in Graz, on the theme "Reconciliation – a gift from God and a source of new life". At that same time, Josefstal was celebrating its thirtieth anniversary as a Cross of Nails Centre, with a festival service, to which Paul Oestreicher sent his greetings, and at which the sermon was preached by Karl-Anton Hagedorn, who was at that time president of the German Cross of Nails Centres. During this time, when we were working all across Europe on the theme of Reconciliation, the desire grew in me to carry this theme back home with me to Wurzburg. I used this opportunity to learn as much as I could about the

66 In Part Two, passages that contain the personal thoughts of representatives of the Cross of Nails Centres are visually distinguished from the rest of the text with a tinted background.

Cross of Nails .... In 2000, I visited the first worldwide conference of Centres of the Cross of Nails in Coventry, and came to know many wonderful people who are working internationally "in the spirit of Coventry".'[67]

At long last, after many stages of preparation, a group was found who were 'prepared to pray together and to work together,'[68] and this resulted in the foundation of the association known as the 'Ecumenical Initiative for Peace and Reconciliation'. A grass roots movement had been created, with considerable self-motivation, and close contacts with church and civic institutions. And so, on 16 March 2001, the town and the churches of Wurzburg were accepted into the worldwide Community of the Cross of Nails. Canon Andrew White brought with him two Crosses of Nails. He presented one of these to the town of Wurzburg, which now hangs in the '16 March Memorial Room' in the historic 'Grafeneckart' of the town hall. The other cross was presented to the Ecumenical Cross of Nails Initiative; at the time, it was the first Cross of Nails in the world with no permanent abode, and it is passed on every year from one parish or ecumenical establishment in Wurzburg to another. Pastor Claus Deininger, like Johanna Falk part of the project since its very early days, speaks of the beginnings of the Wurzburg Cross of Nails Centre as 'Kairos' – a decisive and sublime moment in which God's actions and human desires coincide:

'Looking back in retrospect, I feel that my learning about the reconciliation work of the Cross of Nails, when St Sebald's in Nuremberg became a Cross of Nails Centre, and my meeting with Johanna Falk and Canon Andrew White, are for me a part of the "Kairos" predestined by God. The impulse that we received in that first meeting in September 1999 fuelled and directed the entire process of establishing the Cross of Nails work in Wurzburg. It is quite clear to me that our own efforts, our planning and our skills, were insufficient on their own to succeed in making the Wurzburg Initiative for Peace and Reconciliation a going concern. It was rather that this was the perfect moment in time – God's "Kairos", which brought together the right people at the right time and in the right

67 Falk, 2007.
68 Falk, 2007.

place; and this spirit of animation, which was at first no more than a feeling within us, quickly grew to become an external motivating force, which led on to a visible and tangible form: the Wurzburg Ecumenical Cross of Nails Centre.'[69]

Over the years, this Cross of Nails Centre has striven to give a new dimension to the practice of commemorating the anniversary of 16 March. Every year on this day the centre is responsible for organizing the 'Road to Reconciliation'. In keeping with its motto 'preserve the memory, and practise reconciliation', the Cross of Nails Centre seeks today to promote reconciliation and understanding out of remembrance, and to focus people's minds on projects that relate to this theme. To quote Claus Deininger once again:

'Since the first "Road to Reconciliation" in 2001, the focus of our remembrance has moved onward, to the extent that Reconciliation is the important consideration today, and we practise it. With each passing year, the so-called "wandering" Cross of Nails is handed on to a new parish or institution which, in its work, is dedicating itself in some particular way to the idea of reconciliation. In this way, many people come to partake of the special spirit that emanates from the Cross of Nails. Every year there is a renewed effort to fashion the present and shape the future peacefully in the spirit of reconciliation. We aim to use the 'wandering' Cross of Nails to find ways of making contact with many groups of people from very different backgrounds, and with different beliefs and religions. Such people are often cut off from each other by gulfs of ignorance and intolerance. It makes me happy to see how these people are able to come together in the sign of the Cross of Nails, the symbol of reconciliation, meet with each other and respect each other – and thus fulfil the motto "preserve the memory, and practise reconciliation" in a lively and healing spirit. To me, that is the special spiritual gift of the Wurzburg Ecumenical Cross of Nails Centre: the Kairos moves on – yet it always remains tangibly there.'[70]

69 Deininger, 2007.
70 Deininger, 2007.

How is the symbol of the Cross of Nails thought of in real terms? Wurzburg's 'wandering' Cross of Nails bids farewell to its former resting-place in an initial service on the eve of 16 March; then on the following day it takes part in the official act of remembrance of the town of Wurzburg at the mass grave at the public cemetery and moves on through Wurzburg to its new home. A new community or institution takes it into their care, to live with it as a symbol of reconciliation for another year.

The 'Road to Reconciliation', 16 March 2005.

I have twice had the opportunity to accompany the Cross on the 'Road to Reconciliation'. In 2004, during this journey of pilgrimage, Wurzburg children who had been on schools exchange visits spoke about their schools and told of their experiences and impressions, of France and Poland and other countries. In the following year, the Cross of Nails made one of its en-route pauses in the forecourt of the secondary school on the Heuchelhof – in a part of Wurzburg that is home to people from more than fifty different nations. The children of that school had cut sheets of white paper into the shape of peace-doves, and had stuck all their doves to the windows to form the word 'Peace'. In a song about peace composed especially for that day, they reminded us: 'We should recall that violence destroys on every hand; // if we just listen to each other, we shall understand. // It's up to us to reconcile, and heal our every breach; // so let us strive for blessed peace, and keep it in our reach.' And finally, the refrain rang out in German, Russian and English: 'There will be no more war! We have a symbol to remind us of peace – it is the Cross of Nails!'

Since its ceremonial presentation, the Cross of Nails has journeyed to and fro across Wurzburg: from the Lutheran church of St Stephan (2001) to the Roman Catholic church of Stift Haug (2002), on to the Wurzburg Penal Institute (2003), and from there to the Lutheran parish of St Johannis (2004), then to the Wurzburg-Heuchelhof Centre for the Physically Handicapped (2005), onward to be shared by the neighbouring Catholic and Lutheran parishes of St Josef and Thomaskirche in the Grombühl district of Wurzburg (2006), and finally (at the time when this edition first went to press in 2007) to the Christopherus Association, a joint project of the Lutheran and Roman Catholic charities 'Diakonie' and 'Caritas'.

By way of illustration, we will look more closely at a few of these 'stations' in which the Cross has spent one of its years:

- St Stephan's marked its involvement with the Cross of Nails by creating a 'reconciliation memorial' – an ever-changing display in the space in front of the church. The sculptor Thomas Reuter designed a four-part Road to Reconciliation in stone, with a ramp constructed of limestone blocks and rising up to a peak. The stones – which were originally intended for use in Nazi buildings in Nuremberg – now form a symbol against intolerance and contempt for mankind, war and violence. During the years, memorial plaques were added, set into the ground: at the time when the German edition of this book went to press, they included inscriptions in Arabic, Russian, English, German, Swahili, Japanese, Romany (the language of the Romany people), and also Aramaic. These plaques commemorate sufferings due to acts of injustice, and it is hoped that they will help to build bridges in the future.
- Since the Cross of Nails spent its year at the Wurzburg Penal Institution, representatives of the Cross of Nails Centre have provided support to enable children to visit their father or mother in custody, in the house for day-release prisoners, and self-examination days for male and female prisoners.
- Passing on the Coventry Cross to the Centre for the Physically Handicapped led to a year-long focus on the fact that reconciliation also shows how society deals with people who do not correspond to the 'norm'.

The Wurzburg Cross of Nails Initiative also adopted the Coventry tradition of praying the Litany of Reconciliation every Friday – and this gave rise to a third Cross of Nails in Wurzburg, which is kept in the Marienkapelle in the market square. The Cross of Nails Initiative invites all and sundry to come into this church on any Friday at 1.00pm to pray the Litany of Reconciliation. Inmates of the penal institution, representatives of the city, clergy, and representatives of ecumenical institutions, take turns to prepare prayers for peace according to a set liturgy, which includes at its heart the Coventry Litany of Reconciliation. Following consultation with Coventry, a further Cross was produced in the metalworking shop of Wurzburg Penal Institution for this weekly prayer, as a faithful replica of the other two. The duplicate is such a good copy that, for several years now, the Penal Institution has served an important but almost unknown role within the worldwide Community of the Cross of Nails: namely, at the present time, the prison's metalwork shop produces all the Crosses of Nails that are then sent out into the world from Coventry.

7

Germany

There are more Crosses of Nails in Germany than in any other country in the world. The total has increased steadily since the first one was presented to the St Nikolai in Kiel in 1947; and even today, more than sixty years after the end of the war, new centres are still being received into the German Community of the Cross of Nails every year. The majority of them have a similar history of suffering to that of Coventry, for the bombing raids of the Second World War are a part of the collective memory of all these communities. Other centres, on the other hand, bring quite different experiences into the German Community of the Cross of Nails. In total there are more than fifty centres at the time of writing (2008), as summarized in the following list:[71]

Berlin:		
	1. Martin-Luther-Gedächtniskirche (Memorial Church), Mariendorf	since 1962
	2. Kirche zu den vier Evangelisten (Church of the Four Evangelists), Pankow	since 1962
	3. Aktion Sühnezeichen (Action Reconciliation Service for Peace)	since 1962
	4. Kaiser-Wilhelm-Gedächtniskirche (Memorial Church)	since 1988
	5. Jugendbildungsstätte (Youth Education Centre) 'Haus Kreisau'	since 1993
	6. Versöhnungskapelle (Reconciliation Chapel), Bernauer Straße	since 1999

---

71 In addition to these Cross of Nails Centres, there are also a few Cross of Nails 'sites'. These sites have a Cross of Nails, but they have never had any group of people who have undertaken reconciliation work in the 'spirit of Coventry'. One such site is the Dom (cathedral) in Berlin, whose Cross of Nails was awarded in 1990 to the president of the Federal Republic by Queen Elizabeth the Queen Mother; another is the Konrad-Adenauer-House-Foundation, whose Cross was presented to Federal Chancellor Adenauer; other sites include the History of Technology Museum in Peenemünde, St George's Anglican Church in Berlin and the University of Kiel.

Berlin (cont.)	7. Evang. Seelsorge in der Bundeswehr in den neuen Bundesländern (Chaplaincy in the Armed Forces of the new Federal States)	since 1999
	8. St Marienkirche, Berlin-Mitte	since 2005
Cottbus	9. Schlosskirche (Palace Chapel), Cottbus	since 1984
Darmstadt	10. Evangelische Stadtkirchengemeinde (city parish)	since 1976
Dresden	11. Evangelisch-Lutherische Diakonissenanstalt (Deaconesses' Institute)	since 1965
	12. Kreuzkirche (Church of the Cross)	since 1985
	13. Frauenkirche Foundation	since 2005
	14. Maria am Wasser (Mary upon the Water), Dresden-Hosterwitz-Pillnitz	since 2006
Erfurt	15. Evangelisches Augustinerkloster (Augustinian monastery)	since 2008
Essen	16. Evangelische Kreuzkirche (Church of the Cross)	since 2007
Günzburg	17. Freunde der Hofkirche e.V. (Friends of the Chapel Royal)	since 2007
Halle/Saale	18. Heilig-Kreuz-Kirche (Holy Cross Church)	since 1988
	19. Hospice at St Elizabeth Hospital	since 1988
	20. Jugendwerkstatt (Youth Workshop) 'Bauhof' in the Francke Foundation	since 2005
Hamburg	21. St Katharinen	since 1962
	22. Mahnmahl (Memorial) St Nikolai	since 1993
Heilsbronn	23. Kilianskirche	since 2008
Josefstal	24. Studienzentrum für evangelische Jugendarbeit (study centre for youth work)	since 1967
Karlsruhe	25. Katholisches Dekanat (Catholic Deanery) Karlsruhe	since 2007
Kiel	26. St Nikolai	since 1947
Kloster/ Hiddensee	27. Evangelische Inselkirche (Island Church)	since 1999
Kranenburg	28. St Peter und St Paul	since 2003
Lagerlechfeld	29. Versöhnungskirche (Reconciliation Church)	since 1966
Leipzig	30. St Nikolai	since 1995
Lemgo	31. St Nicolai	since 1989
Löwenstein	32. Evangelische Tagungsstätte Löwenstein (Conference Centre)	since 2002
Lübeck	33. St Marien	since 1971
Magdeburg	34. Evangelischer Kirchenkreis (church district) Magdeburg	since 2003

Mahnen-Löhne	35. Evangelische Kirchengemeinde (parish) Mahnen-Löhne	since 2006
Mainz	36. Gossner Haus	since 1971
Mannheim	37. Citykirche (city church) Concordia	since 2006
Meschede	38. Gemeinsames Kirchenzentrum (joint church centre) Meschede	since 1986
Munster	39. Versöhnungskirche (Reconciliation Church), now: Andreaskirche	since 1963
Neuruppin	40. Klosterkirche (Monastery Church)	since 1994
Nuremberg	41. St Sebaldus	since 1999
Nordhelle	42. 'Haus Nordhelle' conference centre	since 1996
Obersulm	43. Evangelisches Paul-Distelbarth-Gymnasium (secondary school)	since 2006
Oeynhausen	44. Evangelische Kirchengemeinde (parish) Bad Oeynhausen-Altstadt	since 2006
Ottobeuren	45. Benediktinerabtei (Benedictine abbey) Ottobeuren	since 1963
Pforzheim	46. Evangelische Kirchengemeinde (parish) Pforzheim-Huchenfeld	since 1992
	47. Evangelische Stadtkirchengemeinde (city parish) Pforzheim	since 2005
Potsdam	48. Stiftung Internationales Versöhnungszentrum Garnisonskirche (Garrison Church)	since 2004
Stralsund	49. St Marien	since 2005
Usedom	50. Nagelkreuzzentrum Usedom	since 2009
Villgst	51. Amt für Jugendarbeit der Evangelischen Kirche von Westfalen (Youth-work Bureau of the Westphalian Evangelical Church)	since 2002
	52. Institut für Kirche und Gesellschaft (Institute for Church and Society)	since 1970
Wurzburg	53. Ökumenische Nagelkreuzinitiative (Cross of Nails Ecumenical Initiative)	since 2001
Wuppertal	54. Vereinigte Evangelische Kirchengemeinde (parish) Gemarke, Wuppertal-Barmen	since 2007

From its foundation in 1991, the German Community of the Cross of Nails attempted to live up to its aim – 'to intensify the work of reconciliation between East and West Germany and also between Eastern and Western Europe and seek for contacts'.[72] Thus, for instance, the society fosters special links with the Lutheran parish in Modra (in the Slovak

---

72 See above, Chapter 5, p. 39.

Republic), the International Youth Meeting Centre of the Krzyzowa Foundation (in Poland) and the Minsk International Education and Conference Centre (in Belarussia). In addition to this joint co-operation work at international level, the individual centres each have their own projects and initiatives at local level.

On the following pages we will now take a closer look at three of the German Cross of Nails Centres.

7.1 Youth Workshop 'Bauhof', Halle

As I was about to present a Cross of Nails to the Youth Workshop 'Bauhof' (Jugendwerkstatt Bauhof), on 9 July 2005, I was startled to observe that there was already one there. In the old barn of the Stichelsdorf estate, now used as an arts centre, in which we had gathered for the service, there stood a Cross of Nails 'enthroned' upon a giant wrought-iron globe – the two objects together bore a strong resemblance to a huge imperial orb. Some years previously Jochen Heyroth, the Bauhof's director at that time, had had the Cross forged in the Bauhof's own smithy. In a similar way to the course of events at Wurzburg, Heyroth had been fascinated by the story of Coventry, which he had encountered during his youth via Paul Oestreicher and the other two Cross of Nails Centres at Halle (Heilig-Kreuz-Kirche and the Hospice at St Elizabeth Hospital). During the service, the 'pirate copy' was replaced by a genuine Cross, which took its place on the altar of the little court chapel, where it now serves to remind the estate's many visitors of the Bauhof's special links with Coventry and the Community of the Cross of Nails.

As a social institution of the Evangelical church district Halle-Saalkreis, the Youth Workshop 'Bauhof' is affiliated to the historic Francke Foundation.[73] In a region where many young people are unemployed, the establishment offers assistance to members of the community who need careers advice or help in meeting job requirements, in the form of projects and training for qualifications to prepare them for employment. The initiative is focused upon young people who, for one reason or another, are no longer in formal education and live part of their lives on the streets, but it also looks after adults with learning difficulties and problems caused by enforced immigration. Here they can have a chance, for example, to obtain secondary-modern school qualifications under the instruction of qualified instructors in woodworking and metalworking. In addition, they have access to workshops that offer further education in trades such as painting, gardening, locksmith's work or bookbinding. On the Stichlesdorf estate a market garden operation has been set up for young people and older job-seekers, where organic crops are grown, and there is also an ecological learning centre catering for children and youth-groups. And finally, the Bauhof also offers intercultural work, to prepare young people for living with others who

---

73 More detailed information is given on the Institution's Internet home page (see 'Jugendwerkstatt Bauhof, 2007', under the heading 'Bereiche unserer Arbeit' [our scope of work]).

come from very different backgrounds. Jochen Heyroth expresses it in these words:

'In addition to our efforts on behalf of those who are victims of society, to help them to regain a sense of purpose in their lives, from the very foundation of our organization we have believed that it is important to ensure that young people of German and foreign extraction come together both in their work and in their free time, so that we deal effectively with feelings of xenophobia.'[74]

'Experience through meeting' is the educational theme of this intercultural work. Youth training projects and travels are just as much a part of the programme as intercultural events and seminars, anti-racist workshops or practical tasks in which Germans and immigrants work alongside each other. The lecture series 'The past is over and done with!' invites participants to deal with the past by such means as discussion with those who were eyewitnesses at the time, and who can talk about the key events of their generation. The young people talked with Paul Oestreicher about his work for reconciliation; with Egon Bahr they discussed the 'Ostverträge' (the political, social and economic agreements that West Germany made with some Eastern bloc countries in the early 1970s), which he helped to negotiate; and with Friedrich Schorlemmer they wanted to hear about his experiences during the re-unification of the former German Democratic Republic. At regular intervals young people also visit places that have become symbols of Nazi war-crimes – as, for example, when a group of youngsters, both from Germany and from other countries, visited Amsterdam together as part of an 'Anne Frank project' on which they were working. Likewise, the project-group 'Strong Girls and Courageous Women' visited the Ravensbrück women's concentration camp in 2005, and the group became closely involved in studying and grappling with the story of the women who were held captive there during the Nazi regime. The impressions, experiences and learning processes of those young girls are captured in a little volume that they put together. Stephanie, one of the girls who took part, summarizes it in this way:

74 Heyroth, 2007.

'The project did not just help me to understand the facts better – it also changed the way in which I looked upon them. As I was writing down my experiences in Ravensbrück I became increasingly aware of how important it is to be sympathetic towards others, and to be brave enough to stand out against those who hate the stranger and against right-wing extremists. I think it's important that we don't just close our eyes, but that we make the effort to deal with what happened in our history, so that we can make a better job of shaping the future.'[75]

Jochen Heyroth also stresses the fact that this intercultural and political educational work at the Youth Workshop 'Bauhof' gives the young people a perspective for the future:

'Whenever we in the Bauhof discussed the Nazi era in our educational sessions with people who had experienced it at first hand, I always tried to say to our young people – who often included some folk who had been brainwashed in the "right wing thinking" – that we should not feel guilt over these terrible happenings, but however that we bear a great responsibility to ensure that such things never happen again.

I remember two specific events that made a lasting impression on me. Every year we include in our educational work someone or something with particular historical significance, and which can help us to learn particular lessons from history, such as Anne Frank or Paul Schneider or the Scholl siblings [who were members of the White Rose, a non-violent resistance movement in Nazi Germany]. This involves eyewitness accounts from people who had direct experience of the person or event, and exhibitions, and also a visit to the relevant location.

Thus, when we were considering the story of the Scholl siblings, we visited Munich and Dachau. On our trip to Munich we had deliberately taken along two young people who had shown themselves to be very right-wing in their attitude – and I was very touched to hear the questions that these two youngsters asked afterwards; their questions were totally different, and it was obvious that the experience had caused them to start to moderate their opinions.

---

75 Jugendwerkstatt Bauhof, 2005, p. 48.

Or here is another example. A teenager who thought of himself as 'right-wing' told me at his graduation party how his attitude towards foreigners had altered. After working for two years in the woodwork school alongside a youth from Mozambique, he had seen good qualities in that young foreigner that he would never have suspected – and they had become friends.

I can only give examples such as these, but I think they demonstrate clearly how important it is to keep on talking about history and learning from it.'[76]

It is obvious that this work is central to the theme of reconciliation. For the former director of the Youth Workshop, reconciliation is an aspect of the coming of God's kingdom. It 'breaks in upon us, here and now, right in our midst, as part of our own individual story here *on Earth*, and it is through us that broken and estranged lives can be healed and can coexist peacefully; and the kingdom of God comes into being wherever the world is made whole'.[77] With this as his background, Jochen Heyroth describes the reconciliation work of the Youth Workshop 'Bauhof' in the following terms:

'Reconciliation, in its many forms, is a key concept in terms of leading broken lives back on to the right path, in the best sense of the phrase. This is ... a beautiful, worthwhile and meaningful way of spending your life. Reconciliation is the conscious aim of the Youth Workshop, and it is achieved between our own people and those from other lands, among the socially disadvantaged and long-term unemployed, between young and old, we support all of these and use the lessons of history to deal with the present and shape the future.'[78]

There are many aspects to the work of reconciliation in Halle: intercultural meeting weeks and history seminars help to integrate foreigners and asylum seekers. Young people who have no chance of employment via the regular job market are helped, via career-preparation projects and education for job-related qualifications, to gain self-confidence,

76 Heyroth, 2007.
77 Heyroth, 2007.
78 Heyroth, 2007.

acquire new skills and open doors to new opportunities. The Youth Workshop 'Bauhof' has taught me that, in a society which tends ever more strongly towards social discrimination, educational training can also be seen as a kind of reconciliation work.

And what does the Cross of Nails mean to the young people? A young Ethiopian named Jonathan helped to make the intercessions at the service in which the Bauhof was accepted into the Community of the Cross of Nails. When asked what the Cross of Nails meant to him personally, he replied:

> 'I lost a hand and a foot in the war in Eritrea. No more war – as far as I am concerned, that is a global imperative.'

7.2 Frauenkirche, Dresden

'Will she get out or not?' This was the question on many people's lips in Dresden on 22 October 1992 when Queen Elizabeth II stopped off in the capital of the federal state of Saxony during a state visit to Germany and the route of her convoy led along the Frauenkirche. Many people had been waiting for just such a gesture. They had hoped that the Queen would get out and lay at wreath at the ruins. However, the royal coach continued on its way without stopping. This was interpreted by some as a refusal to be reconciled – and twelve years later in autumn 2004, when the British Queen visited Dresden again, there was still no official apology for the destruction of the city on 13 February 1945, as some indignant British people had feared, and which many Germans had hoped for.

This story highlights the fact that the Dresden Frauenkirche symbolizes the horror of the bombs that fell on German soil, yet at the same time it is also a place that calls us to reconciliation and peace.

On 13 February 2005, sixty years after the bombing of Dresden, public feelings were running high. In any other year, this day would have been a time for quiet reflection – but not on the sixtieth anniversary. For some months previously, right-wing extremists had been repeatedly referring to the destruction of Dresden as a 'holocaust of bombs' and calling for a 'funeral march' on 13 February; and demonstrations were also planned by the other side of the political spectrum – left-wing separatists wanted to group themselves under the banner 'No tears for the Krauts'.

Both these interpretations of history trivialize and distort the picture – and so, during the run-up to the memorial day, a group of Dresden citizens under the title 'A Framework for Remembrance' had called for a clear signal to be given on 13 February, deploring above all the attempts by right-wing groups to misuse the memorial day for revanchist propaganda and the glorification of acts of violence. They wanted to prevent the victims of Dresden's destruction being misused as accusation of guilt. Those who signed the petition wanted the memory of the victims to focus more upon the events that led up to it – in other words, the Nazi dictatorship and the crimes of the war that Germany started, and the part that the people and the institutions of Dresden played in it. The petition went on to say:

> We are remembering because the events of history constitute a duty and obligation to stand up for peace, against violence and war ...
>
> We want the date 13th February to be the starting point for an ongoing process of learning and commitment for peace and humanity ...
>
> We want to maintain peaceful co-operation with the peoples of our former wartime enemies and to promote even closer partnerships.[79]

Many of the citizens of Dresden responded to this appeal, and gave a clear sign on this day. Fifty thousand of the inhabitants assembled at the Theaterplatz with candles. This sea of lights became the abiding memory of the sixtieth anniversary of the destruction of Dresden, when it appeared in print next day in newspapers all around the world.

And on this historic day the Frauenkirche also gave a clear signal for peace and against violence and war. In a ceremonial service in the crypt, the Frauenkirche Foundation was admitted into the worldwide Community of the Cross of Nails. John Irvine, the Dean of Coventry Cathedral, presented a Cross of Nails to bishop Jochen Bohl. Commenting on 13 February 1945, he said: 'We should not have done it.'

The Cross of Nails stood at first upon the massive black altar-stone of the crypt, since at that time the interior of the Frauenkirche was not open to the public – this did not happen until 30 October 2005. At the beginning of the service of dedication on that day in 2005, the Cross of Nails was brought up into the church in a ceremonial procession, along with other liturgical objects, and was placed on the altar, where it has served since that time as the altar-cross of the Frauenkirche.[80] This altar-cross made from three nails testifies to Dresden's special relationship with Coventry,[81] and affirms the avowed task of the rebuilt Frauenkirche to strive for peace and reconciliation in the world. Jost Hasselhorn, executive secretary of the Frauenkirche Foundation, explains it in these words:

---

79 Printed in: *Amt für Presse- und Öffentlichkeitsarbeit der Landeshauptstadt Dresden*, 2004, p. 54f. (also available via the Internet, see Bringt/Fritz 2004).

80 The Frauenkirche's Cross of Nails was specially made in the metalwork shop of Wurzburg Prison. In order to suit the proportions of the church, a significantly larger altar-cross was required than the normal Crosses of Nails.

81 This special relationship between the two cities, which both act as memorials in their own countries to the destructive fury of the bombing, is also shown by the fact that there are no fewer than four Crosses of Nails in Dresden: in addition to the Frauenkirche and the Diakonissenkrankenhaus (see Chapter 4.2, pp. 29–35), the Kreuzkirche (Church of the Cross) and Maria am Wasser (in Dresden-Hosterwitz-Pillnitz) are also a part of the worldwide network.

'Unlike the Kreuzkirche and the Diakonissenkrankenaus, the Dresden Frauenkirche has always been one of those churches with which the citizens have been closely involved, and one for which they have felt responsible, ever since it was first built in the early 1700s. It has been a central point, with which the citizens could identify. For this reason the Frauenkirche Foundation felt it was very important to send a message of reconciliation from this church, by enrolling the Frauenkirche in the ranks of the reconciliation centres of the Community of the Cross of Nails.'[82]

But would not the ruins – the 'wounded Frauenkirche' so to speak – have served better as a reminder to people of the need for reconciliation? Wouldn't the visible remains of the destruction and the bombs have been much more effective in calling to mind the horror and the fear of war, as well as Germany's guilt? The question of whether the rebuilding would be appropriate, or whether there would be any point in it, was the subject of enormous contention during the 1990s. Those who were in favour of rebuilding argued that it would 'restore the crowning glory, the "stone bell", to one of the most beautiful cityscapes in the heart of Europe, and that without it the rebuilding of Dresden would remain just a patchwork' – and they linked with this argument the hope that the Frauenkirche would become 'a Christian centre for world peace in the new Europe, in which the gospel of peace would be proclaimed in word and deed'[83]. The issue was decided by the symbolic laying of the first stone in 1994 – and Dresden had made the conscious decision to opt for a different solution to that of Coventry. In place of Coventry's 'double solution', embodying the ruins as a monument together with the erection of a new cathedral church, the original 1743 design of George Bähr was reproduced in faithful detail. In accordance with the wishes of the citizens of Dresden, a wound would be healed, using wherever possible the original materials taken from the mountain of rubble – but at the same time, the blackened stones of the building's façade would still act as scars, reminders of the tale of destruction of the Second World War. The altar too, with its great altar frieze, bears the 'wounds of war': the salvaged fragments of the original work were

---

82 Hasselhorn, 2007.

83 Thus ran the 'Call from Dresden' of 13 February 1990, in which the city's initiative for rebuilding of the Frauenkirche was first publicized, and was printed, for example, in: *Dresdner Neueste Nachrichten*, 2005, p. 17.

left in their grey and damaged state, and were set into the otherwise colourful altar wall.

Paul Oestreicher too, for many years the leader of Coventry Cathedral's Centre for Reconciliation, had at first been against the rebuilding, for he – like many others – saw the ruins as an important symbol of peaceful resistance within East Germany's peace movement. In time, however, he came to change his views:

> 'My love for the ruins sprang from my feelings of solidarity with the East German human rights and peace groups ... However, when it was said that the church would be rebuilt and that we, the people of Dresden, would like to have our church again, it became clear to me that we British had no right to question that decision. On the contrary it was our duty, as those who had destroyed Dresden, to take an active part in the work, as a sign of atonement and an act of reparation.'[84]

In fact the call for support for the rebuilding evoked tremendous sympathy within Great Britain. There was great interest in the process of construction, as I found over and again during my time in Coventry; and there was no other topic on which I was so often questioned as that of Dresden. Along with this interest, there was also an earnest (and sometimes controversially led) discussion as to the purpose and the moral validity of the Allied bombings. In this way, the British interest in the Frauenkirche became in itself a kind of reconciliation project.

But there was also a great readiness to finance the project. A total of more than one million Euros was raised by the Dresden Trust, the British support organization for the rebuilding of the Frauenkirche. This organization was given the task of making the cross for the dome of the Frauenkirche. Silversmith Alan Smith, whose father had been a bomber pilot involved in the destruction of Dresden, created an exact replica of the original 18th-century cross. Before being set in place on the pinnacle of the tower in 2004, the dome-cross was carried up and down through Great Britain for two years, during which it also spent some time in Coventry Cathedral. Its first stopping place had been in Windsor Castle, where Queen Elizabeth II presented the cross to visiting

---

84 The Frauenkirche as a world centre for reconciliation. Interview with Paul Oestreicher, leader for many years of Coventry Cathedral's Centre for Reconciliation, in *Dresdner Neueste Nachrichten*, 2005, p. 30.

The Cross of Nails on the altar of the Frauenkirche.

German state-president Roman Herzog. The Queen's personal support for the project is highly commendable – she contributed from her own private funds, and organized a benefit concert for the Frauenkirche in Berlin in 2004 in order to give renewed expression to her interest in the rebuilding. The fact that the royal procession did not pause at the Frauenkirche in 1992, it subsequently transpired, was due to the chief of Dresden's police force at that time, who had advised against it, and had nothing to do with any refusal to make a gesture of atonement.

However, let us return to 30 October 2005, the day when the church was consecrated. It was not only the Cross of Nails on the altar that testified to the special relationship between Coventry and Dresden – the Bishop of Coventry, Colin Bennett, was invited to participate in the service of consecration that morning, and he was even asked to preach at the evening's ecumenical service. The theme of 'Peace and Reconciliation' pervaded the whole of the evening service; in addition to the sermon, the lessons and the Coventry Litany of Reconciliation, it was also evident in the prayers:

> Let us thank God for the gift of reconciliation. Let us thank God for the friendship with former enemies. Let us thank God for healing old wounds.
> For all who support the overcoming of war, racism and violence. For all those with whom we are joined together through belief and the hope for a more human world;
> Let us pray to the Lord:
> Lord, have mercy. Christ, have mercy. Lord, have mercy.[85]

And that is the key to it all: when the Frauenkirche was rebuilt, it was already an established aim that the church should be a centre for peace and reconciliation, and on the day of its consecration this theme was re-confirmed. And now that the Frauenkirche stands there again in all its glory, the Frauenkirche Foundation is aiming to carry out active reconciliation work, and capitalizing on the opportunities offered by its fame and by its incredible stream of visitors. But is there any evidence that this aim will become reality? As a place of pilgrimage, the Frauenkirche is currently in the unique position of being able to address large numbers of people in a low-key fashion on topics such as peace and reconciliation, and to stimulate and encourage them to get involved. Pastor Holger Treutmann, one of the church's two pastors, believes

---

85 Frauenkirche Dresden, 2005, p. 9.

that this special emphasis should not always be evident at first glance, but that the Frauenkirche should nevertheless structure the whole of its daily work around this special responsibility. Work for reconciliation and peace should be seen in four dimensions – spiritual, intellectual, historical and empirical. [86] Thus, for example, the daily service begins with ringing of the Peace Bell, the significance of which is explained to those who are present; on Friday at 12.00 noon the Coventry Litany is prayed; and baptism or confirmation services dwell upon the special thematic alignment of the Frauenkirche. These are all examples of the *spiritual* embodiment of the theme of reconciliation. At the *intellectual* level, lectures and readings continue the theme, including invitations to monthly readings of 'Literature in the Crypt'; the choice of authors is always based on the charter of the Frauenkirche Foundation, as a European centre of culture, to promote tolerance and peace for peoples and religions. A further example is the literary and musical soirée 'Peace is not the final word' that was organized for 13 February. Church guides draw attention to the *historical* dimension of the duty to promote peace; and finally, in order to bring the spirit of reconciliation to life in an *empirical* sense, the Frauenkirche constantly promotes meetings of all kinds, such as by organizing a Festival of Youth in 2008, by inviting the Pfarrkonvente (clergy deanery meetings) to meet in Dresden, and so on.

In all this, for Jost Hasselhorn the Frauenkirche is a place which can initiate and give rise to tales of hope – tales of hope that open the way to peace and reconciliation:

'Figuratively speaking, human consciousness is like a wardrobe; we clothe ourselves, and cover our souls, with the garments that we keep on the hangers in the wardrobe. For many people, these are penitential robes or dark suits with high-collared shirts. But it is good to have a few colourful clothes hanging in our wardrobe, too. Tales of hope clothe our souls, allow us to breathe, and relax the muscles of our faces. When we listen to tales of hope, we can take new courage, smile and start out on a fresh path. I would like to recall two such tales from the time when the Dresden Frauenkirche was being rebuilt:

In June 2003, the "year after the floods", the first "Night of the Churches" took place in Dresden. In a city in which about eighty per cent of the

---

86 See Treutmann, 2007.

population did not belong to any Christian confession, the 'barriers' were lowered for the evening – the interiors of the churches were opened freely for visitors to wander around and appreciate them, with no compulsion to donate to the collection-box. Catholic and Free Church communities alike had taken up and embraced the idea, which was initiated by a few Lutheran Christians. In the undercroft of the Frauenkirche (which only accommodates a maximum of three hundred people), this "Night of the Churches" was the first opportunity to allow visitors free access to the four remodelled chapels that are contained within the crypt.

By 5.40pm, about five hundred people were already assembled outside the fence enclosing the building site. Just before 6.00pm we opened the doors, and they streamed inside. Down below, a "Devotion of the Cross" had been prepared, with two readers and the songwriter Matthias Trommler. We had deliberately avoided using a service sheet, nor were the visitors invited to join in with singing or with spoken responses. We wanted to make our church accessible to those who had had no upbringing in the church. The songwriter sang a little prelude, and the readers read out a short meditation:

"Here in this place, is where all experiences meet and come together. The beginning of life – the midst of life – the end of life; first awakening and final collapse, continuity and change, wartime and peacetime, injury and reconciliation, wounding and healing.

Here in this place, is where all hopes meet and come together. Health and well-being, pomp and circumstance, diversity and understanding, quiet and reflection, justice and peace."

After the twenty-minute devotional service came to an end, a man aged about sixty-five stood next to one of the columns, tears flowing from his eyes. One of the readers went up to him, and this is what the visitor told him: "Almost sixty years ago, when I was a little child, I was sent away from here to the west, after the bombing of Dresden. Today I am back here, for the fourth or fifth time since the Reunification of Germany – and just by chance, I heard a few hours ago that there would be a "Night of the Churches" tonight. Throughout my life I have had virtually no links with the church, but the Frauenkirche was always an important place to my mother. And then I heard the song that the pianist sang, and I heard your text – and it was as though a knot had been loosened. The fact that I was able to be here today, while all this was happening – it seems to me, as though my mother had sent me a fond greeting.'

'It was 13 February 2005, the sixtieth anniversary of the bombing of Dresden during the Allied air-raid ... As a visible expression of remembrance by the inhabitants of Dresden, and one that could not be associated either with the right-wing or the left-wing radicals, ten thousands of lapel pins in form of a "white rose" were distributed in the city.

The Frauenkirche was still not finished, but for one group of eyewitnesses to the original events, the executive secretary of the Frauenkirche Foundation provided a special guided tour. About thirty individuals, aged seventy and above, were standing in the nave below the dome – many of them strangers to each other. Alongside one of the staff of the Frauenkirche stood a solemn-looking man who must have been born somewhere around 1930. His uncle had been killed in the bombing in 1945; and he himself, just a youth at that time, was evacuated a few days later to the Ore Mountains. His whole life had been affected by that air raid and he had never been able to put it behind him. He was wearing a white rose in his lapel. Elsewhere in the group, an old lady and a well-dressed old gentleman were standing a little apart from the rest, they were obviously well over eighty years old. The lady kept whispering something in the old man's ear, and the others in the group were staring at them – obviously wondering why they insisted on talking whilst the guide from the parish office was trying to tell the group about the internal and external rebuilding of the Frauenkirche, and about the desire for reconciliation.

The lady finally noticed that she was attracting indignant glances, and turned to speak aloud to the whole group: "Please excuse me – but this gentleman is Major D; he was a British pilot, and he wanted to see for himself how the city remembers this day sixty years ago when it had been his duty to drop the bombs." There was dead silence in the nave. Then the man with the white rose, the former inhabitant of wartime Dresden, walked over to the British soldier, said a few quiet words to him, took the white rose from his lapel, and handed it to his former enemy. Bomber pilot and victim of the bombing – they took each other by the hand, and knew in that moment, there in the rebuilt Frauenkirche, that they wanted no talk of guilt or retribution, but simply to bring about a reconciliation.'[87]

As a Cross of Nails Centre, the rebuilt Frauenkirche would like to help to promote more such tales of hopefulness.

---

87 Hasselhorn, 2007.

8

Great Britain

8.1 The Cornerstone Community, Belfast, Northern Ireland

Seldom has there been a more symbolic tearing down of the wall between two halves of a divided house than at Advent 1982, when the Cornerstone Community set up its residence directly on the front line of Belfast's two conflicting parties. This was a significant step forward, in view of Northern Ireland's troubled history. If we recall some of the stages of this story, it will illustrate clearly how far back the roots of the conflict stretch.[88]

In the second half of the twelfth century, the English king Henry II imposed Norman feudal lords upon Ireland. However, England's influence remained limited until a massive and deliberate influx of loyalist Protestants in the seventeenth century, many of whom were puritanical Scots, commencing in Ulster (the so-called 'Plantation of Ulster'). In 1690 the troops of William of Orange defeated the Catholic army under King James II in the Battle of the Boyne.[89] As a result of this victory, King William succeeded to the throne of England and also to that of Ireland. In the nineteenth century, Irish nationalists began to fight for the independence of their island. After Ireland's War of Independence, the British Parliament finally agreed in 1921 to the formation of the Irish Free State, in which Ireland became a free state within Great Britain, with limited sovereignty.[90] The six counties in the north of Ireland however, at their own wish, remained under the direct rule of Great Britain, so that Northern Ireland thus became separated from the rest of the island. About two-thirds of the people there were pro-

---

88 For more details of the conflict in Northern Ireland, see McKittrick/McVea, 2001; Tonge, 1988; and Arthur, 2000. The historical summary given here is based on these published works.

89 In 1795 the Peep O'Day Boys founded a group whose aim was to terrorize Catholics, calling themselves the Orange Order, after their hero William of Orange. The Orange Order soon attracted Protestants from all kinds of diverse backgrounds, and it still exercises authority today within the group of Protestant Loyalists.

90 In 1949 Ireland then declared itself a republic and seceded from the Commonwealth.

British Protestants (Unionists), and the Catholic Nationalists were in the minority. During the decades that followed, the Protestant majority consolidated its political, economic and social domination in Northern Ireland, with assistance from successive governments in London. The newly created Parliament of Northern Ireland, which meets in the Palace of Stormont, was dominated by the Unionists, and the Catholics felt themselves to be second-class citizens.

A powerful civil rights movement arose in the late 1960s, which focused international attention on social and economic discrimination against Catholics in Northern Ireland by a series of planned protests. The conflict escalated from 1969 onward, as civil rights marches were frequently blockaded and obstructed by Unionists, which led to the police being called in, so that time and again the British Army was forced to intervene.

The 'Troubles', as these armed conflicts were euphemistically known, quickly spread across the whole of Northern Ireland. Between 1969 and 1998 more than three thousand people were killed in bomb attacks, street fighting, retaliatory measures and executions, and most of them were civilians. On the Republican side, the IRA (Irish Republican Army) and their splinter groups tried at first to focus the eyes of the world upon Northern Ireland by a series of hunger strikes, and to damage the economy by bomb attacks – later on it was the British Army and the government who bore the full brunt of these attacks. On the opposing side, the Loyalists organized themselves into paramilitary units such as the UVF (Ulster Volunteer Force). Events such as 'Bloody Sunday',[91] or the bomb attempt on the Grand Hotel in Brighton,[92] became part and parcel of the collective memories shared by the Nationalists, the Unionists and the people of Great Britain alike.

A period ensued during which there were various attempted cease-fire agreements and secret talks, and this led in 1998 to an all-party agreement brokered by former US senator George Mitchell. The people of the Irish Republic, together with the people of Northern Ireland, then

---

91 On Sunday 30 January 1972, thirteen Catholic civil rights activists who had been taking part in an unofficial demonstration against the Laws of Internment (which imposed imprisonment for up to a year without the right to appeal, or to legal representation or a trial), were shot and killed by British paratroopers. A further demonstrator died later of his wounds.

92 In October 1984 five people were killed and a further thirty were injured when an IRA bomb exploded in the hotel where the UK Conservative Party was holding its congress. The Prime Minister, Margaret Thatcher, narrowly escaped the attack.

established the so-called Good Friday Agreement in a referendum.[93] The main achievements of the Agreement were a cease-fire, the disarming of all paramilitary groups, and a reform of the Northern Irish police force. On 2 December 1999 the British government brought to an end their direct government of Northern Ireland and formally handed over the reins of authority to a General Assembly of Unionists and Nationalists. However, the situation was still fragile – the question over the disarming of the IRA led to one new crisis after another. Since both sides were not able to build a stable government, London was obliged once again to take over direct control. The elections in 2003 strengthened the radical forces on both sides, namely Sinn Féin and Ian Paisley's Democratic Unionist Party (DUP), which had rejected the Good Friday Agreement. The election in early March 2007 brought a similar result. However, there was a surprising agreement between the two parties, which was hailed as an important breakthrough in the peace process – the DUP and Sinn Féin came together in an all-party government. Since 8 May 2007, hopes have been pinned on this new Northern Ireland regional government under the leadership of Ian Paisley as its First Minister.

Looking at this story, it quickly becomes clear that Northern Ireland was a deeply divided society with two competing communities, and that it still remains so: there is a Protestant/Unionist/Loyalist community that wishes to retain political links to Great Britain, and a Catholic/Nationalist/Republican community that feels itself to be Irish and wishes to have a united Ireland.[94] The members of both groups are overwhelmingly aware of belonging to a group that is markedly different from 'the others', and each feel themselves to have the better claims in terms of religion, customs, historical mythology and territory. Although they are obliged to share the same land and the same resources, the two groups exist for the most part quite separately alongside each other. They live in separate districts, go to different schools, and drink in different pubs. This segregation leads to a lack of communication between the entire communities, deepens the chasm between them, and only serves to reinforce their perception of themselves and their 'enemies'.[95]

---

93 A copy of the Agreement was distributed to every household. The referendum was held in May, in both the north and the south. Even the Unionist voters of Northern Ireland gave their support to the Agreement, though only by a narrow majority.

94 This synonymous usage of the adjectives is of necessity a simplified picture. To be more precise, the Unionists and the Nationalists represent the two sides of the more moderate tendency, as distinct from the extreme Loyalists and extreme Republicans.

95 See Tonge, 1998, pp. 90–94. For a discussion of images of enmity, see Chapter 16, pp. 173–5.

The songs that are sung in pubs in Protestant Ulster, or the famous murals in Belfast, give a clear impression of these two opposing and self-reinforcing communities. Songs and wall paintings send out the message: who are we? what makes us unique? what distinguishes us from our enemies? One Protestant drinking-song, for example, still proudly celebrates a victory in battle in the 17th century:

> Now here's to good King William, for all the deeds he's done,
> For saving us at Derry and making us his sons.
> He gave us all our freedom, to him we must give praise.
> It's great to be a Protestant and high our banner wave.[96]

Some songs even brutally glorify the destruction of the foe. The most famous example is the song published in 1971, *I was born under the Union Jack*, in which the hate of Catholics is expressed in all its repulsiveness:

> Falls was made for burning, taigs are made to kill …
> If guns were made for shooting, then skulls are made to crack,
> You've never seen a better taig than with a bullet in his back.[97]

In the songs, fantasies of superiority are linked with the recurrent feeling of being threatened by the pro-Catholic Irish; the freedom that was bought at such a price must be defended with all the means at their disposal. The same pattern can be seen on the Catholic-Nationalist side, albeit under opposing banners. Here too, murals can be used for propaganda and political indoctrination, to foster and consolidate a standard social identity that is different from that of the enemy. The walls of houses in the Catholic quarter carry pictures of the 'martyrs' of the hunger strikes or murdered IRA heroes; the message is, that the fight must go on in their names. Other paintings show Republicans who, though oppressed, are continuing the anti-imperialist fight for freedom.[98]

---

96 Quoted by Rolston, 1999, p. 49. King Billy, pictured crossing the Boyne, is the oldest of the Protestant mural motifs, and still popular today (see Rolston, 1992). This historical battle has remained in the folk-memory, and in this way it serves to maintain old divisions. Pictures can be found in Rolston, 1992. Rolston has also made some of the images available on the CAIN website (see Rolston, 1998). CAIN (Conflict Archive on the Internet) is the most detailed collection of information on the conflict in Northern Ireland that is available on the Internet.

97 Quoted by Rolston, 1999, p. 34f.

98 Rolston, 1992; and Rolston, 1998.

There is no place for any differences of opinion on either side, everything is turned into a simplified black-and-white image. The murals and the songs speak eloquently of the collective accusation in which all Catholics or all Protestants are held to be equal, or to speak more precisely, equally bad.

Various 'cross-community initiatives'[99] attempt to fight against this continuing tendency. They try to bring together representatives of both communities across the gulf and on to neutral ground, to overcome their lack of two-way communication and remove the images of enmity. Mari Fitzduff, in her *Typology of Community Relations Works*, speaks of eight characteristic features of this kind of work: mutual understanding work, anti-sectarian[100] work, anti-intimidation work, cultural traditions work, justice and rights work, political options work, inter-church work and conflict resolution work. [101] G. Spence sums it up in these words:

> 'A lot of the good work that has been done in Northern Ireland has been done by those nameless people who just keep plodding away in both Protestant and Catholic working class districts, where they do meet across the divide on matters of mutual interest ... I would say this is the one bright star on the horizon of Northern Ireland.'[102]

Another part of this glimmer of hope on the horizon is the Cornerstone Community, which was accepted into the Community of the Cross of Nails in May 2004. The Cornerstone Community is a small group of

---

99 The Community Relations Council, created with the help of the government, is an independent committee charged with promoting and supporting cross-community work at all levels. Lampen, 1995, published by the Community Relations Council, is a practical advice sheet for those interested in this kind of work, which also gives a good overview of the way in which these kinds of initiatives operate.

100 Sectarianism is the name given to the deep political–religious divide that permeates the whole of the Northern Ireland community. With its complex combination of attitudes, actions, convictions and structures, sectarianism leads to destructive relationship patterns at both the personal, communal and institutional levels, including demonization, power struggles, and the dehumanization of others. See Liechty and Clegg, 2001.

101 Fitzduff, 1991. Mention should also be made of some of the problems of such cross-community work. The groups that are involved meet on the one hand with inertia and lack of interest in the local communities. Many of the people have become so used to the ghetto conditions and the violence that they accept both of these things as realities that cannot be avoided. Moreover, there is the danger that each group that is formed to deal with the division and sectarianism will only create further divisions and fresh sectarianism, in that they break off contact with their own groups and people get left behind. Finally, the projects often have to struggle against a shortage of funding and resources, as well as the absence of political support.

102 Quoted in Lampen, 1995, p. 38f.

inhabitants of west Belfast, who come from different religious and polit-ical backgrounds. The foundation of an established community was preceded by seven years of learning together and getting to know each other. An ecumenical group met once a fortnight in Belfast's Clonard Abbey to study the Bible together, to discover the differences in their beliefs – but much more, to discover all the articles of faith that they have in common. During this time there was a growing desire to build a more binding kind of fellowship – and thus eventually the Cornerstone Community was founded. Candidates are accepted into the community after a probation period, and they promise to live in the spirit of recon-ciliation. Each person remains an active member of their own church community, and is involved within the community in which they grew up. Cornerstone is first and foremost a community of regular prayer, in which the members come together for prayer once a week.

The two main objectives of the Cornerstone Community are there-fore:

- To bear witness that people from different religious, social and political backgrounds can live and work in peace, and without losing their own identities.
- To maintain a community that prays for peace and reconciliation in Northern Ireland.[103]

Since 1982 some of the members of the Community have been living together in a community house on the Springfield Road, right on the so-called 'peace line' – a wall up to four-and-a-half metres in height that separates the Protestant-Loyalist Shankill Road from the Catholic-Republican Falls Road. Thus the Community's home is situated in one of Belfast's most strongly polarized and heated districts during the time of the 'Troubles'. To the people of Belfast, Shankill and Falls represent their city at its worst. Paramilitary groups were very popular here on both sides – and in addition, the region is known for its high degree of social tension (chiefly induced by an unemployment level of up to sixty-five per cent). Bill Jackson, who was formerly the priest at the Shankill Road Mission, recalls that memorable day in 1982:

---

103 Thus, according to Fitzduff's typology, Cornerstone may be described as an inter-confessional community that strives for mutual understanding. Fitzduff defines the building of mutual understanding as 'work designed to decrease ignorance, suspicion and prejudices within and between communities'; she regards inter-church encounters as 'theological work which can facilitate the development of pluralism and co-operation' (Fitzduff, 1991).

'On 18/12/1982, we took possession of the two semi-detached, three storey houses, on the front of Springfield Road, on the interface between two communities. The first three residents were Sister Mary Giant, Sister Gladys Hayward, and Hazel Dickson, a Methodist. Inevitably there were jokes made about which house would be for the Protestants and which for the Catholics! But we avoided this problem by breaking holes in the dividing wall on the ground floor and the third floor and putting in doors. To me it is another reminder of our Lord breaking down the wall of hostility between us.'[104]

Over the years, the Cornerstone Community has organized or taken part in countless cross-community events and meetings.

During the 'Troubles', Methodist minister Sam Burch and Roman Catholic priest Gerry Reynolds began paying joint visits of condolence to relatives of the victims of violence. Sam Burch recalls the situation:

'The first home that we visited together was on the Shankill, where a Protestant member of the Ulster Defence Regiment had been shot dead on the pavement in front of his teenage son who was delivering papers. His parents received us warmly, deeply moved that a local priest should visit them at such a time. He gave them a gift, a carved face of Jesus in his agony. As the mother held this gift, her tears flowed freely down on the face of Jesus, and we felt that our Lord, too, was weeping for the agony of Ireland.'[105]

Later on, other members of the Cornerstone took up this duty of inter-confessional visiting, for this simple but courageous idea left behind a deep impression upon the families concerned. The visits showed that people from 'the other side' were sharing in the loss of a loved relative – and thus, the anonymous foe came to have a face.

Symbolic gestures were also important to the community. For instance, members of Cornerstone, accompanied by fifteen hundred sympathizers, carried a huge wooden cross in a long procession along the line of confessional and political demarcation between Falls Road

---

104 Jackson, no date, p. 4.
105 Burch, 1988, p. 22.

and Shankill Road. On another occasion, women from both sides of the divide planted a tree together in a park in what was at that time the 'hostile' residential quarter.

The Cornerstone Community has acquired the reputation of a much-valued arbitrator between the Catholic and Protestant peoples of the area, the Orange Order and the police. The Community's house is a neutral and a safe place, where people from both sides can meet and discuss their problems. Once a month people from both sides of the 'peace line' meet for a communal lunch, and local priests also meet regularly at the Cornerstone for an informal chat. In addition, parent-child groups, pensioners' groups and a youth club offering after-school activities and assistance with homework are organized in the Methodist Church on Springfield Road in collaboration with other organizations.

I have found the Cornerstone Community, which has dedicated itself to peace and reconciliation, to be a wonderful sign of hope in the midst of a divided city. By its mere existence, its ethos, its unceasing prayers for peace, and its ecumenical latitude, the Community demonstrated during the 'Troubles' that the citizens of Belfast could be reconciled with one another, and that peace is achievable. Despite the promising fresh start that was made in Northern Ireland early in 2007, the members of the Community are convinced that their work and their prayers will still be needed in the future – and so, the Cornerstone has set about 'reinventing itself', reflecting upon what has been achieved so far and preparing itself for the future. The first result of this re-evaluation process is a new 'motto', which retains the enduring value of their existing convictions. It is appropriate to close by quoting this new version of the old theme:

Cornerstone is an inter-church community of reconciliation based in North and West Belfast, seeking through witness, prayer, outreach and hospitality to be a healing presence and sign of hope.[106]

---

106 *Cornerstone Contact*, 2007, p. 2.

8.2 Lagan College, Belfast, Northern Ireland

It is worth taking a further look at Northern Ireland. In addition to cross-community projects, the school system is also an important point from which to begin to break down segregation and sectarianism. For Northern Ireland's educational system has been subject to religious segregation in the past, and in many areas it still is even today. When the state of Northern Ireland was first formed, the Unionist parliamentary majority dominated the state's educational system, with privately operated Catholic schools setting up in opposition.

The first integrated school in Northern Ireland (i.e. a cross-confessional school) was Lagan College,[107] which was founded by parents in 1981, at the height of the 'Troubles'. Sister Anne Kilroy, the school's Roman Catholic chaplain, recalls that:

> 'It was felt strongly that if children from both traditions could be educated together, it would help to break down the barriers between the two main communities, and contribute to a more peaceful future.'[108]

The project was an unusual one, and unique at that time; it was started with twenty-eight schoolchildren, two full-time and a few part-time teachers. The motto that they chose for the school was 'ut unum sint' (that is, 'so that all may be one'). In a time of violence and tension, the foundation of a new kind of school was a courageous step for both teachers and parents. They risked total incomprehension by their friends and acquaintances, and the danger of becoming the victims of attacks. Added to this, the school's academic standard was at first uncertain, and the project was on a very insecure financial footing, so that the parents had to finance the costs of the school chiefly out of their own pockets. Campbell Mulholland, who was one of the schoolboys of that first year, recalled that turbulent and modest beginning in the jubilee issue of the school's magazine, *Voices*:

---

107 According to the information from the Northern Ireland Council for Integrated Education, there were fifty integrated schools by 2003, thirty-two of which are primary schools and the rest are secondary schools. Despite the growth in this type of school, it is still only 5% of Northern Ireland's schoolchildren who are educated in cross-confessional schools. This data, and much more information about Northern Ireland's educational system, is regularly updated in the Internet information service CAIN: see McKenna and Melaugh, 2007.

108 Kilroy, January 2007.

'Twenty-five years later, my first day at Lagan College is still a very clear memory. I can remember twenty-eight of us – new first form pupils – being shepherded along a woodland path and in a hidden back entrance to Ardnavalley Scout Centre, to avoid the world's media camped at the front gates of the school. It became immediately obvious that our school, the school that we had just become, was something a bit different, and would be seen as such. There was a massive interest in what we were doing. In the early days, many of us were interviewed by radio, television and newspapers ...

Pupils travelled from far and wide to attend the school, and this required a great deal of organization. The school bus travelled to various pick-up points to get us to and from school. Being a bit strapped for cash, it is only fair to say that our school bus had too many miles on the clock. It was old and borrowed and blue. The bodywork was rusty and it rattled a lot. I can remember sitting in one of the brown leather seats and rattling out of the school gates, hearing the bus backfiring and shuddering to a halt, as the smoke rose up past the windows.'[109]

The school has long since moved to a new site, on its own grounds at Lisnabreeny in the south of Belfast, though not all of the phases of construction are completed as yet. Today Lagan College has more than eleven hundred pupils and one hundred and thirty teachers and specialist staff.

On 6 May 2002, during the celebrations of its twentieth anniversary, Lagan College was accepted into the Community of the Cross of Nails. Since that time, the school's two full-time chaplains, Sister Anne Kilroy and Helen Killick, have been responsible for relations with the international Community of the Cross of Nails. Sister Anne writes: 'The fact that children from different backgrounds are educated together can itself be an instrument of reconciliation. But on its own, this is not enough.'[110] Many further building blocks can be added to this. A central role is played by the school's chaplaincy, which is managed by a joint Catholic-Protestant school pastoral team, and this is still a unique situation for a secondary school in Northern Ireland. Religious Education is also taught together at Lagan, to a common curriculum, and visits to both Catholic and Protestant churches form part of the teaching. The school's daily morning service tackles current and global issues as well

109 Quoted in *Voices*, 2006, p. 19.
110 Kilroy, January 2007.

as themes taken from the ecclesiastical year. Remembrance Day, which is more significant among Protestants, is commemorated in equal measure with Ash Wednesday, which has more meaning for Catholics. The chaplains are available during the lunch break and after school to various different interest groups. One of these is the 'Justice Group', which has been meeting once a week for the last seven years. 'Make Poverty History', the initiative for the worldwide struggle against poverty, was the topic that the group studied in 2005. In the following year they organized an AIDS/HIV Action Week at their school, to draw attention to the pandemic in the developing countries and also in Ireland.

Every year the children in the school's final-year class visit the Peace Line, along with any teachers who are new to the school. This gives those children who have never been in west Belfast their first opportunity to see at first hand the place that was such a tormented area during the 'Troubles'. Sister Anne ensures that the visit programme also includes the Cornerstone Community of which she is a member. After one such visit, one of the schoolchildren recorded their impressions:

'We were able to see the hard work which is going on at the heart of the conflict, which tries to bring Unionists and Nationalists together. I never would have believed that such commitment and kindness could be seen in an area which is more commonly associated with violence and segregation.'[111]

Sister Anne sums up her pastoral work with the schoolchildren, which includes a measure of reconciliation, as follows:

'The pastoral side of my work is very satisfying. This is especially so when young people are reconciled as a result. There may not be a denominational factor, but a challenge to dialogue, and to ask for and grant forgiveness. It usually happens like this: a student comes to talk about falling out with a friend, or being hurt by another student. If they are willing, I arrange for the other person to come to the Chaplaincy, where a difficult but healing conversation can be enabled to take place. Feelings are expressed on both sides, and after some honest sharing, there is usually a recognition

---

111 Kilroy, February 2007.

of culpability on both sides and a gesture of reconciliation. While there may or may not be a sectarian element, the process of reconciliation is nevertheless a central part of our school ethos.'[112]

Lagan College also provides a good illustration of yet another aspect of the Community of the Cross of Nails. Large establishments that either are or will become Cross of Nails Centres, are confronted with the task, as and when they are able, to inspire and motivate all their members in Cross of Nails work. When I enquired what significance the Cross of Nails has for Lagan College, I received the following frank and honest answer from Sister Anne:

'It reminds us that we are part of an international community. Our school has visited the Blue Coat School in Coventry [also a Cross of Nails Centre]. The Chaplains and another member of staff have attended the national and international conferences in Coventry, and have made presentations. The Principal has visited St Cyprian's in Cape Town [another Cross of Nails school] during her sabbatical year, and Sister Anne came across the Cross of Nails in the Cathedral of Kolkata.

Two years ago a group called 'The Link' was formed among a small group of students who met at lunchtime to explore contacts with other Cross of Nails schools. Contacts were made with St Cyprian's, the Blue Coat School, and the Rainsbrook Secure Training Centre in Rugby. Unfortunately the group faded away after six months.

The Cross of Nails is displayed in the school foyer, and brought to special assemblies. The story is told to all first-year students. In the month of March, the Chaplains have a 'Cross of Nails' Assembly around the time of the anniversary. The Litany of Reconciliation is recited or referred to on occasion, but is not used on a regular basis.

Membership of the Community of the Cross of Nails means more to some staff than to others, and means most to those who are committed to the Christian and Integrated ethos of the school.'[113]

112 Kilroy, February 2007.
113 Kilroy, January 2007.

This response shows that Cross of Nails Centres of this size have an ongoing task, to be continually motivating everyone to the Cross of Nails work, passing on the Coventry story to the new generations that are coming along, and establishing a committed core-group of colleagues to carry on the work and keep up the links with Coventry and the Community of the Cross of Nails.

I will bring this section to a close by quoting Helen Killick, Sister Anne's Protestant colleague, who comments on her work at Lagan College in these words:

'Prayers have been spoken, debates have raged, and silence has been kept. Conversations and dialogue have taken place, some leading to greater understanding between people, some leading to reconciliation. There is no doubt that the Chaplaincy is a special place. We trust that God will continue to guide us, as we play our part in answering the prayer of Jesus, which is also our school motto: Ut Sint Unum.'[114]

---

114 Quoted in Kilroy, February 2007.

8.3 Rainsbrook Secure Training Centre, Rugby, England

The focus is also on young people at the Rainsbrook Secure Training Centre. Here, just as at Lagan College in Northern Ireland, education and training are of central significance. However, the education and training concerns a totally different kind of conflict that is in need of reconciliation; Rainsbrook is a penal institution for young offenders between the ages of twelve and eighteen.

On 11 September 2003, Rainsbrook became a member of the Community of the Cross of Nails. The service at which the Cross of Nails was presented, which included young people from each of the residential units, was an unforgettable experience for me – and I hope it was also unforgettable for the young people. We prayed the Litany, there was loud and powerful (and occasionally rather offbeat) singing, and after the Cross had been presented it was passed around through the ranks of young people. The teenagers were surprised to hear that Rainsbrook is not the first 'Cross of Nails prison', and they were still more affected when they learned that their Cross of Nails had been made in the prison at Würzburg.[115]

In order to understand why Rainsbrook became a Cross of Nails Centre, it is necessary to know the role fulfilled by this prison in the Coventry area. Rainsbrook is under private management by Rebound, and takes up to eighty-seven boys and girls who have either already been sentenced or are under custodial arrest. A look at the statistics reveals that 21% of them have committed break-ins, 34% have used violence (e.g. muggings), and 12% were sentenced for car theft; 36% of the teenagers are serving less than six months, 49% between six and twelve months, and 14% have been in Rainsbrook for over a year.[116]

The goal of this rather unusual prison is to provide the young people during their enforced stay with new insights into their own capabilities and strengths, so as to break the disastrous spiral of violence into a career of crime. The Anglican priest Susan Hardwick, who has the charge of pastoral care over Rainsbrook, knows that many of the young people come from the poorest and most needy levels of Great Britain's society:

---

115 See Chapter 6.1, p. 54.

116 These statistics are for 2003; see Rebound, 2007, under the heading 'Why do they come to us?'

'Rebound's whole endeavour is to give the young people in our care the opportunity to reflect on their lives to date in a variety of ways, to plan creatively for the future, and to give them the tools with which to try to turn their lives around, in order to live out those plans and dreams.'[117]

According to Susan Hardwick, Rainsbrook sees itself as being committed to offering homeliness and a safe environment to the juvenile offenders, in which they receive respect, a sense of their own worth, and some private space. The young people are housed in groups of up to eight. Within the high prison walls with their supervisory cameras, the residential blocks, a learning centre and leisure rooms are grouped around a central inner courtyard. The school is giving top priority at Rainsbrook – for in addition to promoting the further social and emotional development of the young people, a solid education is an integral part of their time in detention.[118] Each of them receives full-time schooling for twenty-five hours a week, in which groups of no more than six pupils are taught according to the National Curriculum. The school-children are promoted according to their individual strengths and weaknesses. The regular teaching is supplemented by programmes on management of aggression and so on, and by courses to prepare them for getting a job. Susan Hardwick summarizes it in this way:

'Our approach is holistic, seeing the young people's needs as physical, mental, emotional and spiritual, and trying to provide diverse opportunities to address all these areas.'[119]

Susan Hardwick was ordained priest at Coventry Cathedral and thus became familiar with its reconciliation work. When asked why the theme of reconciliation is such a central aspect of the work at Rainsbrook, she replied:

---

117 Hardwick, April 2007.

118 According to statistics, 38% of the young people gave up attending school in the two years before they came to Rainsbrook, or were expelled from their school; 41% have the reading ability of an eight-year-old or below; in mathematical ability, 79% are no better than an eight-year-old, and 11% have only reached the level of a five- or six-year-old (see Rebound, 2007, under 'Why do they come to us?').

119 Hardwick, April 2007.

'Many of our young people are alienated, either from their families, their local communities, or society as a whole – or all of these. They are also often alienated from themselves: between the different aspects of their understanding of who they are ...

I had not been at Rainsbrook for long before I began to realize, more and more strongly, that what we do here with the young people, is so similar in so many respects to the work of the Community of the Cross of Nails: helping the disparate elements of the young people to be reconciled, and helping them to be reconciled with their local communities and the wider society.

Reconciliation comes through better understanding of others and relating to their lives and their sorrows and joys. Encouraging our young people to be other-centred is an important part of our work here.'[120]

Thus, Rainsbrook's care for the young people can be seen as practical reconciliation work which encompasses four aspects: the teacher, the social worker, the residential housemaster or housemistress, and the chaplains:

a) Reconciliation between the young people themselves, to counteract gang-culture etc.
b) Reconciliation between the young people and the environment that they come from.
c) Reconciliation between the young people and their victims; and finally
d) The personal reconciliation of each person with himself or herself.

In more concrete terms, Rainsbrook sets great store by the key concept of 'restorative justice'. The important point here is not the question of what laws have been broken, but of what damage the victims have suffered, and what was the cause that led to the crime. In trying to restore the situation as closely as possible to its original state, it is a central requirement that the victims, the perpetrators and the environment should be brought together, so that victim and aggressor can talk freely about the parts that they played, and that they should be placed in a new and healing relationship. Howard Zehr, the leading pioneer of this concept, defines it as follows: 'Restorative justice is a process to involve, to the extent possible, those who have a stake in a specific

---

120 Hardwick, April 2007.

offence and to collectively identify and address harms, needs, and obligations, in order to heal and put things as right as possible.'[121] And so, at Rainsbrook the attempt is made to bring young people face to face again with all those who were affected by their crime, and to re-examine what took place and try to find a perspective for the future. And in addition, the attempt is to resolve by mediation and arbitration any conflicts between the young people or between the staff that they cannot resolve for themselves. Susan Hardwick reports the following case: Haley, a female member of staff, came to the prison authorities with a complaint against her direct superior Veronica, by whom she felt herself to have been unfairly treated. This was not the first time that this complaint had been made, so it was decided to set up a meeting for the purposes of restorative justice. The mediator gave both women the opportunity to put their side of the story. Both of them talked about an incident in which Veronica had sent a young girl back to her living quarters because she had behaved badly in the dining room. Haley tried to calm the teenager down, and told her that she did not agree with Veronica's decision. Veronica came to hear of this, and felt that Haley had undermined her authority. And that was the start of the conflict, according to both their statements. When the mediator made further enquiries and asked whether there had been any other tensions, neither of them would say anything at first; but when the mediator persisted, it was finally disclosed that five years earlier, Haley had shown an interest in a man who at that time had been the boyfriend of Veronica's best friend. Ever since that time Haley had had the feeling that Veronica had held it against her. Veronica did not deny this, but said in return that in her opinion Haley had frequently not been up to standard in her work. On the other hand, Haley felt herself to be just as well qualified as Veronica, and had repeatedly sought promotion, but without success.

This case, which Susan Hardwick reports as a typical caste study, illustrates what the chaplain refers to as the 'onion effect' of a process of restorative justice. The more layers that are peeled away, the more information comes to light:

'The meeting went on for approximately one-and-a-half hours. It exposed the fact that jealousy and mistrust had existed between these two that had not been resolved, making the relationship almost untenable. Had

---

121 See Zehr, 2000, p. 37.

it not been for the Restorative Justice conference, where they eventually agreed to respect each other as people and as professionals and to move on from the incident of five years ago, the situation would have continued for very much longer.'[122]

We have seen that, for Susan Hardwick, conscious awareness of other people and their needs is a part of the process of reconciliation. Regular fund-raising campaigns are also an important building block in the pastoral work at Rainsbrook – they help the young people to compare their situation with that of others in the world whose predicaments and problems are often much greater than their own. After the Tsunami catastrophe in December 2004, the inmates and staff at Rainsbrook donated more than £1000, which was raised via numerous fund-raising activities and special events. The staff also gives its support to the Syrian Orthodox School in Jerusalem, a Cross of Nails Centre with which Rainsbrook maintains constant contact. Each staff member who

Fun Day in the Rainsbrook Secure Training Centre.

122 Hardwick, October 2007.

travels during their holidays can have the privilege of taking with them the Rainsbrook Teddy Bear, in return for a donation. Thus, every time the prison mascot takes a trip, the school receives financial support.

The big annual Multi-faith and Multi-cultural Day that is held within the prison walls also serves to cut down on xenophobia, to celebrate different cultures and religions, and illustrate to the young people how boring society would be if all people were the same. All day long there are artistic and musical projects on this theme – on the Multi-faith and Multi-cultural Day at which I was present, there was a drum workshop, body-painting with henna, and Buddhist monks talked about their life in an English 'monastic' community. Every year the young people decorate tags with peace symbols and send them up on hot-air balloons.

Over the year, attention is drawn to the various festivals that are at the heart of different religions, such as the Chinese New Year, Diwali, Easter and Christmas etc., and the customs and backgrounds of these events are explained. Muslims are encouraged to celebrate Ramadan, and to explain to the other young people the significance of Ramadan fasting.

Susan Hardwick feels that the Coventry Cross of Nails constantly inspires and motivates the prison management, the chaplaincy team and the young people themselves not to lose hope, despite the often dismal reality of life, even when everything appears hopeless:

'The starkness and directness of the story of the Cross of Nails, with its message of hope over despair, of resurrection over death, of love over hate, and of forgiveness and reconciliation, is one that very much resonates with many of our young people.

As I said at the beginning, we have a holistic approach to the care and nurture of our young people, where the physical, mental, emotional and spiritual aspects are all given importance. The Community of the Cross of Nails is a powerful way in which we can encourage our young people to see themselves as an essential part of a local, national and world community; as "us" rather than as "me and them".'[123]

This motif is also taken up in the Cross of Nails leaflet that was specially designed in and for Rainsbrook and made available to all the young inmates. Its pictures and text make it clear to the young people

---

123 Hardwick, April 2007.

that they are part of a larger community, in which other people are faced with problems and conflicts – just like them – which have to be solved by peaceful means. The leaflet tells them:

As young people and staff at Rainsbrook STC, you are part of two communities:

1. all who live and work here at the Centre,
2. a wider community called the International Community of the Cross of Nails.

What is it all about?

Resolving differences between individuals, family members, rival groups and gangs, and nations.

It's called Reconciliation.

9

'Johannes Rau' International Education and Conference Centre (IBB), Minsk

On the night of 22 June 1941, three million German soldiers invaded the Soviet Union. From the Baltic to the Black Sea they advanced, crouched in ditches and tanks, and then made a surprise attack just before 3 a.m. It was a display of armed force involving more than three thousand tanks, six hundred thousand motor vehicles, six hundred thousand horses, seventeen thousand goods trains and two thousand seven hundred aircraft. 'Operation Barbarossa', which Hitler had ordered in December 1940, became a gruesome campaign of annihilation unimaginable in its extent, in which millions of innocent lives were lost.

Fifty years later, it was only a single train that crossed over the River Bug. At the same point on the river where the 130th and 135th Infantry Regiments crossed over on their way to storm the citadel of Brest-Litovsk, four hundred German people were now passing by on a journey to Minsk – men and women, old and young, Christians and atheists, left-wing and conservative alike; and for the first time, a group of handicapped people were among them. Germans of all ages who had set off from the Ruhr, travelling in order to express their desire for reconciliation. It was no small thing, given that the horror had been started in Germany's name. In Belarus alone six hundred and twenty-nine villages had been razed to the ground, and one quarter of all Belarussians had been killed. In Chatyn, symbol of the murder of these villages, there stands a memorial to that unimaginable deed. All the inhabitants of the village, including seventy-six children, were herded together into a barn and burned alive.

For the four hundred travellers, this was the first stage-point on their journey to commemorate the fiftieth anniversary of the invasion of the Soviet Union. 'Can there be any forgiveness here, for what the Germans did to the people at that time?' asked Dr Herbert Schnoor, who was at that time the deputy first minister of North-Rhine Westphalia, in an address. 'I do not know,' he continued, 'however, I beg forgiveness for what your people were forced to suffer in the Second World War. That is why we are reaching out our hands to you, in the hope that you will not strike them away.' On the afternoon of that same day, the German party was present when the foundation stone was laid for a new international centre for education and meetings, on the outskirts of Minsk. The laying of that foundation stone was the focus of attention not only throughout Belarus but also throughout Germany. The newspapers carried stories of a 'sign of hope', alongside lengthy editorials on the invasion of the Soviet Union and Germany's war of destruction. 'The grief of the guilty is a part of rec-onciliation' proclaimed the heading in the German daily paper *taz* – it was a free translation of a Jewish saying, which had been taken up six years earlier by a small group of West Germans as their motto, in order to pro-voke as many people as possible into reflecting upon the consequences of Germany's recent history. 'The secret of reconciliation is remember-ing' – it is with this oft-repeated thought that the story of the International Education and Conference Centre in Minsk begins.[124]

Thus ran the introduction to an article about the history of the Inter-national Education and Conference Centre in Minsk ('Internationale Bildnungs- und Begegnungsstätte', or simply the 'IBB'), to celebrate the tenth anniversary of the centre. The article was quick to explain the historical background against which the joint German-Belarus project was to make its contribution to reconciliation. The whole thing began with a small group of people in Westphalia, who had been working together since 1985 to record for posterity this tale of suffering, and this had developed into the International Education and Conference Centre in Dortmund, a co-operative venture which organized visits to Poland and the Soviet Union, and associated meetings. In 1986 they paid their first visit to Minsk – and in time the idea took shape of building another education centre there, a work in which Soviet citi-zens and German people would share equally; and with the advent of *perestroika* and *glasnost*, it suddenly seemed that a bold undertaking such as this would be possible. The laying of the foundation stone on 22 June 1991, described above, marked the beginning of the construc-tion phase, which even the collapse of the Soviet Union and numerous financial difficulties were unable to halt. Finally came the dedication of the IBB on 4 September 1994, and the conference centre commenced operations – as a place for free and open dialogue and meetings between

124 Internationale Bildungs- und Begegnungsstätte, 2004, p. 14f.

people from all kinds of different backgrounds and cultures, for Belarussians to meet with one another and with their European neighbours. Seminars, workshops, further education, language courses, symposiums and conferences and study trips are all part of the programme.

The IBB succeeded in establishing itself as a forum for exchange and freedom of speech – despite the undemocratic developments in the country under the authoritarian rule of President Lukaschenko. In November 2001 the Minsk IBB was presented with the Coventry Cross of Nails, in recognition of the establishment's involvement on behalf of peace in the country. On 11 September 2006, the name of the institution was changed to the 'Johannes Rau IBB', to commemorate the outstanding services to the centre by the former federal president who, in his time as first minister of North-Rhine Westphalia, had staunchly supported and promoted the German-Belarussian project.[125]

'The secret of reconciliation is remembering' – this motto of the IBB, already quoted above, runs like a silken thread through the conference centre's many programmes and projects. The central theme of the events and conferences is always Remembrance – together with the hope that this will lead on to reconciliation, and learning how to make a better future. Thus, for example, visits to Germany were organized for those who remember the former times first hand. Former inmates of concentration camps, forced labourers and inhabitants of the ghettos all came to Germany in order to tell their tales of suffering to children in German schools. By direct contact with the survivors, these young people were encouraged to stand up for justice and peaceful coexistence, and to set their faces against fear of the stranger and the foreigner. Professor Olga Nechaj, a survivor of the Ravensbrück concentration camp and president of the association of former concentration camp detainees, describes her experiences with German children:

'Do I find it difficult to answer the questions of German schoolchildren? No. I am over eighty years old now, and I am no longer afraid. I tell my story – speak out about what I saw with my own eyes – and I give the answers that I have worked out for myself to many questions. But if you are asking me whether it has become something commonplace for me, to talk with these young German children – well, even today, I can still remember the face of every single child.'[126]

125 See Internationale Bildungs- und Begegnungsstätte, 2007.
126 Quoted in: Internationale Bildungs- und Begegnungsstätte, 2004, p. 57.

Another project that focuses upon remembrance is the Minsk History Workshop, as it is called. The biggest ghetto in the whole of the Nazi-occupied Soviet Union was in Minsk; thousands of people were killed in that ghetto, and in the nearby death camp at Trostenez. The Dortmund IBB, the Minsk IBB and the association of the Jewish community have set up the history workshop in one of the few remaining buildings of the ghetto. 'The building in which Jewish families hid during the occupation, and managed to survive it, is today a place where the questions prompted by history can be researched and shared, with the involvement of contemporary witnesses and other interested parties. Belarussian and German historians work together in their research. Belarussian youngsters and international visitors can discover the facts for themselves by "live teaching" on the spot, and there is a place for stories from contemporary witnesses, displays and other public events.'[127] In this way, the 'Place of Remembrance' plays its part in rounding out the story of the time of the Nazi occupation; but at the same time, it allows the people of Minsk 'to obtain new access to their own past history, after the Soviet Union's ideologically influenced history books'.[128]

An important area of the IBB's work is promoting 'partnership in the common house of Europe'. Many German-Belarussian initiatives and projects have had their beginning in the IBB. The initial focus was on humanitarian and medical aid, but since that time other joint topics have been introduced, such as education, health, economic qualification and ecology. In addition, German-Belarussian police conferences have been organized; and a media academy has been founded, so that through exchanges with European media people a new and independent journalism will be promoted in Belarus.

Finally, mention should be made of a further area of work; in April 1997, the Inter-Confessional Working Group of the IBB was founded. Dr Alexander Ladissow, leader of this group and the point of contact for Cross of Nails work, describes the origins and aims of the group in these words:

'Our inter-confessional working group was founded eight years ago, with the blessings of the patriarchs of all four confessions. And for eight years, representatives of the Russian Orthodox, Protestant, Roman Catholic and

---

127 Internationale Bildungs- und Begegnungsstätte, 2004, p. 55.
128 Internationale Bildungs- und Begegnungsstätte, 2004, p. 41.

Baptist communities have been meeting in the Inter-Confessional Working Group of the Minsk IBB, to talk together about current topics relating to beliefs, social life, morals and ethics. Despite the differences in beliefs, dogma and the communion, there has been a growth in understanding of all that which is held in common and which binds and unites, for the common mission of the church – the proclamation of the holy gospel. It is the purpose of the regular meetings of the Inter-Confessional Working Group to deepen and extend the ecumenical dialogue between the different churches. During the meetings of the Working Group, topics for inter-confessional seminars and conferences are discussed, along with the practical details involved in staging them. The Inter-Confessional Working Group of the Minsk IBB focuses on extending and intensifying the ecumenical dialogue between the representatives of the main confessional groups in Belarus. It holds conferences and round-table talks on current problems regarding the belief and the diaconal activities of the involved churches, organizes Christian summer-camps (in which Christians from Germany also take part), and so contributes to the beneficial exchange of views and experiences and reciprocal understanding among the Christian Churches. In the Working Group meetings, they prepare and carry out programmes for joint seminars and conferences about problems that affect our society, and visits to the most significant places of pilgrimage in Belarus.'[129]

In 2004, the Working Group organized a series of seminars on the country's different churches, commencing with the Protestant churches. The second seminar looked at Belarus's Orthodox church. Each seminar portrayed the churches by means of displays, stands, artistic offerings and discussions, and reported on the changes that they had each undergone since the turning-point in Belarus, and on the issues that they see themselves as being confronted with at the present time.

In 2006, in the twentieth anniversary year of the catastrophe at Chernobyl, the Inter-Confessional Working Group planned two seminars on the theme of 'Chernobyl and the Integrity of Creation'. One purpose of these seminars was to keep the deadly legacy of Chernobyl fresh in everyone's memory and stop people from making light of the consequences. Another aim was to allow each of the different churches to comment on what they had learned from the nuclear accident, what consequences they drew from it, and how God's Creation can be pro-

---

129 Ladissow, 2007.

tected. In one of the conferences there was a round-table discussion on the topic of 'the Integrity of Creation' between the Metropolitan Filaret (patriarch of the Belarus Orthodox church), church president Alfred Buss of the Evangelical Church of Westphalia, and a group of students.

When the IBB was renamed as the 'Johannes Rau IBB' in 2007, the Inter-Confessional Working Group organized a two-day seminar on the theme of 'Co-operation between Church and State: experiences and perspectives from Germany and Belarus'. This tackled the topic of col-laboration between the church and the state in the two countries, but also considered how to involve the churches in the discourse on the important ethical and social issues of the day.

From these examples it is clear that there is a second topic, in addition to *Remembrance*, that is central to the work of the Minsk IBB – namely the *Encounters* that are arranged and enabled by the German-Belarus project, both between the different denominations in the church and between the victims and the descendants of the perpetrators. Johannes Rau, who later gave his name to the establishment, described the IBB thus:

The Minsk IBB stands for openness and dialogue. It acts as a light-house in Belarus, casting its light upon the people. It promotes discussions, in which different opinions can be aired, and in which people can speak with one another who perhaps would otherwise have no opportunity to do so. Here they can come together ... and sometimes they can also converge![130]

---

130 Opening address in Internationale Bildungs- und Begegnungstätte, 2004, p. 6.

North America

10.1 Christ Church Cathedral, Cincinnati

Just as in Germany, the Cross of Nails Centres in the USA have banded together in a national association, which since 2006 has extended to cover the whole of North America, including the Canadian and the two Cuban Centres. 'Truth + Forgiveness = Reconciliation' is the motto of the North American Community of the Cross of Nails. In addition to the specific work of each individual centre, in recent years the whole organization has agreed upon a threefold focus – ethnic reconciliation, religious reconciliation, and also the reconciliation that is required regarding the question of sexual orientation. The Episcopalian[131] Christ Church Cathedral in Cincinnati, for example, is a Cross of Nails Centre that has devoted itself especially to the first of these goals, which will now be described in rather more detail.

'Christ Church Cathedral in Cincinnati, Ohio, became a Community of the Cross of Nails Centre in the early 1970s. Our archives have photographs and articles about the visit of Provost Bill Williams when he visited here to create a Cross of Nails Centre in Cincinnati. The cathedral's archival records indicate a much earlier relationship between the two congregations; in the early 1940s, i.e. well before the end of World War II, Christ Church in Cincinnati began to send financial assistance to Coventry Cathedral. Then, just after the dedication of the new cathedral in Coventry, the congregation in Cincinnati commissioned the sculpture "The Plumb Line in the City" (symbolizing the reference to a plumb line in the seventh chapter of Amos) similar to the one in Cincinnati, but reflecting a "city" composed of buildings in Coventry and Jerusalem.'[132]

---

131 The Episcopalian Church of the USA is one of the thirty-eight autonomous churches that belong to the Anglican Communion, the worldwide Anglican community.

132 Diamond, 2007. The sculpture may still be admired today, in the nave of Coventry Cathedral.

Thus writes James Diamond, Dean of Christ Church Cathedral, and until December 2007 also the president of the North American Community of the Cross of Nails, describing the special relationship of his cathedral with Coventry.

The cathedral's engagement in the fight against racism comes about partly for historical reasons. The city of Cincinnati extends along the banks of the Ohio River, which separated the northern and southern states in the American Civil War (1861–65). Crossing the river from Kentucky into Ohio was one of the routes by which slaves from the south fled to the 'free north'. Today, the National Underground Railroad Freedom Center is a reminder of that secret network (symbolically referred to as the Underground Railroad) that devoted itself in the 1800s to enabling slaves to flee to the safety of Canada or the northern states. Well over a hundred thousand slaves used this 'underground to freedom', which was composed of those who helped the fleeing slaves, safe houses and a secret means of communication.

Unfortunately, at the same time Cincinnati has a long history of 'racial disturbances'.[133] The latest riots came in April 2001, when a white policeman, without provocation, shot an unarmed black teenager Timothy Thomas, who was wanted for a traffic offence. There were several days of protests, excesses and looting. The whole city was affected by this exceptional situation, and police and National Guardsmen confronted the citizens with tear gas and rubber bullets.

---

133 In recent years, many voices in Germany's academic circle have wished to see the term 'race' entirely abolished (for instance, in biological terms: Kattmann, 2003). The critics of the word argue that all biological or sociological criteria for defining a race are completely subjective and therefore quite arbitrary. The term had been used in order to provide a 'scientific' justification of the greater or lesser worth of people, and thus to provide a basis for misuse of the power and authority that some people have over others.

In 2005 this debate was taken up by the general member' meeting of the German Community of the Cross of Nails in Löwenstein: one centre submitted the request that the term 'race' as used in the Litany of Reconciliation ('The hatred that divides race from race') should be replaced by an alternative phrasing. James Diamond was present in Löwenstein, as the representative of the American Community of the Cross of Nails. He reported that in Cincinnati and in his cathedral, the term 'race' is used deliberately and consciously, because in the English language it is possible to use it in a neutral sense (e.g. in the sense of 'racial reconciliation', see also below). Moreover, a word is still required that can describe the major distinguishable groups of mankind. Not using particular terms will make no difference to the existence of racism, and doing away with the word will open the door to much greater misuse, was Diamond's line of argument.

The steering committee of the German Community of the Cross of Nails finally decided, on the one hand, to keep to the wording used up to that time, insofar as it relates to the official translation of the Reconciliation Litany of Coventry Cathedral. On the other hand, the centres are free to choose different versions, as long as it is made clear that these are solely based on the Coventry Litany.

In October 2003, when I visited Cincinnati and its cathedral, the events of 2001 were still very fresh in the minds of the people that I came to know. The unrest was still a matter for daily discussion, such as in the 'lunchtime lectures' regularly held in the cathedral. During the week when I was there, the candidates for election to the city council were presenting their programmes and visions for Cincinnati in these lectures. The undercover racism in the city was mentioned several times (for example, the intimidation methods used by the police, and computer surveillance). James Diamond also took me to Over-the-Rhine, the sector of the city in which Timothy Thomas was shot. Originally founded by German settlers, Over-the-Rhine is now one of the poorest areas of Cincinnati, with a high rate of crime, but at the same time a dynamic and pulsating African-American quarter. James Diamond arranged a meeting with ReStOC, a kind of housing association with which the cathedral occasionally works. ReStOC is involved in providing affordable housing in this underprivileged part of the city, refurbishes historically important houses, and supports various community projects that promote the citizens' feelings of unity with each other and their involvement in Over-the-Rhine.

However, to return to 2001. For Christ Church Cathedral, one of the first consequences of the unrest was that James Diamond convened a committee, 'The Cathedral in the City', with members of varying ages, both sexes, and various ethnic backgrounds. The committee was asked to evaluate relations between people in the cathedral from different ethnic backgrounds, and check whether there was any hidden racism even in the cathedral. As long as the cathedral did not pursue these questions in an offensive manner, and worked on them internally, the cathedral should not raise its voice in public – that was the Dean's opinion. The committee met once a week for several months. African-American members of the community were invited to describe their experiences with the cathedral.

> 'These were [some] difficult discussions about truth, before it was possible for reconciliation to occur. Spreading out from the work of the committee were various configurations of meetings and discussions involving more than two hundred members of the congregation as people came to understand the dimensions of racist attitudes and actions, however unconscious, within the cathedral.'[134]

---

134 Diamond, 2007.

The Cathedral Racial Reconciliation Initiative was created. With collaboration and theoretical support from Harvard University's Kennedy School of Government, this reconciliation initiative spent two years in trying to bring together people from all sectors of society and all parts of the city, to build new trust in Cincinnati, and to seek a common future for all the city's inhabitants. Leading members of the local community were identified and encouraged, who were thought to be capable of bridging the gulf between the two sides – the aim was to form small groups at a local level of committed citizens from different ethnic backgrounds, in which trustworthy co-operation would be possible.

In addition, the cathedral created its own Racial Reconciliation Institute, to be a place where central and controversial social topics could be discussed openly and without stress. The Institute set up a Truth and Reconciliation Hearing, based on the model used in South Africa, and a judge from the Ohio Supreme Court was enlisted as moderator of the sittings. Interested parties were invited to give evidence and tell of their experiences. A DVD was produced to explain the work of the Racial Reconciliation Institute, and this also contained some of these stories. One of them is particularly moving – the testimony of an old lady, whose father had been a member of the Ku-Klux-Klan. With a catch in her voice, she told of how she had tried all through her life to reconcile to herself the horror of her father's membership of a racist secret society, with the love that she felt for him. She had been plagued by shame and feelings of guilt for forty years – and now that the truth was out, she hoped that she might perhaps be able to feel God's love and mercy once more. By contrast, an African-American told of how members of the Klan had stormed around his father's house near Birmingham, Alabama one evening with a rope in their hands, to drag his father out. The father only survived because, by good fortune, he was not at home that evening, and the family moved up north to Cincinnati. The man ended his testimony with the words: 'Our lives are all intertwined together. And as long as we share these kinds of stories and talk about the history, then we can begin to heal.'[135]

The Institute is currently preparing to call together a forum of experts, composed of legal experts and teachers, to discuss the landmark case of 'Brown versus the Board of Education', in which the US Supreme Court outlawed the practice of segregation in schools in 1954. Some recent judicial verdicts have called into question one or two of the decisive points in the jurisdiction of that former time. The Racial Reconciliation

---

135 See Racial Reconciliation Institute, 2005.

Institute is also preparing a sponsorship programme through which special African-American candidates can be selected to train for ordination in the Episcopalian Church.[136]

Dean Diamond's understanding of the work of reconciliation is clearly expressed in the work of the Racial Reconciliation Institute. For him, the projects are a way of expressing in practical terms the motto of the North American Community of the Cross of Nails: Truth + Forgiveness = Reconciliation. The act of forgiveness is especially important to him, because that is precisely where the spiritual difference to normal mediation is found. However, the process of reconciliation between blacks and whites in the USA is especially difficult. Whilst reconciliation is often seen as 'the restoration of broken relationships', it is immediately evident that such a definition cannot be applied in this case. There was never any common ground of relationship between slaves and their owners, so that for James Diamond this case must be referred to as 'forming a new relationship'. The basis for doing this is to expose the unvarnished truth about the history of slavery and its consequences right up to the present day, and to talk about what both sides have done. This is the only way in which, it is hoped, forgiveness may finally be granted and accepted.[137]

To the question of how the efforts of his cathedral against racism may be set within the wider context of reconciliation work within the Community of the Cross of Nails, Dean Diamond gives the following surprising answer:

'The spiritual dimension of the reconciling work of the Community of the Cross of Nails is immediately evident to Americans, especially since the attacks and destruction in New York, Washington and Pennsylvania on September 11 2001. Whereas the Dean of Coventry once called for the British to pray for the Germans, it has been our task to pray for Osama bin Laden and all those who seek to harm us. We believe that one of the hardest but most significant teachings of Jesus is to pray for one's enemies and those who wish us harm, and to pray for the grace to love those who see us as their enemies.

---

136 Almost 90% of the members of the Episcopalian Church are white Americans of European origin. Only 3.8% are African-Americans (see The Episcopal Church in the USA, 2005, p. 2)

137 James Diamond, in Racial Reconciliation Institute, 2005.

The war in Iraq gives Americans specific cause to pray for and seek for-giveness from those whose lives have been lost as a result of this war. To that end, we pray each Sunday, by name, for those Americans who have died in the war in the previous week, and for the Iraqis by the number of citizens and soldiers who have also been killed in the past week. It has been further necessary for us to pray for the leadership of our own country (with whom many of us profoundly disagree), both for instigating this war and for our conduct in pursuing it.

Americans who are disciplined by a spiritual practice that includes prayers for forgiveness and reconciliation are far better prepared to travel outside the United States, where our reputation has been so severely compromised by our current leadership. We also understand the great value of the concept of a truth and reconciliation not only regarding race but also on the topics of war and peace and economic justice both within our own country and in the global economy. Finally we embrace the idea of God reconciling the world through Christ to have a manifestation in our care for the earth and its environment.'[138]

---

138 Diamond, 2007.

10.2 St Paul's Chapel, New York City

'Coming to work on that eventful Tuesday that we all remember entirely too well, I arrived at the Chambers Street subway station at about 8.45am to make the switch from express train to local. As I walked across the platform to wait for the #1 train, the conductor yelled, "Get off the train – there's been an incident at the World Trade Center. Get off the train." The people started fidgeting, whispering, becoming agitated. The conductor then reversed his directive and screamed, "Get back on the train." The train engineer then whisked us speedily from Chambers St. to Rector St. without stopping as he normally did at Cortlandt: the station stop directly beneath the South Tower of the World Trade Center ...

When I walked up the steps at Rector St., the heavens were raining debris, and a sizeable crowd of people were running down Greenwich St. towards Liberty St. People were shouting that a jet had crashed into the North Tower of the WTC, but that it was probably just a little plane, even though we could see an enormous gash in the building – one that was oozing smoke and flame. I jumped right into the commotion; joined the runners who got closer to see what was happening; and soon stood at the corner of Liberty and Greenwich – right across from what was the Sam Goody Music Company – when the roar of another low-flying, full-throttled Boeing 767 jet flew over, and did something unimaginable. The jet rammed the Tower head-on, and triggered a massive explosion, an ear-splitting noise, and another cloudburst of fire and debris. It was an incomprehensible sight. The collective denial was in such full force that we all just stood there, trying to assess, to comprehend; trying to apprehend what we had just seen. The woman standing next to me said: "Do you think this is a movie set?" And I said "You know, it probably is." Both of us no doubt expecting Bruce Willis to arrive and to set things right ...

Moments later I heard someone scream that part of the building was coming down on our heads, and that we should run for our lives. I did – as did everyone else standing right there on the plaza under what had become sheer holocaust just above us. We literally witnessed a rain of fire, as jet fuel and fuel-soaked portions of the building fell to the street. I high-tailed it for Trinity's office building ... [The Rector of Trinity Church] said to me: "People are streaming into the church, seeking shelter. Go over there and do something." The church building itself is across the street. I grabbed the organist-choirmaster, we donned cassocks and surplices, and within a matter of minutes we very hastily assembled an impromptu service of prayers, readings from Scripture, and hymns.

People were indeed streaming through the doors of the church nave; they were quiet, but obviously frightened out of their wits; they were desperately seeking the very thing the Church is known to provide when she is at her best – sanctuary, safety and hospitality for anyone and everyone ...

I read the words of Jesus. I was reading the Beatitudes from the fifth chapter of Matthew, when all hell broke loose at precisely 9.59am. A sound like no sound that any one of us had ever heard, or ever want to hear again, forced us to our knees. Bam, bam, bam, bam, bam, and it continued for what seemed an eternity. The impact was so great, Trinity Church shook violently – almost a four on the Richter scale, we later heard. The South Tower [of the World Trade Center] was collapsing in on itself, it was imploding. No one in the church had any clue what was happening. If you happen to have been watching television at that moment, you knew so much more than we did. We thought that the Bank of New York and the New York Stock Exchange right across the street were being bombed repeatedly by blast after blast after blast. The lights went out in the church, the place immediately filled with smoke and debris, and some of the congregation fell to the floor and hid themselves under the pews. One prominent member of the congregation was sitting on the front row. In the midst of all the commotion, she yelled out a particular prayer often heard in New York City and said with a characteristic inflection, "Jesus! Jesus!" And I thought to myself, what an appropriate petition to be making in the midst of what was surely to be our end. "Maranatha, come Lord Jesus".

I kept right on reading the Beatitudes, which of course begin: "Blessed be the poor in spirit, blessed be the meek, blessed are the peace-makers ...". And they continue: they move into a realm of ethics I wasn't completely recollecting when I hurriedly turned to them and started reading. As I continued, I found myself stunned, more precisely, utterly flabbergasted, by Jesus' words and the most amazing, the most uncanny juxtaposition of those words with the unimaginable, incomprehensible events that were taking place just four hundred and fifty feet away. I hope you can appreciate this anomalous picture. Here we were, reading verses from the fifth chapter of St Matthew's gospel, as we prepared ourselves to surrender the gift of our lives: "You have heard that it was said, 'You shall love your neighbor and hate your enemy', but I say to you, Love your enemies and pray for those who persecute you, so that you may be children of your Father in heaven. You have heard that it was said, 'An eye for an eye and a tooth for a tooth.' But I say to you, Do not resist one who is evil. If anyone strikes you on the right cheek, turn to him the other also".

This message jarred everyone in that church house, especially me. We had just heard the rumour that all of Manhattan was under siege, and that the Empire State Building had been vaporized along with the United Nations [building]. So to hear "Love your enemies and pray for those who persecute you" was extraordinary. Our managing editor of Trinity Communications [which is the church's media department] was in the congregation that day. Later he commented: 'In my opinion, the first strike in the war against Terrorism occurred when the priest persisted in reading the Beatitudes before that shocked and dismayed congregation. Against the background of smoke seething from the wreckage of the towers, hearing Jesus' exhortation to "turn the other cheek" was absolutely monumental. The moment has stayed with me, and will continue to do so. That moment has now taken on a life and a momentum all its own, and perhaps it will live on in God's economy as our nation's very first strike in this new and insidious war against Terrorism – and quite a different kind of strike than those that succeeded it.'[139]

This is how Stuart Hoke experienced that Tuesday, September 11 2001. Stuart Hoke is an Anglican priest in the big parish of Trinity Church on Wall Street, with special responsibility for the little chapel of St Paul which is a part of Trinity parish. St Paul's, built in 1776, is the oldest public building in continuous use in all Manhattan. It came through the American War of Independence unscathed, and also survived the various great fires that have raged in Manhattan. St Paul's is the church in which George Washington held a thanksgiving service following his election as the first President of the United States. It stands today, surrounded by skyscrapers, between Broadway and the block in which the World Trade Center formerly stood. By some miracle, the church was the only building in the neighbourhood that was not damaged during the attack on September 11 – and it is less than one hundred meters from the site of the Twin Towers. Just one or two gravestones fell over in the church's tiny graveyard, and a hundred-year-old sycamore was uprooted.

---

139 Hoke, 2005, pp. 1–4. In answer to my question as to what he especially remembered of September 11 2001, Stuart Hoke sent me this extract from the 'fire sermon' of 2005. The 'fire sermon' has been preached in the church of St Magnus the Martyr every year for more than three hundred and fifty years, to commemorate the preservation from the Great Fire of London. Stuart Hoke was invited to give the sermon in 2005.

September 11 2001.

By Sunday, just five days after the catastrophe, St Paul's had already re-opened its doors. For eight months the church was a drop-in centre, in which members of the rescue services could get a little peace and quiet and renew their strength. All round the clock, volunteers from all over America assisted the rescue services, the police and the firemen. Food was available twenty-four hours a day – beneath the church's portal, hamburgers were grilled and hot dogs were handed out. Later on, restaurants began to deliver free meals – three thousand meals a day were served. Department stores donated blankets, sheets and pillows, and camp beds were set up on the church gallery, on which the rescue workers could get some rest. There was an information centre for the relatives of those who were missing. School classes and groups from all over America sent cards and letters with words of comfort and encouragement, which eventually covered every inch of the walls and columns in the nave of the church. Counsellors were on hand at all times to talk and pray, and also masseurs, physiotherapists and musicians. Podiatrists treated the burns on the rescue workers' feet – they set up a tiny treatment point in the same pew in which George Washington prayed after his inauguration as president.[140]

A dedicated community grew up among the volunteers. Class differences had no meaning; ethnic background, religion or gender no longer played a part. Californian bikers in leather jackets worked side by side with the members of a well-to-do East Coast parish. One day a fireman was preaching at the front of the church whilst just in the back a bishop was scrubbing out the toilets. At Christmas, some Jewish communities took over the work, so that the Christians could attend their Christmas service. Stuart Hoke looks back upon this time:

'This respite ministry of hope and healing – radical hospitality as someone deemed it: creating a warm and open space for the stranger, of such warmth that the stranger comes in, sits down, becomes an honoured guest, and begins to open his/her gifts – this radical hospitality continued at high pitch until the first of June 2002, when the city declared that rescue work had come to an end. In just a few days, the redemptive nature of this crisis had transformed St Paul's Chapel from something of an ecclesiastical museum into the most vibrant experience of ecumenical Christian community that I, or anyone else I know, has ever seen in years of ministry.'[141]

Since that time, St Paul's has come to have an important and unique role in the spiritual healing process for the citizens of New York. Almost a million people a year from all over the world come to visit St Paul's and the poignant exhibition 'Unwavering Spirit: Hope and Healing at Ground Zero' – at holiday times there can be over ten thousand visitors in a single day. One small thing that sticks in my memory is the many

---

140 Sanderson, 2004 gives a moving account of the work of St Paul's following September 11. See also the DVD: Trinity Television and New Media, 2002.

141 Hoke, 2005, p. 7. For 'radical hospitality', see also the appropriate section in: Trinity Television and New Media, 2002.

boxes of tissues that are distributed all around the church, and which are constantly in use. The church is now, as it was before, a protected space in which visitors – many of them relatives of the victims – can give vent not only to their grief but also to anger and questions.

St Paul's is involved in other activities:

- There are prayers in the church every day for peace and reconciliation, and the victims of war and terrorism all over the world are remembered. The Prayer for Peace commences with five times four strokes upon the Remembrance Bell that stands before the church door leading out into the cemetery. This traditional firemen's summons is to commemorate all the emergency services (not only those of September 11, but also those in all current catastrophes) who have lost their lives in the service of others. The Prayer for Peace then follows in words attributed to St Francis of Assisi: 'Lord, make me an instrument of your peace; where there is hatred let me love; where there is injury, let me pardon … .' And on Fridays, the noonday service is followed by the Coventry Litany of Reconciliation.
- Every evening, St Paul's opens the gallery to the city's homeless, who can find there a clean and safe lodging for the night.
- Study materials and work-packs are produced, that aim to indicate ways in which the catastrophe can be turned to spiritual ends.[142]
- The church community involves itself in organizations such as the New York Coalition of Religious Leaders, and arranges many ecumenical events and conferences that focus and work upon the theme of Reconciliation.

On the fourth anniversary of September 11, I travelled to New York with John Stroyen, the Bishop of Warwick, to receive St Paul's into the Community of the Cross of Nails. At 8.46am, the time of the first strike upon the towers of the World Trade Center, the Bell of Hope was struck in the church's cemetery. The service began at 9.30am. Bishop Stroyen passed on greetings from the diocese of Coventry and from Rowan Williams, the Archbishop of Canterbury. It was my task to deliver the sermon – a German telling the story of Coventry, and reporting on the reconciliation project with Dresden. And finally Dean James Diamond, as president of the North American Community of the Cross of Nails, handed over the cross from Coventry.

Much of that weekend will remain in my memory: the way in which Bishop Stroyen and I were made welcome gave me a good idea of what

---

142 An example of this is the DVD: Trinity Television and New Media, 2002.

Ground Zero with St Paul's Chapel, 2005.

St Paul's had practised during their eight months of 'radical hospitality'. Another memorable and striking moment came as we stood outside after the service, with snatches of words constantly wafting over from the far side of Ground Zero, where all day long the names of the victims were being read out aloud. But most of all, my deepest impressions were of the many people and their own individual tales of September 11. Stuart Hoke has already been mentioned. There was also a teacher from the parish kindergarten, who told me how she had led her children through streets darkened with dust and ashes and brought them to the southernmost tip of Manhattan Island, to be taken from there to safety. And then there is the story of one of the producers of the church's own television and media station – September 11 was his very first day at work for the parish, and without any warning he was suddenly faced with the task of documenting the awful events and their effects on the community.

If you ask people such as Stuart Hoke what the Cross of Nails will do for St Paul's, their answer will be: It is our hope that the Cross of Nails will be an inspiration and a motivation for St Paul's, to work for reconciliation in an American society that is deeply divided within itself, and which is still trying to understand what led to the attacks on September 11 2001, and what can be learned from this for the future.

I want to end with some words of hope that were spoken in that Cross of Nails service on September 11 2005: the phoenix, which sprang up again from the ashes, the old symbol of Christ, the heraldic beast of Coventry, was the basis for an unusual choral work. The words of the work are from the fourth century, attributed to Prudentius, and set to contemporary music by Peter Hallock:

As the Phoenix wings from the woodland tree swift of pinion, soars to the sky, so will I rise and give thanks to you … Let thy handiwork mount up on high as that blessed bird, when a thousand winters have waxed and waned and life ends the balefire burns that blessed bird, rises again out of ashes transformed, restored. Saviour of souls, speak; with the sounding trumpet awake. Thy bitter passion by the Father's grace was given new life. As the Phoenix with youth refashioned out of the ashes wakes again, to the life of life by God's grace (the body's death). Our eager flight, our hymns, our songs rise, rise to praise the Lord in his glorious kingdom, that lovely city, world without end.[143]

---

143 St Paul's Chapel, 2005, p. 7.

10.3 St James the Apostle, Montreal

Cross of Nails at St James the Apostle.

The story of St James the Apostle is the story of a Cross of Nails Centre that drowsed for decades like the Sleeping Beauty. It is also the story of a very ordinary parish, searching for a way to contribute to the spiritual and social wellbeing of its city. St James the Apostle lies right in the heart of Montreal on St Catherine Street, the bustling main shopping street in this big city in the French-speaking part of Canada. The church first opened its doors to worshippers in May 1864, and at that time it stood in the middle of what was still a largely undeveloped building site. On 30 April 1964 St James marked its centenary with a celebratory banquet, to which Provost Bill Williams was invited as the guest speaker. On the following morning, the Provost of Coventry preached at the commemorative service, and presented a Cross of Nails to St James.[144] The Cross took a place of honour on the wall of the sanctuary, where a bronze tablet beneath it explains its significance:

> This Cross of Nails, made from 14th century hand-forged nails from the roof of the Cathedral of St Michael, Coventry, England, destroyed by aerial bombardment in November 1940, is the symbol of the ministry of International Christian Reconciliation centered upon Coventry Cathedral. Its placing here brings the church of St James the Apostle into close fellowship with Coventry Cathedral in the search for the relevance of the Christian faith to the international needs of the world.

---

144 Exactly how Provost Williams came to be invited is no longer clear. But at any rate, Coventry Cathedral had already had contacts with Canada prior to his visit. Provost Howard had visited Canada together with Basil Spence, the architect of Coventry's new cathedral, on a lecture and fund-raising tour in 1953 (see Spence, 1962, pp. 78–83). During this trip he presented Crosses of Nails to several Canadian cathedrals, such as Christ Church Cathedral in Vancouver.

The Cross and its tablet remained hanging there, but its story and its significance were largely forgotten, which is evidence of the fact that in the early years many crosses of nails were presented more as 'souvenirs'. It intended to invoke a certain solidarity with Coventry, but this was not linked with any specific criteria or duties.[145] And so the connection with Coventry soon lapsed into slumber. Parishioner Deborah Hinton recalls that:

'By the time my husband Michael and I had joined the community, the Cross of Nails had faded quite literally into a dark corner of the church ... Some time in mid 2004, I'd been a member of the St James the Apostle community for over a year. And I was curious. What was this "close fellowship with Coventry Cathedral" about? My questions came at an opportune time. We had a new rector, Linda Borden Taylor, and it turned out she was as curious as I was.'[146]

Deborah Hinton's research among older members of the parish and on the internet led to an e-mail addressed to the International Centre for Reconciliation in Coventry. From there she discovered that the opinion in Coventry was that St James was one of those Cross of Nails centres with which all contact had been lost. Moreover, Deborah Hinton was amazed to find that there is an international Community of the Cross of Nails with more than 160 centres worldwide. This discovery provided the incentive for St James to look for ways in which the Cross of Nails could acquire some significance in terms of the life of the parish. After some preliminaries and preparatory work, the Cross of Nails was rededicated, in a service in autumn 2005, and confirmed as a symbol of reconciliation. Since the Litany of Reconciliation was pronounced for the first time at St James during this service, it has been used again and again on particular occasions (e.g. at the weekly Communion service and healing service on Thursday evenings, at Easter, and on Remembrance Day).

But what is it like, when a 'normal' church parish sets out to track down the Coventry spirit of reconciliation? Deborah Hinton asked a few members of the parish what significance the Cross of Nails already had for them, or what significance it might have in the future.[147] These

145 See Chapter 3, pp. 19–20.
146 Hinton, 2007.
147 All the quotations that follow in this chapter are taken from Hinton 2007.

statements will now be read in connection with some of the initiatives undertaken by the community. I would like to begin with a fairly general reflection, one that made a particular impression on me. The head of the Sanctuary Guild, which is concerned with looking after the interior of the church, said of the Cross of Nails:

'Every time I look at the Cross of Nails, or clean the plaque, or hear about the Ministry, I am reminded of that very dangerous petition in the Lord's Prayer, "as we forgive those who trespass against us". It reminds me that I had better make sure that I truly forgive, and move on into a new relationship of truer love with those who I think or I know have offended me. It also reminds me that I had better make sure that I have apologized to those whom I have offended. And, in doing so, I am not only reconciled with other people, but also grow in my relationship with God ...

For me, reconciliation is about moving on from 'wickedness' – be it the sin of commission or the sin of omission, or the refusal to forgive – to a fuller life in Christ. I have no right to refuse the petition of one who seeks forgiveness – think of Jesus' ministry, as well as one of the greatest acts of forgiveness ever, the forgiveness of Saul of Tarsus who sent Stephen and other Christians to death. And look at the result, the ministry of Saint Paul!'

It seems that being involved with the Cross of Nails has caused St James to be more dynamic in looking outwards beyond the confines of its own parish, and in grappling with the social issues of the city. Writing about this, Deborah Hinton says:

'We're a very diverse community in terms of race and sexual orientation, surrounded by a university with a very strong and visible Islamic student population ... We're searching for opportunities to build relationships beyond our garden. We expect that in doing so, we will gain deeper understanding of inter-faith issues, racism and sexual orientation.'

By the time of the interregnum in the parish (2002–03), the parishioners were already firmly of the opinion that the huge nave of St James no longer met the needs and requirements of the services and of the life of the parish in general. What was wanted was a flexible place of worship, in which on one hand the now smaller congregation would feel comfortable, and which on the other hand could also be used for other purposes, whilst somehow retaining the beauty of the spacious nave. This led to a number of conversion projects, which were completed by early in 2006. The re-awakened interest in Coventry became clear when the church was rededicated at Easter 2006: musical items were performed which also have a special significance for Coventry. The parish choirmaster and organist explains it like this:

'Our work with the Community of the Cross of Nails connects us concretely with our world communion, lifting us out of our insularity, and helps us to see our own challenges more objectively. Following the suggestion [from Deborah Hinton], we researched what music was sung at the re-consecration of the newly built Coventry Cathedral, and used this "Coventry Antiphon" by Herbert Howells at the re-dedication of the transformed nave at St James. The Litany of the Cross of Nails was coupled with "A Prayer for Peace" by David Lord, written for the Coventry Cathedral Choir in 1971. This experience coupled us directly with a somewhat parallel situation, thus for me, raised us up and increased the relevance of our expression of faith on that day.'

In addition to this transformed church nave, St James now also has a large parish room. Although this has occasionally been hired out in the past, the parish has recently started a deliberate policy of opening its rooms to others, as part of what might be called a parish outreach concept, allowing them to support and promote other groups and their aims. Thus, the Ethiopian Orthodox Church regularly holds its services here, as does the Impact Church, a cross-confessional church for young people. Alcoholics Anonymous meets there, and so does Women Aware (an organization for women and children who are victims of domestic violence), Action Réfugié (an aid organization for refugees) and Circle of Support (a self-help group for those recently released from prison).

The topic of reconciliation has been a particular focus, in accordance with a long-term tradition within the parish. Every year, St James puts on a series of lectures after the Sunday service during Passiontide – and the rediscovery of the Cross of Nails has given these lectures a new orientation in recent years. The theme for the lecture series in 2005 was 'Under the Cross of Nails: exploring the promise of justice, peace and reconciliation'. Representatives were invited from the Montreal

Institute for Conflict Management, McGill University's Middle Eastern programme 'Civil Society and Peace Building', the above-mentioned refugee organization Action Réfugiés Montréal, the Canadian Human Rights Foundation, and the Native Friendship Center (a society with the self-appointed task of improving the standard of living for native Indians in the state of Montreal).

Two years later, the focus of the event was 'Journeys of Hope and Reconciliation'. For example, a Hungarian survivor of the Holocaust told the story of her life; and a young woman from Uganda was invited, whose parents both died of AIDS when she was thirteen, was brought up by relatives who mistreated her, won a scholarship to an international school in Norway based on her school results, and eventually came to Canada to study politics and economics – always seeking for a better understanding of the world so as to be able one day to sponsor AIDS-assistance and development projects in Africa. That evening's lecture, and subsequent further contact with the young African woman, led St James to seek contacts with her former parish in Uganda. In view of the schism within the Anglican community,[148] there was a hope that both sides could learn from each other, and that perhaps a small contribution could be made to avoiding a complete breakdown in the exchange between the North American and African 'camps' of the Anglican Communion.

The significance of the series of talks and the discussion with the invited speakers is confirmed by the rector warden of the church and its choirmaster:

'For me, the Cross of Nails was only a symbol of war and re-growth until [a new parishioner] took an interest and researched it. Then the reconciliation aspect came to the fore. I would say that all the work ... to make the congregation is evident if you compare last year's Lenten program attendance to this year, more and more people are interested, and some perhaps are spiritually moved.'

Regarding reconciliation at St James, certainly the Lenten Speaker series of the past couple of years and field trips to various social agencies have raised consciousness through the stories of others. This sows seeds of understanding, empathy, and reconsideration of opinions.'

---

148 Following the consecration of Gene Robinson as Bishop Coadjutor of the diocese of New Hampshire (the first bishop to be consecrated in the Anglican Church who openly lives in a homosexual relationship), some Anglican churches in Africa broke off official contact with the Episcopal Church of the USA.

However, it is not just looking outwards that is important; the parish is also faced with the difficult task of reconciling itself with its own past. The people's warden draws attention to this point:

'At first I thought that we should be figuring out clever ways to deal with major problems of forgiveness and reconciliation in the world around us: racism, sexism, the Middle East, Northern Ireland, child abuse, what have you.

But it seems to me this is an opportunity to start with ourselves. To reach out to one another, to find forgiveness and reconciliation. There are things that have happened in this parish for which we might seek forgiveness and reconciliation, if we have the strength to do so.'

The people's warden is referring to the year 1993, when the rector of St James at that time was found murdered in his own rectory. Accusations were levelled against a drug-dependent male prostitute whom the rector had taken into his home. There followed a very difficult time for the parishioners, who felt themselves humiliated by the reporting in the national gutter press. The accused man was released from prison a few years ago; 'He has asked at least twice to meet with members of the congregation, to undertake the reconciliation process. We believe that the community, or at least part of the community, are now ready to begin this process of healing,' says Deborah Hinton. The rector also left a large sum of money to the parish in his will, which was used at the time to purchase new computer equipment as well as a pedestal for the paschal candle – but it was not permitted to make an inscription to commemorate the donor. Efforts are being made now to correct this.

We will let Deborah Hinton have the last word in this chapter:

'I think the rediscovery of our Cross of Nails has given me a focus for the things I do at St James the Apostle, and an opportunity to make an important contribution by helping to bring the Cross of Nails to life in the community.

But this is a journey that is having impact in other ways. I'm gaining deeper understanding of the meaning of reconciliation in my own life, and in the life of the community and the diocese.

And, this exploration has introduced me to ideas, people and organizations I would never otherwise have reason to be in touch with ... And in one instance that relationship has developed into a formal volunteer position. I am now on the Communication Committee of the board of Equitas (the International Centre for Human Rights Education, an organization I met in the planning for the first Lenten Series on reconciliation). It's also given me a chance to meet more members of our own community than would otherwise have been possible. I feel that doors are opening.

The connection with Coventry – no matter how limited – reconnects us to our past (the British military) and our future (as an English language parish in a predominantly French and Arab community), in a way that is hard to explain. And I believe the Cross of Nails and its message of hope and reconciliation is opening doors to reconciliation within our community that wouldn't have been possible to even consider just a few years ago.'

11

Musalaha, Jerusalem

In the Arabic language, *musalaha* means 'forgiveness/reconciliation'. It is also the name of a programme and the name says it all – the Musalaha organization, run by Christians, has devoted itself to reconciliation between Israelis and Palestinians.[149] The death and resurrection of Jesus Christ is the accepted starting-point of Musalaha, as the only means of achieving reconciliation and peace. [150] In accordance with this theological conviction and alignment, Musalaha seeks to address and reach out to a very specific section of the population in Israel and Palestine – Palestinian Arabic Christians and messianic Israeli Jews. Although both groups share the same beliefs, they are on different sides of the multi-layered Middle Eastern conflict, and they are not immune to its effects,[151] since most Palestinian Christians and messianic Jews share the political, ethnic and cultural views of their respective ethnic groups. As a result, they are confronted by great cultural, linguistic and historical barriers. For over fifteen years, Musalaha has been attempting to create opportunities for reconciliation between Palestinian and Jewish believers in Jesus. Salim J. Munayer, founder and director of the Musalaha organization, puts it like this:

---

149 To use a Western/European categorization, in terms of its piety and theology Musalaha would be classified as evangelical. Musalaha's European-American support groups are also drawn mostly from the evangelical and free churches. Musalaha maintains contact with the Lausanne Convention on Jewish Evangelism (LCJE), an offshoot of the Lausanne Committee for World Evangelism that was founded by Billy Graham in 1974. As its name implies, the LCJE is concerned with spreading evangelism among Jews (see the Willowbank Declaration: Lausanne Consultation on Jewish Evangelism, 1989). On the other hand, the Evangelical Church in Germany and its member churches no longer see any call for a church mission among the Jews ('We trust, that God will let His people see the completion of His salvation; our missionary work is not needed for that.' *Evangelische Kirche in Deutschland*, 2000, p. 60), instead they focus upon Christian-Jewish relations via meetings and dialogue.

150 For Musalaha's theological interpretation of the reconciliation, see the appropriate passages in the two anthologies: Munayer (ed.), 1998; and Munayer (ed.), 2002.

151 For the Middle Eastern conflict, see also Section 14.2, pp. 153–7.

'Believers can play an important part in this conflict, because as a result of their faith in the Messiah they are one body. Because of Christ's death on the Cross, believers are given the tools required for a transformation of hearts, and can answer hatred and bitterness with the message of forgiveness and love. In the current political conflict and division, we can be examples and models that it is possible to live side by side, free of the bondage of hatred.

At the same time, believers disagree on many issues, especially political and theological. Our board presents the spectrum of opinions within the body of the Messiah. As we founded Musalaha, we knew that we had to deal with those issues, but we also understood that Musalaha had to find a safe forum where people could develop relationships, and then express, exchange, learn, and debate the issues that divide us.'[152]

'To develop relationships' – that is the key phrase. Musalaha has found that topics such as identity, unequal division of power, justice or attitudes to one another can best be addressed and handled if they form part of a process in which relationships and friendships can come about. Therefore the central aim of the work is always to enable encounters to take place. One particular method of achieving this is the so-called 'desert encounters', to which mixed groups of Israelis and Palestinians are invited. Musalaha believes that the desert is a special kind of neutral and impartial place where the participants will be removed far away from the comfort of their own familiar environment. Moreover, they soon discover that, in the solitude, they are directed towards each other. The challenges of a journey in the desert offer opportunities for building personal relationships, talking openly with one another, and praying together. The possibilities of such a desert trip are described in Musalaha's quarterly newsletter:

'Thirty-eight Palestinian and Israeli teenagers spent their spring holidays trekking through the sand dunes of the Negev desert this year. On the first day, they pretty much stuck to their own, not even helping one another up the steep cliffs and rocks we hiked. That night, after sharing a meal, some opened up enough to share a bit about their backgrounds: where they come from, who their parents are, etc. But not everyone felt comfortable sharing.

152 S. J. Munayer, 'On the Road to Reconciliation', in Munayer (ed.), 2002, p. 83.

This was the beginning of a four-day, first-time encounter whose specific intention was to make the youth confront their own identity issues as individuals and, through that exercise, to show them that they are all in the same boat – both in the world and in Messiah. Most Musalaha participants will agree up front that we are all one in Messiah. It is our worldly identities that create problems, and so we started our reconciling there, even though it's the less comfortable choice.

That first night, we did an essentially Middle Eastern thing. We revealed to each other which "box" we belong in. In the Middle East, identities are largely forced upon us by the groups we are born into: our nations, our ethnic groups, our religions, our families, even our schools. We call this phenomenon the "box mentality". Everybody has a box – "Jew", "Arab", "Palestinian", "Israeli", "foreigner", etc. – and when people know which box you belong in, they feel more comfortable ... or not. Anyway, they always like to know.

The problem is, that not everybody fits so cleanly into one of these boxes. And that is one of the primary reasons why, our first night in the desert, some preferred not to share. We know very well that, among our participants, nobody belongs one hundred per cent in any one box – that is precisely what they all have in common! – but they don't all know that about each other the first time they meet. "Jew", to the average Israeli mind, rules out "believer in Jesus". You can't be both, according to mainstream Israeli society. And one thing Israelis and Palestinians agree on is that both "Arab" and "Palestinian" imply "Muslim". Christian Arabs and Christian Palestinians are an anomaly that largely gets ignored, swallowed up by the larger Muslim bloc on both sides of the wall. In short, both Palestinian and Israeli societies can make believers feel like they are nationally and ethnically inferior, like they don't belong and are just being tolerated. When that's what you're used to, you're not going to perk right up and offer personal information.

So the second night we started by defining identity, specifically what it means to be Israeli, Palestinian, Israeli Arab, Arab, Jewish, Messianic Jewish, and Christian. Then we opened the floor for people to share how they see themselves as opposed to how other people see them. As they saw others from different boxes struggling with the very same issues, they began to realize that those "others" were not really different from them. It called forth in them a deep-rooted empathy where before they had felt there was nothing in common. Suddenly everybody had something to share. People were asking questions about identities they were unfamiliar with, about why one identifies as this as opposed to that, about why people with this identity behave this or that way. The atmosphere had changed completely from the night before: everyone was interested, listened carefully, and answered respectfully.

The next evening we began to discuss the possibilities of changing our identities – according to our own will, not society's pressures. We found that every single one of the youth had found some way to deal with the tension between their nationality/ethnicity and their faith in Messiah, aspects of their identity deemed incongruent by the societies around them. Each one shared his/her personal challenges, failures, and victories in this struggle. In doing so, they unconsciously encouraged one another to struggle on in Him.

After these exchanges, the box walls came crumbling down. In fact, you'd never have even known they were there. Israelis hiked with Palestinians, Palestinians rode camelback alongside Israelis ... nobody thought twice about it. Now that we all know one another – and know ourselves better – we'll be preparing a follow-up within the year to strengthen the bonds. In the meantime, we've all got a lot to digest back home. At least now we know we're not doing it alone!'[153]

Musalaha organization's Israeli-Palestinian 'desert encounter'.

The follow-up meeting is not just intended to further the process that was begun in the desert, but is designed so as to take the experiences

153 *Musalaha Newsletter*, 2007, p. 3. Two further first-hand reports may be found in Munayer (ed.), 2002, pp. 93–100.

that were gained and bring them into the home environments of the respective participants, so that they bear fruit there.

Another important field of Musalaha's activities is the 'women's work', in which the building of relationships is once again a key aspect. 'Musalaha recognizes that women have a unique impact in society and thus provides conferences that will enable building relationships between these two groups of women ... [We] wish to provide a platform for addressing some of the intrinsic subjects concerning daily life and family issues.'[154] The society also organizes conferences and theological seminars, with a programme that includes topics such as prophecy, peace in the Bible, and anticipation of the Latter Days.

To Salim J. Munayer, the Cross of Nails has a role to play in the work of Musalaha:

'The Cross of Nails was presented to Musahala in November 2001, in recognition of our work to promote reconciliation between Israelis and Palestinians, and the unique approach that we have developed towards reconciliation. It was a great encouragement to receive the Cross of Nails at that time, and an inspiration to hear what others are doing around the world. It is always good to meet other people who are similarly inspired towards reconciliation, and to hear their stories of how God is working to bring reconciliation to their communities. The Cross of Nails reminds us that the Cross of Christ is the central and the only true way to reconciliation.'[155]

---

154 S. J. Munayer, 'On the Road to Reconciliation', in Munayer (ed.), 2002, p. 87.

155 Munayer, 2007. It remains an open question as to whether all those who are involved in a conflict must recognize the healing significance of Jesus Christ before reconciliation is possible, or whether the 'Cross of Christ' is merely the motivational force for the Christian participants. In case of the first option the question arises, how it is possible for Christians to be reconciled with Jews and Muslims, and whether Jewish-Islamic reconciliation is possible in the Holy Land. See also Section 18, p. 182.

12

South Africa

In addition to Germany, Great Britain and North America, South Africa is a further focal point for the Community of the Cross of Nails. Here, with a few exceptions, the centres are mainly Anglican, as can be seen from the following list. There are Coventry Crosses at:

- The Anglican Cathedral of the Holy Nativity in Pietermaritzburg.
- The Anglican Cathedral of St Michael and St George in Grahamstown.
- The United Reformed township community in KwaMakhuta, together with the white Suidkus Nederduitse Gereformeerde Kerk (Dutch Reformed Church) in Amanzimtoti.
- The Anglican diocese of Christ the King, south of Johannesburg.
- The retreat centre 'Volmoed Healing Community' in Hermanus.
- The Anglican Cathedral of St Mark in George.
- The Anglican St Cyprian's girl's school in Cape Town.
- The Anglican Cathedral of St George in Cape Town.
- The Anglican Church of St Saviour in Cape Town, and its affiliate church.
- The Anglican Church of the Good Shepherd in Cape Town.
- HOPE Africa (the social development programme of the Anglican Church of Southern Africa).
- The Anglican Church of the Ascension in Klein Drakenstein.

The six Centres of the Cross of Nails in the Western Cape region have now united in a loose network, with regular meetings and occasional community activities.

Before giving a more detailed account of the last three centres in the above list, a brief summary of the history of South Africa may help the reader to gain a better understanding of their work:[156]

---

156 For a detailed account of the history of South Africa, see Davenport and Saunders, 2000.

c.1000 BC	Hunter-gatherers from the Botswana region develop into nomadic herdsmen (known as Khoikhoi) and migrate southwards.
300–1000 AD	Bantu-speaking people migrate into the territory known today as South Africa.
1652	Jan van Riebeeck settles at Table Bay (below Table Mountain).
1795	The British bring the Dutch Cape Colony under their rule.
c.1835	The Great Trek: the so-called Vortrekkers (Boers) spread into the northern Bantu region, outside of British influence.
1910	The Act of Union: the British colonies (Cape and Natal) form a union, together with the Boer Republic (Transvaal and Orange Free State).
1912	Foundation of the Native National Congress, later renamed the African National Congress (ANC).
1914	Foundation of the National Party (NP).
1948	The NP comes into power and introduces the policy of Apartheid.[157]
1950	People are classified by race: the Group Areas Act forces Blacks, Coloureds and Indians to re-settle; the beginning of civil disobedience, led by Nelson Mandela and the ANC.
1960	The Sharpeville Massacre, in which sixty-nine black demonstrators were killed; the ANC is banned.
1964	Mandela is sentenced to life imprisonment.
1976	Soweto uprising: in the aftermath, more than six hundred are killed in the black townships.
1984	Bishop Desmond Tutu is awarded the Nobel Peace Prize.
1984–9	The country is in a state of emergency.

---

157 Apartheid (Afrikaans for 'Separation') is the name for South Africa's former political system, in which white supremacy was ensured by the strict separation of whites and non-whites. A Christian-nationalist ideology – based upon Dutch neo-Calvinism, German romanticism and Anglo-Saxon racial theories – provided the theoretical support for racial segregation (see Dubow, 1995, pp. 246–83). Omond, 1985, gives a comprehensive overview of the effects of the Apartheid laws on all aspects of life (health, education and upbringing, place of residence, means of transport, etc.). In my opinion Sparks, 2003, gives the most readable account of the story of Apartheid.

1986	Desmond Tutu becomes archbishop of Cape Town.
1989	F. W. de Klerk succeeds P. W. Botha as state president; segregation in public establishments is ended.
1990	The ban on the ANC is lifted; Mandela is set free.
1991	Multi-party talks commence; international sanctions are lifted.
1993	Mandela and de Klerk are jointly awarded the Nobel Peace Prize.
1994	The ANC are victorious in the first free elections; Mandela becomes president.
1996	The Truth and Reconciliation Commission is set up, under the presidency of Tutu.
1999	The ANC wins the election once again; Thabo Mbeki becomes president.

Desmond Tutu, Nelson Mandela and F. W. de Klerk,[158] the miracle of free elections in 1994, the Truth and Reconciliation Commission – rarely has any country been so strongly associated with the word 'reconciliation' as South Africa. The change in the country is quoted regularly as a shining example of successful reconciliation. However it is a fact that, during the years of Apartheid, 'reconciliation' was by no means the solution for which everyone was striving – this idea was only formulated by the progressive element among the white South Africans, whilst on the opposing political side it was only black South Africans with an international reputation (such as Desmond Tutu) who were permitted to speak about reconciliation without having to fear repression from the ruling regime. It was those in power who decided what could be said, and when – and for the black and coloured majority of the population, the question of reconciliation might as well not have existed. For them the first step to be achieved was the removal of the system of suppression. Only after Nelson Mandela was set free did the idea of reconciliation or rapprochement begin to take on, and that was chiefly for purely pragmatic reasons. Blacks and whites both recognized that peace must be achieved in order that the new South Africa could function, and President Mandela made an exceptional contribution to uniting the country, by means of symbolic gestures of reconciliation.[159]

---

158 See the (auto)-biographies of the three Nobel Peace Prizewinners: Allen, 2007; Mandela, 1994; and de Klerk, 1999.

159 Mandela's symbolic appearance in a Rugby shirt with the colours of the South African Springbok team during the 1995 Rugby World Cup opened, for example, the way for

However, it was not only in the political sector that ways were sought to contribute to reconciliation in the country, but also of course in the church. We will now look at the work of three Cross of Nails Centres.

the black population to unite behind the team in what had until then been a 'white' sport, so that the whole nation could support their national team in the World Cup.

12.1 Church of the Good Shepherd, Protea

For most Cross of Nails Centres in South Africa, reconciliation also always includes the question of justice. Protea is especially worthy of mention, with its Church of the Good Shepherd, below Cape Town's Botanical Gardens at the foot of Table Mountain. Beside the entrance to the church is a tablet that reads:

TO THE GLORY OF GOD
Church of the Good Shepherd, established circa 1884, in which the people of Protea Village worshipped until they were displaced by the Group Areas Act of 1950.
I give to you a new commandment: love one another as I loved you.

The village of Protea was originally a little settlement of former slaves of the estate that bears the same name.[160] With the foundation in 1848 of Bishopscourt, the official residence of the Anglican Archbishop of Cape Town, the nearby village of Protea came under the responsibility and supervision of the Anglican Church. In about 1880, a group of little stone houses was erected, to provide homes for local road menders and their families – and soon afterwards the church was also erected, built with stones from the Liesbeeck River. When the botanical gardens were first created in 1913, many of the inhabitants of these houses found employment there, and a few of them played an important part during the construction of the facility. Protea developed into a tight and closely linked village community, with the church at the centre of its social structure. Children were brought to be baptized and confirmed, people met after a service in the church, the whole village community came together for weddings and funerals. A little church primary school was attached to the church. 'Protea was a community of saints and sinners, of joy and sadness, but it was a community.'[161]

The criminal law-making of the Apartheid regime put an end to all this.[162] In 1957, based on the Group Areas Act of 1950, a large area around Table Mountain was declared to be a region in which only

---

160 Named after the protea plant, which has flowers resembling thistles. The King Protea is the national flower of South Africa. The nearby botan'·al garden is home to the world's largest collection of proteas.

161 Thus wrote Bishop Christopher Gregorowski, w'   ·st responsible for Protea in the 1960s (in *From Protea to Coventry*, 2000).

162 See *From Protea to Coventry*, 2000. This collection .   by some of those who were involved was produced for the First Intern.   ʻ the Community of the Cross of Nails in Coventry in August 2000, and is document.

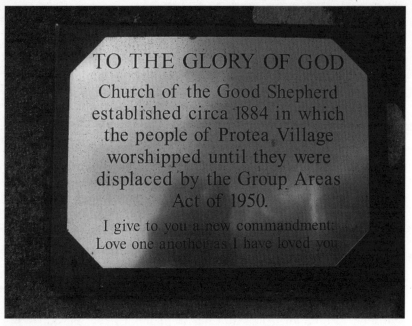

Memorial tablet at the Church of the Good Shepherd.

whites were allowed to live. And so the inhabitants of Protea, labelled as 'coloureds', were driven out and re-settled in the Cape Flats, the sandy windswept plain outside of Cape Town that had been allocated to the non-whites. In 1968 the last families were forced to leave Protea – without any kind of forewarning or time to prepare themselves.

> 'Many of the older people, who had lived in Protea Village all their lives and had firm family roots there, were the most traumatized by their uprootment and forced removals, so much that many of them gave up hope. Having to live in the dreary sandy wastelands of the Cape Flats, with no garden, tree or river, and amongst total strangers, some simply died of a broken heart.'[163]

The Good Shepherd Church was shut up and most of the houses, more than a hundred of them, were destroyed. The plan to build an elementary school for whites was never put into practice, however – and so the land became a sort of park, in the midst of one of Cape Town's most

---

163 McLean and Nomdo in *From Protea to Coventry*, 2000.

Church of the Good Shepherd.

attractive areas. Three of the stone houses along with the Church of the Good Shepherd escaped destruction by the bulldozers – and this turned out to be a big 'error' on the part of the ruling regime, for soon afterwards, the people who had been driven out attempted to hold services once again in their beloved home church – initially it was only once a month, since Advent 1978 every Sunday. One of these was 'Hatta' Frances van Gussling, born in 1909, who until her death in January 2008 was the oldest member of the Good Shepherd's congregation. She had always remained true to 'her' church and had never joined any other church community at her new home. Other people, on the other hand, found it too painful to travel back again to Protea. However, people like Hatta Frances had kept the memory alive over the years for the next generations. Thus, some of them had a long journey to make back to Protea each Sunday – but they received support from the parish of St Saviour's, under whose jurisdiction the Church of the Good Shepherd comes;[164] as a gesture of faith against Apartheid, they paid part of

164 St Saviour's contacts with Coventry go back to 1989. In 1991 Canon Paul Oestreicher visited the community, and later on the boy choristers of Coventry Cathedral paid a visit. In 2000 St Saviour's became a Cross of Nails Centre, and in April 2004 its associate Church of the Good Shepherd received its own Cross of Nails.

the displaced villagers' travel costs to their church services, and from 1983 onwards bus transport was organized from the Cape Flats to Protea and back. In time, the Church of the Good Shepherd grew into a multi-ethnic congregation, composed of former village inhabitants and visitors to the service from the nearby well-to-do 'white' districts of the city, who attempted to live together in accordance with Christ's Commandment, which is commemorated on the tablet at the entrance to the church. Archbishop Desmond Tutu, who took up his official residence at Bishopscourt in 1986, also occasionally found the time to take part as a visitor to the Sunday services in the Good Shepherd.

The Apartheid regime finally came to an end in 1994, and South Africa now had a black president. Under these new conditions, the first official meeting of the Protea 'family' was held in March 1995 – a meeting that was destined to become a decisive event in the history of Protea. About three hundred people came to a service of thanksgiving, with a barbecue afterwards at the stone houses facing the church. Jenny Wilson, one of the 'white' members of the church community, gave a speech at the barbecue:

'Last Sunday's theme was about "Taking Risks". Today I'm about to take a large risk, in telling you my story.

During my school years, I worshipped at St Saviour's. We used to pray regularly for Good Shepherd, Protea. At that stage I never knew where it was. But in 1979 I moved to this area and the bell of Good Shepherd called me, and I returned to regular worship at this little church …

In 1991 I had a vision. A vision of houses on the Protea village land. This vision I shared with Father John Goliath, and he encouraged me to pursue the vision. However, at that stage [i.e. before 1994], the legal implications seemed impossible.

But since then, I have always had a nagging passion that something can be done. I have watched the newspapers with great interest, following the developments of land claims in the other areas. However, the institution of the Land Restitution Act of 1994 gave me a further encouragement to pursue the matter. But I have always been rather cautious and nervous about it.

At the beginning of 1995, making New Year's resolutions, I prayed to God to give me some direction for this year, and to specifically give me concrete evidence that the matter must be pursued. On 26 January 1995, God directed me to read Psalm 37, and this is what it says:

v3:   Trust in the Lord, and do good; dwell in the land, and enjoy safe pasture.

v9:   Those that hope in the Lord will inherit the land.

v11: But the meek will inherit the land and enjoy peace.

v22: Those the Lord blesses will inherit the land.

v29: The righteous will inherit the land, and dwell in it for ever.

v34: He will exalt you to possess the land.

This has challenged my faith incredibly, but as a Christian I have to accept God's word. The mixed emotions of excitement and fear have been tremendous. I shared this revelation with a few people, and with their encouragement I contacted an organization called Lawyers for Human Rights. What I gather from them is that the community of Protea Village has the right to make a claim for their land.

Lawyers for Human Rights are prepared to come and tell you about your rights, and so a meeting has been planned for Sunday 26 March 1995, at 3pm in the St Saviours Church Hall. I encourage as many of you as possible to attend this meeting so that a united Protea Community can go forward to bury the wrongs of the past and to ensure that justice is done.'[165]

At the meeting that had been called, the former inhabitants took the decision to reclaim their land. It was decided to submit the application for compensation not as individuals but as a community, which led to the inauguration of the Protea Village Action Committee (PROVAC). On 15 September 1995 the elected board of PROVAC submitted the claim for restitution. The long and rocky road to seeking justice together was consciously perceived as a process of actively coming to terms with the injustice that had been done and the injuries that had been inflicted. This is how Jenny Wilson describes it:

'The achievements we have accomplished have been a group effort ... Most of all, we have seen a community coming together after nearly forty years of living scattered all over the Cape Flats. This has all been

---

165 Wilson, Address Given at the First Protea Village Reunion, 5/3/1995, in *From Protea to Coventry*, 2000.

> an amazing healing process, which continues daily as the people grow in stature and spirit. I have been honoured and humbled to have walked this path with them.'[166]

In May 2002, the first forty-six claims for compensation were paid. However, the remaining eighty-six families that were affected had decided not to accept the financial compensation but to wait for their land-rights to be returned – and this finally happened on 26 September 2006. A service of thanksgiving in the Church of the Good Shepherd was followed by the formal signing of the agreement between the Protea Village Action Committee and the officials responsible for restitution of land.[167] Symbolically, the ceremony took place in a big marquee in front of those same three stone houses that had escaped the levelling work in 1968; and among the guests was Frances van Gussling, ninety-seven years old at that time, and the *grande dame* of the Protea community. Cedric van Diemen, the president of PROVAC, was asked repeatedly by the press why he had not taken the money, and why he had never thought of selling the valuable land as soon as it was in his hands. His answer was short and to the point: 'You can sell anything else, but you don't sell your heritage.' With the return of the land, the Protea community has finally recovered their history, their inheritance.[168]

Protea's struggle to regain their land is a story of rapprochement – and also of reconciliation – between people from two ethnic groups in a country where for decades everything possible had been done to keep these people segregated from each other. Jenny Wilson looks back on this:

> 'Through my membership at the Church of the Good Shepherd, Protea over the past nineteen years I have got to know the community, listened to their stories, shared their pain, learned about them and from them, worshipped with them and tried to help them wherever possible. Our relationship has grown from being a distant one of mutual respect, calling me madam or Mrs Wilson, to being accepted by them, calling me Jenny

---

166 Wilson, 2007.

167 See the live recording of the celebrations: Valentine 2006. The agreement also included plans for a museum of the history of Protea.

168 Valentine, 2006.

and being able to hug and kiss each other. I have visited their homes, prayed with them, attended their family celebrations and funerals, shared my home and garden with them, supported them wherever possible, grown close to them, championed their cause and honoured God's instruction that "those that hope in the Lord, will inherit the land" (Psalm 37.9), by motivating their legitimate Lands' Claim. I have acted as facilitator, mentor, guide and friend. For me this has been a great learning experience, giving me much joy in seeing God's people affirming themselves and growing in spirit.'[169]

---

169 Wilson, 2007.

12.2 HOPE Africa, Cape Town

Without a doubt, Cape Town is one of the world's most beautiful cities. The metropolis owes this to its topological position, between the sheer face of majestic Table Mountain and the deep blue of the Atlantic Ocean – and the climate and vegetation do the rest. However, if you set out from Cape Town airport on the N2 heading towards the centre of the city, the first thing that meets your eye is quite a different picture. To the left and right of the city motorway you see the tiny corrugated iron and clapboards huts of the so-called 'informal settlements' – that is, unapproved and unauthorized settlements. The huts are huddled closely one upon another, most of them with no running water or electricity. The dusty, unmade lanes that lead into the poor quarter are not shown on any map of the city. On account of the high rate of drift from the country into the town, the city administration and the health authorities do not have the problem under control. Scarcely has one set of corrugated iron shanties been replaced with simple stone constructions and the district connected to water and electricity supplies, when the next shanties are already springing up out of the ground.

Children at the kindergarten in Khayelitsha, supported by HOPE Africa.

Khayelitsha is one such 'informal settlement' at the Cape. One of its many huts is home to a kindergarten, which we visited in April 2004. There is barely room for forty children in the three-by-six metre room; a few play outside in the hut's fenced-in sandy compound, where a couple of empty water containers serve as playthings for building towers. The rain comes in through the roof, and when it really pours the water floods into the room from the street. Amidst the din of children's voices, the resolute Christine proudly told us how she set up the refuge two years ago. Today it offers a safe home to almost a hundred children, keeping them off the streets so that their parents or guardians can go to work without worrying about them. Many of the children are orphans, others come here to escape the domestic violence at home for a few hours. Christine is especially glad that she can always find mothers or female relatives of the children to support her in this work, and in this way she is able to teach them at the same time a little about child care, nourishment or health care.

Kindergarten in Khayelitsha.

Christine was supported by HOPE Africa, whose workers took us to Khayelitsha and to Christine. On the morning of that same day, HOPE Africa was accepted into the Community of the Cross of Nails. HOPE

Africa is an establishment of the Anglican Church in South Africa, which promotes social development in this territory. The tasks are enormous – from providing village communities with clean water, electricity and medical care, to career training such as computer education for unemployed young people and AIDS projects in the townships of Cape Town, to help for flood victims in Mozambique. That is why the organization is called 'HOPE', which stands for 'Health, Opportunity, Partnership and Employment'.

But what has all this to do with reconciliation? I received the same answer as I had been given in Protea; namely, that reconciliation in South Africa must always include the search for social justice. Reconciliation between the races in South Africa has certainly made good progress already, but the healing of social and economic differences still lags far behind. Only when these conditions change, only when black South Africans can develop self-confidence and have access to education and the necessary economic means to enable them to meet with their white counterparts on an equal footing, only then can real effective reconciliation take place, and the building of a new South Africa – according to HOPE Africa. Petrina Pakoe, one of the organization's project co-ordinators, puts this more precisely into the context of their work, thus:

'The pain and brokenness that HOPE Africa is working with every day, were caused by the Apartheid regime. There is this great gap between the rich and poor of our country, which grows bigger every day, and as a church organization we are trying to assist in breaching that gap. We also attempt to get the rich and poor to work together, not only by the rich giving money to assist the poor, but also by giving their talents and time to assist the poor. We also engage with government to breach the capacity gap that government has in assisting the poor. More importantly, we give the church a voice, with which to speak against the injustices of society, and to ensure that people are treated equally within communities.'[170]

When asked what special significance the Community of the Cross of Nails has for this work, Petrina Pakoe continues:

---

170 Pakoe, 2007.

'The spiritual significance for me is that Jesus died on the cross for all our sins. No matter what the different injustices are that we have suffered in our different countries, we must learn to forgive. It is only by forgiving that we will be able to move forward. However prayer is not enough, it is in our actions that we show forgiveness. The involvement of HOPE Africa in the Community of the Cross of Nails has shown me another aspect of the healing that development work can do for people. Development work provides a platform for people who have the ability to assist to reach out and help. HOPE Africa is that bridge, that assists the one to work with the other. The Community of the Cross of Nails has allowed that bridge to spread as wide as the UK (via donors in Coventry) and the US (via a partnership with St Marks Cathedral, Minneapolis, another Cross of Nails Centre), from which HOPE Africa gets tremendous support.'[171]

Award of the Cross of Nails to HOPE Africa, April 2004.

Thus, by development work and working together in partnerships, HOPE Africa is bringing hope to those people in South Africa who are involved. One of its projects has already been briefly outlined in

---

171 Pakoe, 2007.

the story of the kindergarten in Khayelitsha. Some notes on a couple of other initiatives may give a more complete understanding of HOPE Africa's wide range of activities:

- Several hours' journey by car from Cape Town, on the eastern side of South Africa's southern tip, lies the fishing village of Arniston on the Indian Ocean. The economic changes of the last few decades have robbed the village's inhabitants of their traditional source of income. The fishing of the waters was taken over by large commercial fishing fleets, who own the monopoly on the state's fishing quotas, forcing the fishermen either to work at low wages for these companies or to abandon their traditional livelihood. However, most of them have no other occupational qualifications by which to earn a living for themselves and their families. The consequence is great poverty and high unemployment in villages such as Arniston.

  Working together with the villagers, HOPE Africa carried out a feasibility study for Arniston. This came to the conclusion that peaceful tourism would be the best source of income for the village, with its typical white fishermen's houses and the picturesque beach. HOPE Africa offered basic know-how in bricklaying and plumbing work – and thus some of the long-neglected cabins were transformed into simple but cosy guest-houses, whilst another house right on the beach was turned into a small arts and crafts centre in which the women of the village offer handicrafts and pottery for sale. If required, they will also cook local dishes for the tourists in the evenings. In addition, there is now a small day centre with overnight accommodation facilities, on a plot of land owned by the Anglican Church, where confirmation groups from the surrounding neighbourhood also meet. Some of the fishermen have now found jobs with local builders, while others have undertaken further training in tourism management.

- HOPE Africa has also taken on the task of helping people such as Geoffrey to become self-supporting. Geoffrey comes from Zwelile, and has the talent – quite rare these days – for decorative painting of ostrich eggs; but he had no access to a market for his goods. HOPE Africa enabled Geoffrey to go on a training course in basic business know-how – after which, he decided to open a mobile shop for his ostrich eggs. Now he also supplies his products to several arts and crafts markets, which display and sell them for him. His painted eggs can also be found on several Internet web sites that advertise South African artwork. His business has expanded, and Geoffrey

The fishing village of Arniston, another of HOPE Africa's projects.

has been able to take on members of his family to help him. The young entrepreneur proudly shows a printout of his bank account, in which there is more than 10,000 Rand (about 1000 Euro).

- HOPE Africa also expends much energy in the struggle against the consequences of the AIDS pandemic. In Illinge and Machibini – two run-down townships, created during the enforced resettlement of the Group Area Act – the organization provides basic medical and sanitary materials (soap and hand-towels, disinfectants, rubber gloves, ointment etc.), to make the lives of AIDS victims bearable during the last stages. In Brown's Farm an AIDS self-help group meets regularly, for mutual support and to exchange experiences. Many of the young women who are affected, whose babies already carry the virus within themselves, make traditional bead ornaments at home, which they can sell through such outlets as HOPE Africa in order to increase their income so as to be able to afford the necessary medication.

- And also in Klein Drakenstein near to Paarl, HOPE Africa regularly supports the local church community, and this will now be described in more detail.

12.3 Church of the Ascension, Klein Drakenstein

'God is good! God is so good!' These words from Father Dirk are among the most enduring memories of my visit to South Africa in September 2004. Father Dirk Magerman is the Anglican priest of the Church of the Ascension in Klein Drakenstein near Paarl. Paarl is part of the well-known wine and fruit-growing region, a good hour's drive to the east of Cape Town, which attracts tourists from all over the world. The famous vineyards of Stellenbosch and Franschoek are not far away – but Klein Drakenstein has no share in the financial profits of the wine tourism. The members of this rural parish are poor; most of them work – if indeed they have any work at all – for the white landowners, as seasonal fruit-pickers on the twenty or more fruit farms in the area. The poorest of the poor are supported by the community with boxes of provisions. According to the varying financial situation of the parish, a meal is provided for children in the parish hall once or twice a week – for many of the children, this is their only chance of a hot meal. On my first visit to Klein Drakenstein, well over a hundred children were waiting at the door of the parish room, many of them with younger siblings in their arms; and shortly afterwards, they were all sitting with a plate of rice and vegetable stew in front of them.

In that same room, the parish also runs a pre-school for disadvantaged children. Together with members of the parish, Father Dirk and his wife Ellen also care for about two hundred and sixty victims of AIDS.

However, at the time of my visit in 2004, Father Dirk's greatest concern was for the fate of the families of more than fifty farm labourers within the parish. Some of the white landowners were trying to get a court decision to evict them from their homes. It is true that the houses were built on land owned by the white farmers, but the families had been living in them for over thirty years. Two of the houses had already been set on fire, in an attempt to accelerate the eviction without waiting for a judicial decision. Dirk and Ellen Magerman had looked after those who were affected, tried to negotiate with the landowners, and were now also turning to the law on their own account. In this, they also received legal advice and support from HOPE Africa.

Despite all this misery and care, Father Dirk said more than once during my visit 'God is good! God is so good!' – he was so touched that my colleague and I had travelled all the way from Coventry to Paarl 'just' to present a Cross of Nails to his small and insignificant parish. He was visibly moved at the concern shown by the Community of the Cross of Nails in the fate of his parishioners, and by the support, the prayers, and the more concrete assistance that his parish had already received from other South African Cross of Nails Centres (from St George's Cathedral in Cape Town, in addition to HOPE Africa). It was precisely this mutual exchange of prayer, actions and ideas, that had been for Father Dirk one of the hopes that he associated with the Cross of Nails. During the early preparations for the presentation of the Cross of Nails, he wrote to Coventry:

'Joining the Community of the Cross of Nails would help us tremendously, because we will then be able to learn how other centres deal with problems that may be a major stumbling block to us. And secondly, just to pray the Coventry Litany of Reconciliation is so encouraging that it uplifts us all.'[172]

The service on the occasion when the Cross of Nails was presented was one of the most moving, and also the longest (almost three hours) that I have ever celebrated; hospitable parishioners (well over five hundred attended the service), musical accompaniment, deep spirituality and thick clouds of incense. On that day indeed, we all saw that God really is very good to us.

In 2007, the work with and for the farm labourers of the region is still one of the central tasks of the parish and its priest. On 31 January Father Dirk sent the following circular letter:

'Dear friends,
... [twenty-six families in Luiskamp] lost everything they have in a fire this morning at about 1.30am. Ellen and I were woken by the telephone and by a very early ringing at the door. We went there and the poor people really have lost everything, whilst they were sleeping. Through the grace of God, not one life was lost. Only a mother who had a stroke was taken to the hospital. We made our church hall available, and are hosting all the people to help them with their immediate needs ...
Ellen and I are in dire need of your prayers, as are all these poor people who have struggled for the past seventeen years to make a living.'[173]

---

172 Magerman, 2004.
173 Magerman, 2007.

Luiskamp, before the fire of 31 January 2007.

Luiskamp is a little collection of huts above the Church of the Ascension. The living conditions here are incomparably more wretched than those of the 'informal settlements' at Cape Town. Up to the time of the fire, most of the huts consisted only of wood, reused scrap and plastic sheeting. The only source of water is a tiny stream below the settlement, which is not suitable for drinking. The fire was probably caused by sparks from one of the cast-iron cooking ranges, and it quickly spread to the other huts. Nothing was left but rubble and ashes.

During the first five days after the fire, the families were able to stay in the parish hall. However, in order to be able to continue running the pre-school mentioned previously, the families then had to be distributed among the houses of members of the parish. Thanks to the financial and practical support of HOPE Africa, and of other Cross of Nails Centres, and of the surrounding communities, and through Father Dirk's international contacts, it was soon possible to start rebuilding Luiskamp. The farmer on whose land Luiskamp stood gave the land to its occupants; and the incoming donations were used to buy sand, cement, stone, wood, nails, corrugated iron and so on.[174] Under the

---

174 Schools in the neighbourhood donated new school uniforms for the children who were affected. Others supplied the inhabitants of Luiskamp with food.

Luiskamp, rebuilding after the fire.

direction of experienced craftsmen, the families began to rebuild. This time the huts were erected on concrete foundations, and with spaces between them to avoid the spread of fire. A total of twenty new houses were built in this way, and a big water tank with filtration plant to provide at last a reliable source of clean water. The little community of Luiskamp has now renamed itself as 'New Beginnings'.

Since that time, the efforts have continued – and other farmers have also given their workers the land on which they live, so that eviction complaints are now a thing of the past. From the e-mails of thanks sent by Father Dirk from time to time, to friends and supporters, it is evident how much strength and encouragement in this struggle for justice he draws from the participation and support of the Community of the Cross of Nails.

13

All Saints Cathedral, Khartoum

At the mention of Sudan, most people will probably think immediately of the conflict in Darfur in the west of the country, which escalated in 2003, and whose gruesome images appear from time to time in the news, only to dwindle again soon afterwards in the public conscious- ness. To add to this, civil war raged for a decade in the east African country, between northerners and southerners, until a peace agreement was signed in September 2005, guaranteeing wide-ranging autonomy to the south of Sudan and a referendum on the independence of South Sudan from 2011 onward. The civil war made very evident the tensions between the Islamic-Arabic element in the north and the animistic/ Christian/black African elements in the south. The crisis in Darfur, on the other hand, shows that the outlying regions of the Sudan in general have a greater potential for conflict, because they feel themselves to be marginalized both politically and economically by the Arab-dominated central government.

The early days of the Cross of Nails Centre in All Saints Cathedral, Khartoum, were marked by a story of personal reconciliation. On 22 February 2002 the Provost of Khartoum Cathedral, Canon Sylvester Thomas Kambaya, was the victim of an attack. Angry supporters of a schismatic group around Peter El Beresh, the deposed Anglican bishop of Kadugli, stormed the cathedral and its sacristy, destroying furniture and the computer, and attacked the Provost. His life was saved thanks to the selfless action of a policeman, who threw himself over the body of the priest as he lay on the ground and thus protected him from fur- ther attack. The special relevance of this story, in a country such as the Sudan, was that the Provost's rescuer – Amir Hassan – is a Muslim.

As the diocese of Coventry maintains contact with Khartoum, the incident became known there, and it was decided to present a Cross of Nails to Sylvester Thomas and his community in Khartoum, in order to encourage them in their efforts for reconciliation in a country torn apart by civil war, and for reconciliation between Christians and Muslims on the one hand and between Christians amongst themselves on the other. In November 2003 the Cross of Nails was brought by the Archdeacon of Coventry to the capital of the Sudan and presented ceremoniously to the cathedral. During the service, the Provost called for forgiveness. Prior to this occasion he had already publicly forgiven his attackers and had refused to press any claim for attempted murder. That evening a further service was held, at which Amir Hassan was also present – and the high point of this service was when the Provost and the police officer appeared before the congregation of All Saints linked symbolically arm in arm.

This is not the only remarkable event in the varying fortunes of the cathedral. The original church was built between 1904 and 1912, and came initially under the jurisdiction of Canterbury and Jerusalem, until the Episcopal Church of the Sudan became an independent church province of the Anglican community in 1974. When the state was overthrown in 1971 and some of the revolutionaries sought refuge in Khartoum Cathedral, the building was confiscated and not returned, and it was later turned into a museum. The Anglican Church obtained another plot of land, and in 1983 a new cathedral was consecrated. Since that time, the community has been shaken by further unrest, both external and internal, as illustrated by the example above and those that follow:

- At Whitsuntide 1988, All Saints was stormed by the police using tear-gas. Owing to disputes among the church leadership of the Episcopalian Church of the Sudan, the cathedral remained closed for several years.
- In 2003, four hundred and eighty-six people were attacked and beaten at Khartoum airport by police forces. The fled into the cathedral, where they took refuge for three months. Among the 'church asylum-seekers' was a heavily pregnant woman, who gave birth to her child on the cathedral premises.
- On 31 January 2006, a congregation of over five hundred was attacked again during Midnight Mass by police using tear-gas. Many people were injured, and six of them had to be taken to the hospital. Pews, doors, windows and the loudspeaker system were all damaged, bibles and hymn books were destroyed. No reason for the action was ever given by the Islamic government. Provost Thomas Kambaya later reported:

'We have written a protest letter ... So far now, we have cleaned the cathedral, and resumed our normal activities this week. Nothing will stop us from going ahead with the work of God.'[175]

Amidst these troubled times, even within the Episcopalian Church, thanks to the unswerving desire to do God's work and will, the cathedral continued to show significant instances of peaceful collaboration:

- Christians from the country's different racial groups live in the capital. In order to do justice to the diverse mother tongues of the faithful, the cathedral celebrates six services every Sunday – in Nubo Moro, Zande, Nuer and Dinka as well as English and Arabic. In addition, the community makes its church available to groups of Congolese and Eritrean refugees.
- As already mentioned, Provost Sylvester Thomas had stated publicly on Ash Wednesday 2002, just three weeks after he had been attacked, that he had forgiven the perpetrators. He took up this theme again in May 2004, at a seminar on Reconciliation and Forgiveness that he was conducting with a team in the Kadugli and Nuba Mountains region in the heart of the Sudan. As an outcome of that workshop, two of the schismatic bishops around Peter El-Beresh and one of those who attacked Provost Thomas wrote to say that they were sorry and begged to be forgiven. The two unofficial 'bishops' handed back their episcopal insignia and promised to work as priests under the legitimate bishop of Kadugli.[176]
- In December 2006 a further Reconciliation Workshop was carried out in Kadugli by Khartoum Cathedral. During the week of training, the bishopric of Kadugli was presented with its own Cross of Nails. In the closing service of the ceremonies, there were moving gestures of reconciliation. Provost Sylvester tells of the reaction of an old woman from Katcha, who said: 'You, my children, you have brought us ... a brush, so that we can clean off our dust, the scorpions and harmful insects that have eaten away at our families, church and community.'[177]

---

175 Thomas Kambaya, January 2007. The other details in this section are based on Thomas Kambaya 2004.
176 Both these extracts are from Kambaya, 2004.
177 Thomas Kambaya, February 2007.

- At one of the workshops, there were also three pastors present who were on close terms with the SPLA (Sudan People's Liberation Army) and their political wing the SPLM (Sudan People's Liberation Movement). The rebel group was formed in the 1980s, to campaign for autonomy for the non-Muslim black Africans of South Sudan. Right up until the peace agreement in 2005, there were reports of violations of human rights on both sides of the civil war. At the request of the three pastors, there are now plans to repeat the Reconciliation Workshop in southern Sudan, for the benefit of the families of the SPLA and SPLM.

In conclusion, it is worth taking another brief look at the Litany of Reconciliation, in the form in which it is used every alternate Sunday in All Saints Cathedral. In order to adapt the prayer more closely to the actual situation in the Sudan, the fifth and seventh pleas are extended to refer to the special problems of this country, so that the prayer now runs as follows:

> Our indifference to the plight of the imprisoned, the displaced, the homeless, the refugee, the disabled, the HIV/AIDS victims, the widows and orphans, God forgive us.
> God the Father, forgive us.
> The pride which leads us to trust in ourselves and not in God, to misuse powers, authorities and ideologies, to deprive others of their rights, God forgive us.
> God the Father, forgive us.

14

The Reconciliation Centre at Coventry Cathedral

14.1 Dealing with religious conflict

And what of Coventry itself? How does Coventry Cathedral view its work for reconciliation in the world today, more than sixty years after the end of the war? As already mentioned, the cathedral is linked to the International Centre for Reconciliation (ICR), which, in addition to co-ordinating the Community of the Cross of Nails under the leadership of Canon Andrew White and Canon Justin Welby (see earlier) has striven for reconciliation in Israel/Palestine and in Nigeria. In order to describe this part of the ICR's work more clearly, it will be helpful first to take a quick look at the theoretical debate on the handling of conflict.[178]

'The religious sector may well be the most rapidly expanding in the field of international conflict analysis and transformation today' – thus wrote C. Sampson in an article in 1997.[179] This faith-motivated handling of conflict has been brought forcibly to the attention of the general public in recent decades by prominent individuals such as the former Archbishop of South Africa Desmond Tutu, or by religious NGOs such as the Community of Sant'Edigio. However, in addition to top-ranking leaders such as Archbishop Tutu, religious participants are

---

178 Since I left Coventry at the beginning of 2006, far-reaching changes have taken place in the ICR. For instance, there has been a marked reduction in staffing, and some of the working arrangements have changed significantly. Since two high-profile reconciliation processes were initiated by the ICR during the leadership of Andrew White and Justin Welby, the following illustrative considerations will concentrate on that time period. At the same time, this chapter will also use a rather different method to that in the preceding chapters in Part Two. Up to this point (see above), practical projects and initiatives by the individual centres have been described, and personal thoughts have been cited from the people in the Cross of Nails Centres; but here in this chapter, by looking at Coventry, we will catch up with the theoretical considerations that lie behind the faith-motivated reconciliation initiatives within the wider spectrum of conflict resolution. The following considerations are based in part on the article: Schuegraf 2004.

179 Sampson, 1997, p. 273.

also involved in the middle-range leadership, and also at the grassroots level.[180]

In his study *The Ambivalence of the Sacred*,[181] R. S. Appleby offers a conceptual tool with which to analyse more precisely this phenomenon of religious work for peace. As the book's title indicates, Appleby emphasizes the two-edged nature of religion – on the one hand it can promote and bring forth successful human co-operation, but on the other hand it can become a source of intolerance and destructive force. According to Appleby, religious participants may be described as 'militant', irrespective of the way in which they work – whether as peacemakers or as violent extremists. For both, peacemakers and extremists alike, see themselves as 'radicals'; or in other words, both are convinced of the fundamental truth of their religious tradition, are rooted firmly in it, and are constantly renewing it. In this sense, they differ from those who are not motivated by any religious ties – and they also differ from the great majority of believers (c.f. Appleby, p. 11). However, the decisive difference between the two groups is that 'the religious peacemaker is committed primarily to the cessation of violence and the resolution of conflict: *reconciliation or peaceful coexistence with the enemy is the ultimate goal.* By contrast the extremist is committed primarily to *victory over the enemy*, whether by gradual means or by the direct and frequent use of violence' (ibid, p. 13).

According to Appleby, faith-motivated intervention for peace is centred upon the 'transformation' of conflict, i.e. by 'the replacement of violent with nonviolent means of settling disputes' (ibid, p. 212). There are three aspects to this:

a) *Conflict management*, which develops ways of preventing conflicts from becoming violent or spreading to other areas.
b) *Conflict resolution*, which works towards the ending of a conflict (by the use of mediation, dialogue, negotiation etc.).
c) *Structural reform*, which attempts to address the deep-seated roots of a conflict (c.f. ibid, pp. 213–21).

Finally, Appleby differentiates between three distinct modes of conflict transformation:

---

180 This pyramid-shaped model of the various levels of conflict resolution (top, middle-range, and grass roots) was developed by the American researcher on conflict J. P. Lederach (see Lederach, 2002, pp. 38–55).

181 See Appleby, 2000. The page numbers given in brackets in the following text relate to this book.

a) *Crisis mobilization mode*, in which religious participants mostly react spontaneously to a crisis, and without prior preparation.

b) *Saturation mode*, in which the various local religious participants develop long-term concepts and activities for resolving the conflict.

c) *Interventionist mode*, in which external participants intervene in a conflict situation and work together with local initiatives on the spot (c.f. ibid, pp. 229–43).

If we apply these conceptual considerations to the reconciliation work of Coventry Cathedral, it can be regarded as 'nonviolent religious militant' (ibid, p. 6) in the sense that it draws its spiritual resources from a founding 'myth' that can be described in these terms. The decision to strive for reconciliation rather than for revenge was surely a militant one when it was first taken. Since the end of the 1990s, the International Centre for Reconciliation has tried – as already mentioned – to make a contribution to conflict resolution in Israel/Palestine and in Nigeria as an external religious participant; and this will now be described more fully.[182]

---

182 Unless otherwise stated, the information is based on my own work for the Community of the Cross of Nails, and on numerous conversations with Canon Andrew White and Canon Justin Welby.

14.2 The Peace Declaration of Alexandria

The disputes between Israelis and Palestinians have a long history, which neither can nor should be described in detail here.[183] The summit meeting at Camp David in 2000 failed in its attempt to rescue the peace process that had been initiated in Oslo. The disappointments and frustrations on the Palestinian side finally led to the outbreak of the second, so-called Al-Aksa Intifada, in September 2000 – and this time the level of force employed by both sides was much greater than in the first Intifada between 1987 and 1991. For example, the militant wing of Fatah started using small-arms fire on Israeli troops, whilst the Israeli army attacked installations of the Palestinian autonomous government with helicopters and missiles. The peace process broke down completely and the attempt to get it going again with the aid of the so-called 'roadmap' has met with no definitive success so far.

Despite the significance of the Holy Land to Jews, Christians and Muslims, the Israeli/Palestinian conflict is not fundamentally a religious one. 'However, religious traditions are invoked to justify nationalistic claims and grievances', as Yehezkel Landau, former executive director of the Israeli religious peace movement Oz veSchalom-Netivot Shalom, rightly remarks.[184] During the first Intifada, many religious leaders began to identify with the Palestinian-Arabic longing for a state of their own, and started to call for an end to the Israeli occupation. The Latin Patriarch of Jerusalem Michel Sabbah became a particularly strong advocate for the Palestinian cause and for the promotion of peace and justice in the Holy Land.[185] In his Christmas homily in 2002, Sabbah also addressed the Israeli people and their government directly:

'To you all, peace and security. For you also, there was bloodshed in your cities and your streets, and among innocents. However, we tell you that the ways of peace are not those that you follow. You have power, make it a power for peace and then you will harvest peace and security ... [The Palestinian people] want peace for you, and for themselves, and with the peace they want their freedom and the end

---

183 For the details, see works such as Krämer, 2002; Herz, 2003; Perthes, 2002, pp. 154–87; and Konkel and Schuegraf, 2000.

184 Landau, 2003, p. 11. Landau also draws attention to the fact that across a large sector of Palestinian culture (and also a part of Jewish society) state and religion are not seen as being separate entities, as is normal in Western liberal societies – but rather, religion, in addition to being a private and personal affair, is also a matter of public interest (ibid, p. 11).

185 C.f. Tsimhoni, 1993, p. 170f.

of the occupation. We say no to all violence and terrorism, but we also say no to the oppression that makes it be born'.[186]

Patriarch Sabbah can be seen as a representative of the religious leadership elite of the country, speaking out passionately on behalf of himself and his religious community. The call for peace and reconciliation is more effective, however, if the religious leaders of the various different religions enter into a common dialogue and work together for peaceful management of conflict – and that is exactly what the International Centre for Reconciliation is aiming to achieve.

A meeting of the Alexandria Group.

In the summer of 2001, the Israeli Ministry of Foreign Affairs asked Canon Andrew White if he saw any possibility of involving some of Israel's and Palestine's key religious figures in the search for peace. After a series of consultations, a three-day meeting took place in January 2002 in the Egyptian port city of Alexandria. The talks were hosted by Sheikh Mohammed Sayed Tantawi, Imam of Cairo's Al-Azhar University, and former Archbishop of Canterbury Dr George Carey led the meeting. 'It was an historic occasion; never before had such

---

186 See Sabbah, 2002.

distinguished religious authorities from the region, representing all three Abrahamic traditions, met to talk about ending the violence that has engulfed the Holy Land.'[187] Among those representing the Jewish side were Israel's sepphardic Chief Rabbi at that time, Eliyahu Bakshi-Doron, Rabbi Michael Melchior the Chief Rabbi of Norway and at the time also Israel's Deputy Foreign Minister, and Rabbi David Rosen who was president both of the World Conference of Religions for Peace and of the American Jewish Committee. The Muslim view was represented by, among others, Sheikh Taisir Tamimi who was at that time the presiding judge of the Sharia Court of the autonomous authority, and Sheikh Tal el-Sider,[188] former secretary of state of the Palestinian autonomous authority and one of the most respected religious authorities in the occupied territories. The Christian delegates included Patriarch Sabbah.

The meeting culminated in the signing of the 'First Alexandria Declaration of the Religious Leaders of the Holy Land'. The declaration included:

- a 'commitment to ending the violence and bloodshed that denies the right to life and dignity',
- a pledge 'to continue a joint quest for a just peace that leads to reconciliation in Jerusalem and the Holy Land',
- a call for a cease-fire with religious backing, and for implementing the Mitchell-Tenet plan,
- a call 'to refrain from incitement and demonization, and to educate our future generations accordingly'.[189]

All of the practical preparations and co-ordination, as well as the fundraising for the Alexandria Peace Process, was led by the ICR – and this activity, to use the terminology devised by Appleby, is an example of interventionist peace-building, in which external actors work together with local ones. The follow-up work was also organized from Coventry – a 'permanent joint committee to carry out the recommendations of the Alexandria Declaration' was set up. This committee included some of the signatories to the declaration, together with other spir-

---

187 Landau, 2003, p. 16.

188 According to Landau, the presence of Sheikh el-Sider, a former Hamas sympathizer, was especially significant, since by taking part in the Alexandria talks he was siding with those who see religion as a source of peaceful transformation of conflict (Landau, 2003, p. 16).

189 See Landau, 2003, p. 51f.

itual authorities from the region. It became one of the few remaining networks to keep open the dialogue between Palestinians and Israelis and allow meetings to take place. Members of the working group were actively involved, for example, in defusing the crisis that was triggered in 2002 by the occupation and siege of the Church of the Nativity in Bethlehem. In the summer of 2003, the permanent working party called upon the religious leaders in Israel/Palestine for general support of the road map, and its Muslim members campaigned for upholding the 'hudna' (the faith-motivated cease-fire). Since the end of Canon White's time in office in Coventry in 2004, the Alexandria Peace Process has no longer been led by the ICR – Andrew White currently chairs the Foundation for Reconciliation in the Middle East, which then led the peace efforts for the Alexandria Group.

What are the prospects for such a religious peace process in Israel/Palestine? The Alexandria summit meeting must accept the blunt criticism of Elias Jabbour, a Christian Arab and peace activist: 'We have had so many official meetings and declarations. This is an elitist approach, with little impact on the average citizen.'[190] These misgivings indicate – and justifiably so – the dilemma that peace initiatives by senior leaders and efforts at grass-roots level often have no point of common contact and thus do not come to anything. According to Lederach, this is precisely why participants from middle-range leadership can have a decisive effect – they know the circumstances and the perceptions of the people who are working at the grass-roots level, but they also have access to the leadership elite; they are therefore the decisive link between the two.[191] Elias Jabbour is correct when he suggests that the process launched by the Alexandria summit may easily run the risk of being ineffective in the long run for the great majority. For the initiatives and meetings that emerged of the Alexandria process to become established as visible and influential tools for peace, they must include those important Palestinian/Israeli middle-ranged leadership, in order to maintain contact with the grass-roots level. The committee has the potential to become an important authority, with which the initiatives at the grass-roots[192] and middle-range level can be linked and co-ordinated. At the same time, the involvement of the religious elite will reassure the region that this dialogue is not merely the activity of fringe groups who only attract a few followers and have little influence

---

190 Quoted in Landau, 2003, p. 36.
191 C.f. Lederach, 2002, p. 41f.
192 For examples of inter-faith work for peace between Jews, Christians and Muslims at grass-roots level, c.f. Landau, 2005, pp. 26–34.

over coverage in the media and thence on public opinion.[193] Whether all this will ultimately be accomplished is, in my opinion, still not clear six years after the signing of the Alexandria Declaration.

As a final point, on the whole it would be wrong to think that faith-motivated peace initiatives can achieve the breakthrough to a lasting and just peace in Israel/Palestine.[194] The Middle East conflict cannot be resolved as long as there is no political will to do so. But it would be just as shortsighted to try to dismiss the religious convictions, feelings and commitments of Israelis and Palestinians. All things considered, the Alexandria Group achieves special significance because it can address the subconscious religious dimension of the conflict. For instance, it could be an important mechanism for coming closer to solving the extremely delicate question of the holy places and sites. In addition, a common peace initiative by the religious authorities in the region can make it harder in the future for political extremists to misuse religion as a justification for violence.

---

193 C.f. Rabbi Rosen quoted in Landau, 2003, p. 24.
194 In this connection, it should also be noted that many religious leaders in the Middle East were appointed by political groups and are accountable to these groups.

14.3 The Peace Declaration of Kaduna

According to the Nigerian historian Toyin Falola, the situation in Nigeria 'can only be understood by adopting an eclectic framework that combines relevant elements from history, religion, politics and economics'.[195] From 1906 until 1 October 1960, Nigeria was a British colony, and during this era it was the British who maintained the economic and administrative infrastructure of the country. Since its independence, Nigeria has witnessed no fewer than nine military coups, plus a civil war in Biafra during the late 1960s. There was an election in 1999, from which the former military dictator Olesegun Obasanjo emerged as president. In April 2003 Obasanjo was re-elected, although the election was overshadowed by disturbances due to widespread irregularities in counting the votes. And when the country went to the polls in April 2007 and Obasanjo's favoured candidate Umaru Yar'Adua emerged as the victor, there was renewed violence and accusations of manipulation.[196]

Nigeria does not form a natural state – its borders are man-made, and were drawn up to include a large number of different ethnic groups. In addition to the main groups, Hausa, Yoruba, Fulani and Igbo, the country contains about two hundred and fifty further ethnic groups, many of which have their own languages. The ethnic and linguistic factors in the conflict are further complicated by social and administrative problems. The whole state of Nigeria and its central government depend heavily upon the income from oil production. The oil deposits are all located in the south of the state, however, which has led to fighting over the distribution of wealth between the rich south and the rest of the country. Moreover, the country suffers from one of the highest rates of corruption in the world.[197] The result of all this is that many of the country's inhabitants feel that the government and its authorities do not represent them – instead, they identify themselves with purely local concerns and with the needs of the community in their immediate neighbourhood, which often cannot be reconciled with those of other groups.

Half of the population is Muslim, 40% is Christian (21.4% Protestant, 9.9% Roman Catholic, 8.7% African-initiated), and other

---

195 See Falola, 1998, pp. 12–14.

196 A general overview of Nigeria's history from 1960 to 1996 is given in Osaghae, 1998; and Falola, 1998, pp. 49–68.

197 See the Corruption Perception Index for 2007: Transparency International 2007. A few years earlier, Nigeria even came bottom in the table.

religions make up 8.7% (mainly Animistic).[198] The Muslims live mostly in the north of the country, whilst the south is overwhelmingly Christian. 'Central Nigeria, with its large Christian population, has been the most permanent source of tension. To many Muslim leaders, to yield the central part of the country to Christian control would be to allow the hostile destruction of the north.'[199] These are precisely the conditions that can lead to religiously motivated violence, as will now be illustrated in the example of Kaduna, the main city in the federal state of the same name in the north of central Nigeria.

In February 2000, Kaduna was the scene of violent clashes between Christians and Muslims. More than three thousand people were killed, eighty-five thousand were left homeless and a further eighty thousand were forced to flee. Churches were destroyed. The rioting was sparked off by the announcement in one of the northern federal states that Sharia law would be invoked at all levels.[200] In November 2002, the Muslims staged protests against the Miss World Contest, which was scheduled to take place in the Nigerian capital Abuja, leading to renewed bloodshed between Muslims and Christians in Kaduna. This time the rioting caused the loss of more than three hundred lives. Enraged mobs burned shops, mosques and churches to the ground.

Looking at the history of violence in Nigeria, it is clear that conflict is often inflamed by religious participants and groups.[201] However, up to the present time, hardly any attempts have been made in the country to promote religious tolerance and peaceful conflict resolution. One exception to this has been the Nigerian Inter-Religious Council (NIREC), a committee of key religious figures called together by the government. The group is a valuable forum, in which religious leaders can meet and talk with one another. However, it is not a very effective tool for resolving conflict. It concentrates upon the dialogue itself, and pays too little attention to resolving that dialogue – and in addition, extremists from both sides are excluded, with the result that such people do not feel themselves to be bound by any decisions that are reached.

---

198 Amanze, 1999, p. 228.

199 Falola, 1998, p. 168.

200 For the history of the Muslim insistence on the introduction of Sharia law, see Falola, 1998, pp. 77–93. In 2002 the case of Amina Lawal caught the attention of the whole world. Accused of adultery, the pregnant woman was sentenced to be stoned to death after her child was born. It was not until September 2003 that a court of appeal declared her innocent.

201 A comprehensive overview of the recent history of faith-motivated violence is given in Falola, 1998, pp. 137–225. However, many conflicts in the country are primarily ethnic in source, and examples of this are given in Suberu 1996. But even in non-religious conflicts, religion can sometimes be the factor that sparks off a smouldering crisis.

Words of hate on a church in Kaduna.

On the whole, however, there are very few faith-motivated initiatives in the country to promote tolerance. Falola comes to the conclusion, and quite rightly, that the hopes fostered by the government of resolving conflict by advocating tolerance have 'run into trouble, because of the very basic fact that no one listens to anyone else'.[202]

In such a situation, external mediation can help to overcome the lack of effective communication between the two sides – and this is exactly what the ICR has attempted to achieve, by setting up a process similar to the Alexandria initiative described earlier, with the aim of bringing together the religious leaders from the Kaduna region, the Anglican associate diocese of Coventry. Although several of those invited were actually responsible for the bloodshed, in fact they are the very ones who have the influence with their supporters. It is hoped that involving them in the conflict resolution process will have a positive effect on their supporters.

In August 2002 the 'Kaduna Peace Declaration by Religious Leaders' was finally signed, based closely on the Alexandria Declaration. It addresses all the aspects of conflict resolution as defined by Appleby:

---

202 Falola, 1998, p. 271.

- *Conflict management*: 'We condemn all forms of violence.' 'We call upon all to refrain from incitement and demonization.'
- *Conflict resolution*: 'We announce the establishment of a permanent joint committee to implement the recommendations of this declaration and encourage dialogue between the two faiths, for we believe that dialogue will result in the restoration of the image of each in the eyes of the other.'
- *Structural reform*: 'We pledge to do all in our power to promote greater understanding of the [juridical] reform, so that it can provide a true and respected justice in each of our communities.'[203]

The ICR has undertaken to support this process and to monitor the transformation. It is hoped that, among other things, the permanent joint committee will develop into an early warning system for crisis situations, for religious participants are often the first to recognize the early signs of conflict. The permanent joint committee tries to maintain continuous contact with one another and with other religious participants, to use their influence to ease the tension in a crisis, or to alert the civil authorities at the appropriate time. However, one problem facing the working group is the lack of communication facilities in the region, which makes it difficult to report points of conflict in good time.

The 'top-down' approach of the Kaduna Peace Declaration is complemented by a 'bottom-up' strategy, which targets key groups in order to build mutual understanding and teach basic techniques for conflict management. Thus, for example, the ICR organized a workshop for Anglican priests in the region, to do away with prejudice and hate against Muslims (for example, by re-narrating the biblical story of Jonah chapter 4, the destructive resentment of the priests towards Muslims was put into words and thus it could be dealt with), and to introduce the concept of reconciliation (for instance, via Coventry's own story). In this programme of pacifist instruction, the ICR worked with local partners such as the Muslim Christian Dialogue Forum, a private inter-faith non-governmental organization. And finally, the ICR also supports humanitarian work in the region, such as helping with the building of the Kateri Clinic and raising donations for the continued upkeep of the clinic. Humanitarian help makes it possible to maintain that daily presence over a long period which is so important in building up local trust – and in that sense it also strengthens the efforts to resolve conflicts. Moreover, a humanitarian involvement of this kind can be

---

203 C.f. International Centre for Reconciliation, 2002.

seen as a building block in making the necessary structural reforms. On the other hand, it is more difficult to talk about the reform of the legal system. As far as I am aware, the thorny question of Sharia law has not yet been raised via the contacts initiated by Coventry. The very vague commitment of the Kaduna Declaration has not yet become a reality.[204]

---

204 The ICR's African Team was not only active in Kaduna, but also for example in the Ogoni territory and the region around Jos – and by now some of the projects in Nigeria have been completed. However, Coventry has maintained certain contacts with the partner dioceses of Kaduna and Jos even after the changes in the ICR. Three Peace Centres have been created there, supported by Coventry but managed by local teams, which act as meeting places for Muslims and Christians and serve as early warning systems for any problems that may arise between the ethnic groups.

14.4 Conclusions

It is only half of the truth to say that religious faith inflames and causes conflict. Faith can also be the motivation for seeking peace and reconciliation. Therefore it is helpful when faith-motivated resolution of conflict goes hand in hand with political initiatives and the two complement each other. This is particularly important where the conflict has a religious component. In such cases, if religious participants are involved in resolving the crisis, this can offset the risk that politically motivated violence may be exacerbated or legitimized by religion. Moreover, having support from recognized religious leaders for a peace process also raises the hope that the work to achieve the goals of the process will be shared by those who are the most deeply involved in their own respective faiths.

Since the bombardment of 1940, Coventry Cathedral has developed a unique mission of reconciliation. Because of its historical experience, Coventry Cathedral has always striven to play an active role in areas of crisis, as a moderator and a mediator. As we have seen, over the last ten years the ICR has attempted to bring together religious leaders in Israel/Palestine and in Nigeria, across the front lines of conflict and into discussion. Thus, its work can be viewed as part of the so-called 'track two diplomacy' which – in contrast with 'track one diplomacy' between governments and statesmen – brings together representatives of opposing groups unofficially and informally in order to discuss and explore strategies for peace.[205]

But what metrics can we use to measure the aims and the success of such a service of mediation? The examples quoted above have shown that, both in Nigeria and Israel/Palestine, there are still not enough religious leaders involved in the local initiatives for peace. The 'saturation mode' described by Appleby has not been achieved. In these situations, the 'interventionist mode' by external participants can be extremely useful. One of its advantages is 'the provision of a neutral and secure place where antagonists [can meet], at a physical and psychological distance from the conflict zone and in an atmosphere of civility and mutual respect, to discuss their differences, and discover what they hold in common'.[206] The signing of the Peace Declarations of Alexandria and Kaduna can achieve precisely this aim. Aided by external mediators, religious participants were freed from the violence of their

---

205 See Montville, 1991, p. 162.
206 Appleby, 2000, p. 225.

everyday environment,[207] in order to get to know one another and build up personal relationships of trust – and this then led to a stronger commitment to resolve the conflict by peaceful means.

However, it also shows that the local work requires continued support from the outside, even after the initial success. For one thing, even the bare essentials sometimes cannot be achieved without external financial help: for example, the Kaduna permanent joint committee was unable to assist in a newly arisen conflict because they only learned about it when it was already too late, so they were provided with the funding for a couple of mobile phones as an effective remedy. For another, there is always the risk that the work of putting into practice the two peace declarations will lose its momentum, and that without the impulse from outside the meetings of the working parties will lapse again. Therefore, from 2002 onward, it has been necessary for representatives of the ICR to make regular visits to Israel/Palestine and Nigeria. In all probability, we will only be able to say that the ICR has achieved real success when this service as an external mediator is no longer necessary – when it has made itself superfluous and instead there are local initiatives formed from among the conflicting parties, who can work on their own to reconcile themselves.[208]

As a final consideration: the international 'track two diplomacy' described above is only possible thanks to great professionalism, precise knowledge of the local situation, and moral authority. Because of its history, Coventry has gained a profound knowledge regarding questions of reconciliation, and the ICR has achieved considerable moral authority.[209] Great trust is placed in the cathedral. The work must be planned and carried out by a professionally trained team, such as the one of ICR with its various project officers for the Middle East and Nigeria. However, the disadvantage of this is that the 'ordinary' members of the

---

207 In the case of Alexandria, they even met in a different country.

208 The three Peace Centres in the Jos region are successful examples of exactly this – although admittedly they still receive financial and 'moral' support from Coventry, they are run by local staff and they also organize the content of their work for themselves.

209 In both cases, this is not just important at the institutional level; just as important is the personal skill, and the authority and charisma of the people who are involved. This explains why the cathedral had more than once to find a new focus for its work of reconciliation – for instance, when Canon Oestreicher retired, the focus shifted from Eastern Europe to Israel/Palestine; and also when Canon White and Canon Welby came to the end of their time in office, the ICR lost some of its important personal skills and contacts. To that extent, it is logical that the ICR had to review the content and the geographic alignment of its work, and that the Alexandria Process, for example, which is very closely connected with Andrew White, should remain under his responsibility and no longer be dependent on the ICR.

cathedral community can take no part in such highly professional and internationally aligned reconciliation work, nor is there any possibility of bringing them into such work. Thus, there is a danger of the work becoming divorced from the cathedral, and of the cathedral community becoming cut off from its own heritage. Perhaps it is precisely for this reason, that, as a result of the changes that the ICR has undergone in the last two years, interest has been re-focused on local reconciliation initiatives. For instance, the cathedral is seeking new ways of involving itself in social issues within the city of Coventry (such as the tensions between established residents and new immigrants, between Muslims and Sikhs, the formation of gangs, etc.).

PART THREE

Reflections on a Theology of Reconciliation

Reconciliation statue by Josefina de Vasconcellos in the ruins of the old cathedral.

15

Introduction: Forgive your brother or sister from your heart

The small selection of fifteen Cross of Nails Centres has already made it clear that reconciliation can be experienced in very different ways: some centres can look back on experiences that are similar to those of Coventry, and they have therefore chosen to work for peace between nations or ethnic groups; other initiatives aim to help people to heal the voids and the wounds in their own personal biographies; and then again, there are centres that help to find solutions to the pressing problems of society in their own country or town. There are centres that prefer to work on a small scale and in private; others work more effectively in public, and have access to greater resources both in human and financial terms. All these different individual circumstances and different goals mean that there can be no single fixed definition of what reconciliation means and by what method it can be achieved.

And yet, the Community of the Cross of Nails is not just a random network; the centres are *linked together* via the original history of the founding centre, Coventry. This mutual commitment is maintained in the centres' prayers for one another, by their exchanges of communication, and also in part by their practical support for one another. And finally, my own experiences with the worldwide Community of the Cross of Nails have convinced me that the examples given also allow us to distil something resembling generalized building blocks for a theology of reconciliation despite of the many methods and different goals. The 'parable of the unforgiving servant' may provide a starting point for understanding what is involved:[210]

---

210 In Part Two, passages that contain the personal thoughts of representatives of the Cross of Nails Centres are visually distinguished from the rest of the text by a tinted background. Here in Part Three, boxes are used to mark passages that by their narrative nature stand out from the general flow of the text. These biblical interpretations and observations explain and illustrate the theological reflections. They mostly refer to workshops, bible studies and sermons that originated during my time in Coventry.

Then Peter came and said to him, 'Lord, if another member of the church sins against me, how often should I forgive? As many as seven times?'

Jesus said to him, 'Not seven times, but, I tell you, seventy-seven times. For this reason the kingdom of heaven may be compared to a king who wished to settle accounts with his slaves. When he began the reckoning, one who owed him ten thousand talents was brought to him; and, as he could not pay, his lord ordered him to be sold, together with his wife and children and all his possessions, and payment to be made. So the slave fell on his knees before him, saying, "Have patience with me, and I will pay you everything." And out of pity for him, the lord of that slave released him and forgave him the debt. But that same slave, as he went out, came upon one of his fellow-slaves who owed him a hundred denarii; and seizing him by the throat, he said, "Pay what you owe." Then his fellow-slave fell down and pleaded with him, "Have patience with me, and I will pay you." But he refused; then he went and threw him into prison until he should pay the debt. When his fellow-slaves saw what had happened, they were greatly distressed, and they went and reported to their lord all that had taken place. Then his lord summoned him and said to him, "You wicked slave! I forgave you all that debt because you pleaded with me. Should you not have had mercy on your fellow-slave, as I had mercy on you?" And in anger his lord handed him over to be tortured until he should pay his entire debt.

So my heavenly Father will also do to every one of you, if you do not forgive your brother or sister from your heart.' (Matthew 18.21–35)

Jesus told the story of a king who summons his servants to him; it is the Day of Reckoning. One of the men comes with a particularly heavy heart, for the Lord will soon realize that he owes him ten thousand talents, an enormous sum. The servant cannot pay back this amount, even if he wants to do so, and even if he sells everything that he has. The theme of this parable is the situation of mankind in God's eyes, and this leads us to an initial insight:

1. *We mortals owe to our heavenly Father a debt that can never be repaid.* However, the story takes a surprising turn. The plea for patience is heard – and the king even goes a step further: 'And out of pity for him, the lord

of that slave released him and forgave him the debt.' So, our second insight is that:

2. The basis of every story of reconciliation is God's infinite mercy.
However, the servant shows himself to be unworthy of the fresh start that was granted to him, and shows no pity to his own debtors. He remorselessly demands his money, and has his fellow servants thrown into jail until they can pay him. In the face of such behaviour, the merciless servant is held up to reproach by the king: 'Should you not have had mercy on your fellow slave, as I had mercy on you?'

3. God's mercy must have repercussions among mankind; it longs for that brotherly forgiveness and reconciliation that come from the heart.
And now something is made clear. In reply to the question 'how many times must we forgive?' Jesus answers: 'Not seven times, but, I tell you, seventy-seven times'. Forgiveness does not reckon up or keep score.

4. Reconciliation and forgiveness must continue for the rest of your life.

These four basic biblical tenets can be rediscovered time and again in the various stories from the Cross of Nails Centres. If we expand them with further recurring experiences from the Cross of Nails work, then I believe that the essence of a theology of reconciliation can be summarized as follows:

- Reconciliation requires insight into human guilt.
- Reconciliation is based on God's salvation through Jesus Christ.
- Reconciliation and forgiveness go together, and yet there is a difference between them.
- Reconciliation is based on commemoration and remembrance, which teach a lesson for the future.
- Reconciliation calls for patience.
- Reconciliation is embedded in a community of prayer.

These six theses will now be more fully developed and justified in the following chapters. However, the aim is not to produce a comprehensive definition of what is meant by 'reconciliation'. It will not be a dogmatic lesson on reconciliation, nor will it develop a detailed ethical reflection on that theme – for either one must refer to the relevant dogmatic and ethical literature, some of which will be listed at the end of each chapter. And one further hint on how to read the following chapters: since the reflections have their origin in the time that I spent in Coventry, the discussion tends to focus on the literature of the English language. For those who live in other countries, this has the disadvantage that some of the literary sources are not as easily accessible as might be desired – but on the other hand, they may come across new voices in this way, that they would never otherwise have heard in their own countries.

So, let us now turn to the first thesis – that reconciliation always requires insight into human guilt.

16

If we say that we have no sin, we deceive ourselves

In essence, the whole thing ought to be very straightforward. 'So God created humankind in his image, in the image of God he created them' (Genesis 1.27). That is what it says at the beginning of the Bible. Man is made in the likeness of God. So, one might suppose that this image of God would be reflected in the way that people behave to each other. And indeed, respect for the dignity of every human being is one of the basic lessons in the upbringing of people of all Christian denominations. 'Those who long to be with God, must reflect God's love for the whole of His creation and for all of mankind, they must be understanding, merciful and loving towards mankind, and should use no compulsion' – this is the ideal state summarized by an orthodox theologian,[211] and he quotes a scholar from the first century of the Church's history:

For Maximus the Confessor, no-one was excluded from the community with God. He urged people to 'be zealous to love everyone as much as you are able. And if you are unable to do this, then at least do not hate anyone'. Community with God shows itself in the love that a person lavishes equally upon everyone. 'If you hate some people, and neither love nor hate some others, and love others but only moderately, and love others again excessively – then learn from this inequality, that you are far from the perfect love ... that requires you to love everyone in the same way.' Maximus accepts that the motives for this love may be different in each case, but the intensity of the love should not differ. The virtuous person who follows God's example 'loves all mankind equally – the virtuous for the sake of their nature and their good intentions, the evil for the sake of their nature and for the sake of that compassion that requires the virtuous

211 Clapsis, 2006, p. 185.

one to be merciful to them, as they would be to a fool wandering in the darkness'.[212]

However, reality looks rather different from the traditional calling for mankind that has been prescribed since the beginning of Christianity. For example, in Northern Ireland even the colour of a shopping bag can betray which side a person belongs to, by declaring publicly whether one shops at a Protestant or a Catholic shop. And from that this colour can also decide whether or not someone will be a victim of violence. In the southern states of the USA, the colour of a person's skin could have been a sufficient reason for the hooded members of the Ku Klux Klan to appear at his or her door with a rope in their hand. And in South Africa during the time of apartheid people were separated into strictly defined groups on account of the colour of their skins, so that each group of people could then be allocated to defined residential areas. It is evident that both individuals and groups constantly seek to draw a line of demarcation between 'I/we' and 'the others'. Instead of seeing God's image in the 'others', they see the image of an enemy.

Can the enemy image that is formed in this way, with its highly polarized view of the world, be defined more precisely? According to the political analyst J. Stein the 'image' of others that we have in our mind refers first and foremost 'to a set of beliefs or to the hypotheses and theories that an individual or a group is convinced are valid'.[213] If such images are used by one group to distinguish themselves from another group, Stein maintains that this creates stereotypes. However, this is not to say that all stereotypes automatically lead to a distorted view of the world or an inimical attitude to others; they can often be a necessary organizational aid that helps 'to divide the world into understandable and easily grasped units in order to avoid chaos and make possible an organization built upon common values, expectations and concepts that permit sensible behaviour in a social world'.[214] Stereotypes are thus guides that allow us to get a grasp on a muddled and confused world. However, they can become so firmly embedded and unalterable that even new information that differs from the stereotype does not produce any correction or modification of the stereotype. 'Enemy images' may be viewed as such a kind of extreme and inflexible stereotype. Spillmann & Spillmann see this sort of phenomenon as

---

212 Clapsis, 2006, p. 185.
213 Stein, 2001, p. 190.
214 Spillmann and Spillmann, 1991, p. 70.

a socio-political syndrome, comparable to a disease pattern, with the following seven properties:[215]

1. *Distrust* ('everything originating with the enemy is either bad or – if it appears reasonable – created for dishonest reasons').
2. *Placing the guilt on the enemy* ('the enemy is responsible for the tension').
3. *Negative anticipation* ('whatever the enemy does is intended to harm us').
4. *Identification with evil* ('the enemy embodies the opposite of what we are and what we strive for, wants to destroy what we value most and must therefore be destroyed').
5. *Zero-sum thinking* ('anything which benefits the enemy harms us and vice versa').
6. *De-individualization* ('anyone who belongs to a given group is automatically our enemy').
7. *Refusal of empathy* ('we have nothing in common with our enemy ...; human feelings and ethical criteria towards the enemy are dangerous and ill-advised').[216]

Enemy images thus strengthen the binding energy of the 'Us'-group, and they are often based on subjective impressions rather than on hard facts. Usually the two rival groups lack any kind of communication, or else the information channels are very restricted.[217] As far as information flow is concerned, it is processed in a very simple way – facts are selectively filtered, and perceived according to different standards, on the basis that 'whenever there is ambiguity, assume the worst about the enemy'.[218] All this merely serves to strengthen and cement the opposing enemy images still further, with the net result, as stated by J. Stein, that 'enemy images tend to become self-fulfilling and self-reinforcing'.[219]

The categorizations that arise from this – we are right, the others are wrong; we are the victims, they are the aggressors; we would like to do it, but the others won't let us; etc. – are also pursuing a further strategy,

---

215 Spillmann and Spillmann, 1991, p. 57f. The two authors also give a psychoanalytical description of what happens emotionally and psychologically in a person who exhibits such an enemy-image syndrome, describing it as a process with five stages of escalation.

216 It is interesting, however, that the enemy images held by both sides are often very similar. J. Frank refers to this as the 'mirror image of the enemy': 'The opponents attribute the same virtues to themselves and the same vices to each other' (Frank, 1967, p. 117).

217 See Frank, 1967, p. 125f.

218 Silverstein and Flamenbaum, 1989, p. 53. See also Frank, 1967, p. 126f.

219 Stein, 2001, p. 196.

in addition to the aims already mentioned. Time and again, we are identifying some 'other' person whose behaviour is worse and more reprehensible than our own. Representatives of Northern Ireland's Cross of Nails Centres, for instance, will endorse the analysis made by J. Liechty and C. Clegg, that the sectarianism in Northern Ireland is based on a culture of allocation of blame.[220] This same mechanism can also be seen in many other conflicts. In short: the opponent – the political or ethnic or religious 'other' – is the sole problem. He is declared to be the scapegoat,[221] who must be treated with caution or removed altogether. We ourselves, on the other hand, have no faults at all.

Although we maintain the Christian belief in the creation of mankind in the image of God, the biblical image of mankind is more realistic than our own self-awareness, which is only too happy to point the finger at others. The Bible teaches that we do not live up to the image of God in us. The introductory verse of the Litany of Reconciliation that was quoted earlier – taken from the Epistle to the Romans – reminds us inescapably that:

All have sinned and fallen short of the glory of God.

(Romans 3.23)

A few lines earlier, St Paul had already written 'all, both Jews and Greeks, are under the power of sin' (Romans 3.9). In terms of the all-embracing sin, no one should delude themselves that they are superior, said the apostle. He described mankind's fall into sin in dramatic words. 'All have turned aside, together they have become worthless' (Romans 3.12), 'They use their tongues to deceive; the venom of vipers is under their lips' (Romans 3.13), 'ruin and misery are in their paths' (Romans 3.16).[222]

---

220 Liechty and Clegg, 2001, p. 18.

221 René Girard, in particular, has distinguished himself as a researcher into the scapegoat mechanism. Kearney, 2003, pp. 37–46, provides a worthwhile overview of Girard's work.

222 A glance at the comments in the margin of the various editions of the Bible shows that Paul is quoting many Old Testament passages, particularly from the Psalms of Lamentation and the denouncements of the prophets. However, it is interesting to note that most of the Old Testament passages quoted in verses 10–18 do not relate to the all-embracing sin all mankind is guilty of. Instead they castigate the ungodly, whilst the one who offers up the prayer portrays himself as righteous. The reference texts used by Paul thus appear to be cast in the same 'enemy image' format as described above, in terms of 'me – the others'. However, the Old Testament does know of the corruption of mankind in general, including Israel, c.f. for example Isaiah 59.4–12, 'No one ...', 'we know our iniquities'); Daniel 9.11 ('all Israel has transgressed your law').

And in the great hymn to Christ in the Epistle to the Colossians, there follows the sobering recognition that we 'were once estranged and hostile in mind, doing evil deeds' (Colossians 1.21). And finally, the writings of John also leave no room for illusions:

'Let anyone among you who is without sin be the first to throw a stone.'

(John 8.7)

If we say that we have no sin, we deceive ourselves.

(1 John 1.8)

In the face of this sin that links all mankind, the difference between 'us' and the 'others' cannot be sustained. We are all linked together in a 'solidarity in sin', to quote an apt expression coined by Miroslav Volf.[223] Indeed, the bombing of Coventry, Kiel or Dresden provides evidence of how very much the aggressors and those whom they attack, the instigators and the victims, become lumped together, and how it frequently happens that before long the two roles can no longer be clearly distinguished. How many of the pilots who flew over Coventry came from Dresden or Kiel? Did the inhabitants of Dresden feel shame as the rain of bombs was released over Coventry? And again, had the people of that Midlands town any sympathy, did they show any compassion, as Dresden burned? Boundaries become smudged and indistinct, and no one can claim to be innocent. Even apparent non-participants find it difficult to escape this tragic entanglement in the context of sin and guilt. In God's eyes there was no such thing as a neutral Switzerland. No one can describe themselves as uninvolved and allege that they were merely an external spectator. The New Zealander and Anglican priest Michael Lapsley, who would later lose both his hands to a letter bomb because of his involvement against apartheid, recalls how he first came to settle in South Africa in 1973:

'In my naivety, I had thought that South Africa would be composed of oppressed people and oppressors but that I would belong to a third category called the human community. The all-embracing system of apartheid, however, decreed that my colour would make me a member of the oppressor group.'[224]

223 See Volf, 1996, pp. 79–85. The reflections that follow owe much to the work of Volf.
224 Lapsley, 1996, p. 18.

However, this concept of collective solidarity in sin should not be allowed to lead to the misconception that, in the final analysis, all sins are equal. Quite rightly, Miroslav Volf states that:

> 'The aggressors' destruction of a village, and the refugees' looting of a truck and thereby hurting their fellow refugees, are equally sins, but they are *not* equal sins; the rapist's violation and the woman's hatred are equally sins, but they are manifestly *not* equal sins.'[225]

Even though no one can legitimately claim to be innocent, the failings of the individual must not be translated into some kind of generalized talk about sinfulness that does not really apply to anyone. This would merely give the oppressor another opportunity to shrug off his guilt and avoid taking personal responsibility. Injustice should be labelled exactly as what it is.[226] The Old Testament prophets and Jesus have spelled this out clearly to us.

In summary, from the biblical teaching that all people are linked together in their collective solidarity in sin, I believe that we can draw a threefold insight that has great relevance to a theology of Reconciliation. Firstly, we can see how right Provost Howard was, in keeping the inscription on the chancel wall of Coventry's ruined cathedral to the brief statement 'Father forgive'; he resisted the understandable urge to excuse ourselves and put the blame on 'the others' by adding the word 'them'. Secondly, the 'others' do not need to be innocent and without sin before we can care for them. Reconciliation aims to establish a new community with people who are all sinners before God, just like me. And finally, the gospel teaches us sinful people about the only truly innocent and sinless victim, Jesus Christ. This final point will now be developed in a little more detail.

Suggestions for further reading

Miroslav Volf's *Exclusion and Embrace* is one of the most readable publications on the theme of reconciliation. Those who would like to examine more deeply the question of how our own identity is shaped by differentiating it from 'the others'/'the enemy' will find some thought-provoking and original ideas in Richard Kearney's *Strangers, Gods and Monsters*.

---

225 Volf, 1996, p. 82.
226 See also Chapter 19, p. 192.

17

Be reconciled to God

The Christian message is that death and destruction will never have the last word. As we have seen, this is precisely what Coventry's new cathedral symbolizes, raised up as it is alongside the ruins of the old one; in the words of Provost Howard: the cathedral will rise again.[227] And this is proclaimed in the whole imagery of the new church, with its majestic tapestry in the apse: Jesus Christ is risen from the dead and he will come again in majesty.

This is also the message of the Coventry Cross of Nails. It reminds us of the crucified and risen Christ, in whom God grants reconciliation to sinful man. Friends of my own age sometimes said to me, 'So! – you work for the Community of the Cross of Nails? That sounds pretty warlike.' Yes, in fact the Cross of Christ can be offensive, as Christians we cannot ignore that. And the Coventry Cross of Nails is no mere pretty little item of jewellery on a golden chain – rather, it reminds us of the three nails with which Jesus was crucified. For Christ's death on the Cross brought about God's reconciliation with mankind, and we will now examine this aspect more closely. The biblical *locus classicus* of every theology of reconciliation summarizes what happened as follows:

All this is from God, who reconciled us to himself through Christ, and has given us the ministry of reconciliation; that is, in Christ God was reconciling the world to himself, not counting their trespasses against them, and entrusting the message of reconciliation to us. So we are ambassadors for Christ, since God is making his appeal through us; we entreat you on behalf of Christ, be reconciled to God. For our sake he made him to be sin who knew no sin, so that in him we might become the righteousness of God.

(2 Corinthians 5.18–21)[228]

---

227 See Chapter 2, p. 9.

228 The first Epistle of John also makes it clear that reconciliation takes place in Jesus Christ: Jesus Christ 'is the atoning sacrifice for our sins: and not for ours only, but also for the sins of the whole world' (1 John 2.2).

St Paul is writing about reconciliation here not as an ethical concept, but as something that pre-dates man's attempts to restore damaged relationships. It is not about two partners – or rather, two opponents – struggling for reconciliation, but more a question of one party giving and the other permitting to let it happen. It is God alone who takes the action[229] – reconciliation comes from him, and mankind receives it through Jesus Christ (c.f. Romans 5.11). Mankind must allow itself to receive the gift – hence the plea in 2 Corinthians 5.20, that we should let ourselves be reconciled to God. Man is the recipient of the action, even if he himself is called as a result to be the messenger of the words of reconciliation and has to prove himself in the reconciliation that is granted.

The special significance of the Cross of Christ in this scenario is more fully developed in the Epistle to the Colossians:

> For in him all the fullness of God was pleased to dwell, and through him God was pleased to reconcile to himself all things, whether on earth or in heaven, by making peace through the blood of his cross. And you who were once estranged and hostile in mind, doing evil deeds, he has now reconciled in his fleshly body through death.
>
> (Colossians 1.19–22a)

Just before this point, the New Testament text has already confirmed that in Jesus Christ we have 'redemption, the forgiveness of sins' (Colossians 1.14). And in this respect the Epistle to the Colossians tallies with one of the oldest of Christianity's creeds: that Christ died for our sins (c.f. 1 Corinthians 15.3). His death has iconic power. The New Testament and all subsequent traditions declare unanimously that 'the death of Jesus was not a private death but a vicarious death;'[230] Jesus was crucified *for us*, in order to free us from the captivity of sin.

To return to one of the concepts in the previous chapter: we saw that groups invariably take the bait to portray 'the others' as scapegoats, in order to affirm their own identity and to distract attention from their own failings. If we apply this method of categorization to the salvation story, we can say that Jesus Christ took it upon himself to die upon the cross 'in order to expose once and for all the lie about sacrificial victims, by proclaiming the innocence of the sacrificial victim – the sacrifice to put an end to all sacrifices'.[231] This talk of sacrifices may seem

---

229 See Käsemann, 1964, p. 46.
230 Ritschl, 1987, p. 188.
231 Clapsis, 2006, p. 189.

to us today somewhat difficult to comprehend. The New Testament makes use of it repeatedly, however, in relation to the death of Jesus on the cross. St Paul already speaks of the 'offence of the cross' (Galatians 5.11): the one who is righteous and does not use violence dies a violent and unjust death. Right up to the end, up to his death on the cross, Jesus remained firm in his rejection of any kind of reprisal.[232] In this way, the mechanism of the scapegoat will be exposed, the spiral of violence will be broken, and the obsession with creating enemy images will be dispelled.

> This achieves something quite revolutionary: Christian belief sides with the victim to the fullest extent, sees its own self as represented by this victim, and discovers deliverance through belief in the crucified Christ. And this makes it clear – it is not God who requires sacrifices and violence, but mankind. The sacrifice of Christ comes about for the sake of mankind, not of God. It is not God who needs to be reconciled by the sacrifice, but mankind.[233]

God's strength thus shows itself in frailty, in the final analysis his power is demonstrated in powerlessness. In the person of the crucified and risen Jesus, he stands up for 'the others'. In so doing, he shows his love for mankind – for all mankind, without exception. For the 'other' is not only the victim, not only the one who must be done justice – the perpetrator is also included in the process of reconciliation. To him also, a place is opened up in which he can exist, above and beyond the sinful strategies of sacrifice. In short, in the crucifixion of Jesus sin is cast away, but the sinner is accepted. In the resurrection of the crucified one, God gives new life to sinful man. All-embracing sin is matched by God's desire for reconciliation, and all we have to do is to accept this – 'be reconciled with God'!

Applying this line of thought now to the symbol of the Cross of Nails leads to the following interpretation: the reconciliation described between God and man through Jesus Christ may be symbolized by the vertical nail of the Coventry Cross, whilst the two horizontal nails symbolize the reconciliation between humans (which we will examine in the next chapter). But the first stage of every reconciliation between humans is always – in the symbolism of the Cross of Nails, as well – the

---

232 See the relevant section of the Sermon on the Mount: 'You have heard that it was said, "An eye for an eye, and a tooth for a tooth": but I say to you, do not resist an evildoer: but if anyone strikes you on the right cheek, turn the other also.' (Matthew 5.38–39).

233 Dietrich and Mayordomo, 2005, p. 242.

fact that God has already offered us reconciliation. The words 'Father forgive' in the Litany of Reconciliation remind us that we need the gift of divine forgiveness if our work for reconciliation in the world is to have any lasting value.

This is an outline of the motivation and basic belief that moves Christians to act for reconciliation: they are called to live a life of reconciliation because they have first been loved by God and reconciled with God. However, this is not to suggest that human reconciliation is only possible between people who share these convictions – that is, only between Christians. Christians can (and must) also seek for a common path to understanding and peace with people of other faiths, or with no faith at all. When working together in practice, the convictions and preconceptions that motivate the work of reconciliation are perhaps not the deciding factor – so long as 'non-Cross-of-Nailers' are prepared to respect the motivation that is symbolized in the Cross of Nails, and Christians are likewise prepared to respect the motivations of others as real and sufficient.[234]

This interfaith collaboration is both possible and urgently needed, as was made clear by the political/religious situations in Israel/Palestine and Nigeria, where the International Centre for Reconciliation has fostered collaboration and reconciliation between different faiths. From this background, it is even possible for interfaith initiatives to be accepted as associated members of the Community of the Cross of Nails – and the Muslim/Christian dialogue forum in Kaduna became such an Associated Centre in November 2003. The forum is jointly led by two former militants from the opposing fronts of Nigeria's religious conflict. The initiative set itself the task of promoting friendship between Muslim and Christian young people, and familiarising religious leaders around Kaduna with patterns and methods for dialogue and conflict resolution. Of course, such an associated centre was not presented with a Cross of Nails as a symbol – instead, a miniature copy of the Reconciliation Statue that stands in the ruins of Coventry's old cathedral was given to the interfaith centre.[235]

---

234 An interesting discussion is taking place in South Africa at the time of writing this book. Some representatives of the South African Cross of Nails Centres who are taking an active role in interfaith dialogue have decided to make as little use as possible of the Cross of Nails. Others are unsure whether this hiding of their Christian roots in the interests of being involved is really helping the dialogue, or whether it is not precisely by stating their own Christian convictions and the symbols used to express them that the dialogue will be facilitated.

235 See photo on p. 167.

Suggestions for further reading

All the relevant classical dogmatic compendiums include a chapter on God's act of salvation through Jesus Christ. The most comprehensive account of a theological teaching on reconciliation is surely that from the pen of Karl Barth, who discusses the topic in the fourth volume of his 'Church Dogmatics', dividing it into three parts: Jesus Christ is true God, who humbles himself and thus reconciles; at the same time he is the very man, thus exalted and reconciled by God; and finally in the unity of the two he is the guarantor and witness of our atonement – this is Barth's thesis, which he develops over more than two thousand pages. An approach to this comprehensive work is given by the overview in Barth, 2009, pp. 76–149. A very readable explanation of the significance of the Cross of Jesus may be found in Joest, 1989, pp. 242–69.

18

Welcome one another, therefore, just as Christ has welcomed you

Lord, make us one.
Do not make us like them,
do not make them like us,
but make us all more like you. Amen

This little prayer greets me, framed alongside the Cross of Nails on the wall of the tiny theological reading room of the Cross of Nails Centre in Sibiu/Hermannstadt, Romania. Forgiveness and reconciliation between people means living together in the light of Christ's resurrection and becoming a successor to the Son of God through the presence of the Spirit of God. For St Paul, life according to Christ has consequences. Just like Provost Howard referred to this Christ-Child-like life in his Christmas address in 1940, the apostle writes:

> May the God of steadfastness and encouragement grant you to live in harmony with one another, in accordance with Christ Jesus, so that together you may with one voice glorify the God and Father of our Lord Jesus Christ. Welcome one another, therefore, just as Christ has welcomed you, for the glory of God.
>
> (Romans 15.5–7)

St Paul wrote these words to the new people of God who came together as Christians from both heathen (Gentile) and Jewish backgrounds – two very different groups, who often thought in terms of lines of demarcation and were mistrustful of each other. Paul felt, however, that both sides had been called to overcome conflict and become one in Jesus Christ, for Christ was sent to both – servant of the Jews and ruler over the Gentiles (c.f. Romans 15.8.12). God in Christ accepted Jews and Gentiles alike; therefore we as Christ's disciples should accept and welcome one another. The church thus becomes a new and reconciled community, a foretaste of the eschatological healing of a mankind that was divided by sin.

Forgiveness is all about the individual aspect of these events. Only 'I' can forgive, no one else can do it for me, or in my name. One can even forgive someone else without the participation of the other one being necessary. Normally, however, forgiveness is something that is begged for, as in the Old Testament story of Joseph and his brothers in the last chapter of the book of Genesis:[236]

> Realizing that their father was dead, Joseph's brothers said, 'What if Joseph still bears a grudge against us and pays us back in full for all the wrong that we did to him?' So they approached Joseph, saying, 'Your father gave this instruction before he died, "Say to Joseph: I beg you, forgive the crime of your brothers and the wrong they did in harming you. Now therefore please forgive the crime of the servants of the God of your father.' Joseph wept when they spoke to him. Then his brothers also wept, fell down before him, and said, 'We are here as your slaves.' But Joseph said to them, 'Do not be afraid! Am I in the place of God? Even though you intended to do harm to me, God intended it for good, in order to preserve a numerous people, as he is doing today. So have no fear; I myself will provide for you and your little ones.' In this way he reassured them, speaking kindly to them.
>
> (Genesis 50.15–21)

The story of forgiveness begins with the death of a father. Jacob has been buried – and now that the burial is over, Joseph's brothers fear for their own welfare. For better or worse, they are handed over to Joseph when they seek refuge in Egypt because of a famine in their own land – and it is to Joseph of all people, whom they had sold into slavery, that they owe their thanks for a safe refuge. How will he react, now that their father is dead? Their common father, or rather the love between Jacob and Joseph, had always been the brothers' safety net. What will happen, if Joseph now sees this as his chance of revenge? At last one of the eleven brothers has an idea: 'Say to Joseph: I beg you, forgive the crime of your brothers and the wrong they did in harming you' – and the brothers put

---

236 For this interpretation of Genesis 50.15–21 I am grateful to Müller-Fahrenholz, 1996, pp. 101–6. See also in more detail, Schuegraf, 2006.

these words into the mouth of their dead father. But Joseph's reaction is surprising: 'Joseph wept when they spoke to him.' No one cries without a reason. Perhaps his brothers' words brought back afresh the painful memories of slavery – there must have been times when Joseph's eyes had been filled with tears of anger and aggression.

Forgiveness should never be confused with suppressed anger or bottled-up aggression. Those who have suffered and have been victims are angry, and they have a right to be angry. The Epistle to the Ephesians also teaches this – but it makes the following condition:

Be angry, but do not sin; do not let the sun go down on your anger.
(Ephesians 4.26)

There are times when anger and pain are appropriate and necessary. But painful memories, whether individual or collective, can destroy the individual or the group. Only those who are able to express their anger are able to overcome it and open themselves up to new experiences. Michael Lapsley, who we have already met earlier in this book, testifies to the truth of this from his own personal experience. Shortly after the letter bomb was sent to him, he realized that:

'If I became filled with hatred, bitterness, self-pity and desire for revenge, I would remain a victim for ever. It would consume me. It would eat me alive. God and people of faith and hope enabled me to make my bombing redemptive – to bring life out of death, the good out of the evil … I am no longer a victim, nor even simply a survivor, I am a victor over evil, hatred and death.'[237]

Forgiveness can open up to victims the freedom of no longer being held captive by the power of the past. The readiness to forgive cannot be

237 Lapsley, 1996, p. 21. Michael Lapsley certainly does not view the overcoming of hate and thoughts of revenge as forgiveness. In his specific case, he feels that forgiveness is not possible until he knows who did it: 'I haven't forgiven anyone, because I have no one to forgive. No one was charged with this crime, and so for me forgiveness is still an abstract concept. But if I knew that the people responsible for the letter bomb were prisoners in themselves because of what they'd done, then I'd happily unlock the gate.' (The Forgiveness Project, no date, p. 18). Based on his own experiences, Michael Lapsley has developed the model of the 'healing of memories', and he now works all around the world with groups of people who are suffering the traumatic consequences of conflict.

compelled, however, it is a gift from God. It is possible for Joseph to forgive his brothers, not because he is without sin, or because he is better than them, but rather because he recognizes that all men are fallible in the eyes of their Maker: 'Do not be afraid! Am I in the place of God?'

However, one should not harbour the delusion that words of forgiveness come easily to the lips – they are not easy to speak, and call for courage. They should never be spoken unwillingly, or merely to please the other person; and above all, they cannot be forced or demanded from the aggressor. To expect such a thing would quickly devalue the theology of forgiveness. Because forgiveness is not an exact science, L. G. Jones once referred to it as a 'craft'[238] in two senses of the word – as an 'art' in which one must be skilled, and as a 'lifelong learning experience'. And this 'craft' that we call forgiveness aims at more than the mere retrospective absolution of guilt – it also includes hope for the future restoration of community spirit.

Reconciliation between people helps to achieve this hope for the future. In contrast to forgiveness, I see it as a process that actively involves *all* the parties in a conflict. Its goal is the restoration of broken relationships, in accordance with the words of the Sermon on the Mount: 'So when you are offering your gift at the altar, if you remember that your brother or sister has something against you, leave your gift there before the altar and go; first be reconciled to your brother or sister' (Matthew 5.24). And thus for the Mennonite J. P. Lederach, a leading mediator in international conflicts, reconciliation most of all involves relationship and meeting:

> Reconciliation can be ... understood as both a *focus* and a *locus*. As a perspective, it is built on and oriented toward the relational aspects of a conflict. As a social phenomenon, reconciliation represents a space, a place or location of encounter, where parties to a conflict meet. Reconciliation must be proactive in seeking to create an encounter where people can focus on their relationship and share their perceptions, feelings, and experiences with one another, with the goal of creating new perceptions and a new shared experience.[239]

This concept of reconciliation provides the space in which to open oneself up to others without losing one's own identity, to listen to the other party's story, to talk about the painful past, and at the same time to begin the search for a shared future. This is considered in more detail in

---

238 See Jones, 1995, p. 226f.
239 Lederach, 2002, p. 30. See also Lederach, 2005, p. 34f.

the following paragraphs, and applied to the earlier considerations on the subject of 'enemy images'.

If it is possible to create the 'space of encounter' described by Lederach, then it might also be possible to break down these rigid enemy images. The hardest task for the parties in a conflict is to overcome their purely egocentric viewpoints and recognize that there are other possible emotional and rational points of view and attitudes. J. P. Lederach refers to this requirement as 'paradoxical curiosity', by which he means not forming over-hasty judgements, allowing contradictions to persist, and appreciating and examining the other side's view of the truth.[240] The path to be followed is usually anything but straight and smooth. Frequently it is only by prompting that each party recognizes that they cannot simply dominate or browbeat the other party. This realization can be the first step towards accepting the existence of another identity-group and their needs. It may then be possible to take a further step and get away from 'zero-sum' thinking (one of the characteristics of enemy-image syndrome that were listed earlier) to a point where we start to look for a solution that is beneficial to all parties. Instead of looking for victory at the expense of the others, we start to look for victory for everyone. A key aspect of this process is 're-individualization' – that is to say, it is specific individuals that have to meet each other, not just two abstract identity-groups. This takes place in two ways:

> inwards, meaning within the own group, where early in an escalation of conflict an intolerance to different evaluations and perception in the group develops, and outward, towards the enemy, who as a stereotyped category has lost not only his individuality, but also his humanity.[241]

The joint work carried out by Germans and British in the ruins of Dresden's Diakonissenkrankenhaus (deaconesses' hospital) was surely just

---

240 See Lederach, 2005, pp. 35–7. Absorbing new facts about the other party into our preconceived notions of them takes time, for – as we have seen – enemy images are generally deeply entrenched, and new information is not absorbed impartially. Therefore Stein feels that it sometimes helps to produce a large quantity of inconsistent data: 'Important beliefs can change dramatically when there is no other way to account for 'large' amounts of contradictory data. Greater change will occur when information arrives in large batches, rather than bit by bit' (Stein, 2001, p. 197).

241 Spillmann and Spillmann, 1991, p. 71f. The preparations to initiate personal relationships must be carefully planned in order not to seem counter-productive. These will preferably be accompanied by a targeted information policy, training in the ability to communicate, and by clearly defining what should be the objective of initial talks and what each side should expect from them (see Spillmann and Spillmann, 1991, p. 72f).

such a meeting space for reconciliation. Anyone who works for weeks or months on end with the 'enemy' on a joint project, spends their free time together and goes together to Bible study and church services, finds it impossible to dwell upon abstract enemy images – the 'other one' now has a face. When one plays football together or prays together, it is no longer possible to see things in terms of black and white, for many shades of grey appear. And if friendships are formed across the border-lines, then perhaps all the colours of the rainbow may become visible. I imagine that those young adults got to know each other as real human beings – with all the strengths and the weaknesses of humanity. The Germans must surely have been confronted with the uncomfortable question of how such injustice could have taken place in their names; and the British, in their turn, may have learned that not all Germans were entrenched Nazis, even if they had all been part of the iniquitous Nazi system. During the clearing-up work in Dresden, the young British may also have discovered the damage that the carpet-bombing had caused in the German city. I am certain that all the young people began to understand why Provost Howard insisted on the words 'Father forgive'. Further examples can be seen in the Cornerstone Community in Belfast and Musalaha in Israel/Palestine – for both these cross-community projects are trying to make visible the individual people behind the opposing identity-group on the other side of the fence, and to seek for and promote person-to-person dialogue.[242]

In the Dresden–Coventry project and also in the Cornerstone Community, it became clear that the virtue of seeking for relationships and meetings can come to have a special role – and it is a role that was venerated both in the ancient Orient and in Greek antiquity, and that also has a special importance both in the Old Testament and the New Testament; it is known as hospitality. It provides, as one might say, a 'non-violent way of dealing with the fear that can be triggered by the arrival of strangers'.[243] By means of hospitality, the stranger – the 'other' – is transformed into a fellow lodger, if only for the moment. It is an important form of Christian fellow-love with great potential for reconciliation, when in Belfast doors are open to people, who after all just live on the other side of the street and yet are such infinite strangers! And I believe that hospitality also plays a decisive role in

---

242 In addition to the national political level and the social level between alienated communities and groups (see under the earlier detailed descriptions of the groups described), this process can also take place at the interpersonal level between individuals – for example, in a marriage. See De Gruchy, 2002, p. 26.

243 Dietrich and Mayordomo, 2005, p. 135f.

the special relationship between Coventry and Germany. Many of the older members of the cathedral community had Germans lodging with them after the war, so that they were suddenly faced with having to get to know real live representatives of the wartime enemy. They began to tell their own stories, and to listen to one another – and in this way, friendships grew up that have endured right up to the present day.

Let us now turn back again to the story of Joseph, in order to highlight another important aspect of reconciliation between people: *repentance and penance.*

> Although the brothers tell Joseph a white lie in order to lull him, neverthe-less for the first time in their lives they are facing up to their misdeed. Now that they are potential victims in a strange land, they acknowledge that they had previously been the culprits. It becomes clear to them that the circle of injustice and violence cannot go on like this. They appear to recognize that only repentance and penance could break the circle. They fall down before Joseph; this takes great courage, as do the words 'We are here as your slaves'. However, Joseph can no longer rejoice at this gesture, though it is exactly what he had dreamed of when he was a young man (c.f. Genesis 37.1–11). We have already heard his initial reaction: 'Am I in the place of God?' And then we are told that he comforts his brothers and speaks kindly to them: 'Even though you intended to do harm to me, God intended it for good, in order to preserve a numerous people, as he is doing today.'

The Old Testament story leads us to suspect that reconciliation, as a relational process a space of encounter, promotes a series of events, in which repentance and confession of guilt lead to forgiveness, which leads in turn to reconciliation. Archbishop Tutu also writes of this: 'True reconciliation is based on forgiveness, and forgiveness is based on true confession, and confession is based on penitence, on contrition, on sorrow for what you have done.'[244] R. Schreiter, however, suggests the following connection, and I think he is right:

God initiates the work of reconciliation in the lives of the victims. Ordinarily we would expect reconciliation to begin with the repentance of the wrongdoers. But experience shows that wrongdoers are rarely willing to acknowledge what they have done ... God begins

---

244 Tutu, 2004, p. 53.

with the victim, restoring to the victim the humanity which the wrongdoer has tried to wrest away or to destroy.[245]

Given this prime initiative from God, reconciliation may therefore develop in totally different ways. One has just been described above, but sometimes the process of reconciliation is only triggered when the victim forgives the aggressor, and this experience then gives rise to the latter's repentance and admission of the painful truth.[246] What matters is that during the course of the process the guilty behaviour of all those involved should be put into words, and that they should show repentance and regret.

As stated before, reconciliation aims at the restoration of broken relationships. But to be more precise, this complex process of repentance, forgiveness and reconciliation aims at more than the mere restoration of previous relationships. Joseph and his brothers surely had no interest in going right back to the time when they were growing up, the time when they were competing for their father's attention. 'So have no fear; I myself will provide for you and your little ones.' Joseph's closing words show that reconciliation is leading to a new future. Under the heading 'Rememberance' we will now take a closer look at the significance of the past (acknowledgement of guilt/telling the truth) in relation to the opening up of this new future.

Suggestions for further reading

Müller-Fahrenholz, 1996, pp. 87–171 offers nine very graphic examples of biblical stories of reconciliation, under the heading 'Recommended for imitation'. The theme of forgiveness is treated in detail by L. G. Jones in *Embodying Forgiveness* (Jones, 1995).

---

245 Schreiter, 2002, p. 14f. See also ibid, pp. 63–6.

246 Forgiveness without prior repentance is also a recurring theme of Jesus according to St Luke, see Jones, 1995, p. 102. Desmond Tutu also recalls Christ on the cross, who was ready to ask for forgiveness without waiting for his tormentors to beg for it themselves. As the above quotation shows, Tutu believes that the aggressor's repentance is highly desirable, and a helpful starting point for the victim in the process of reconciliation, though he adds: 'If the victim could forgive only when the culprit confessed, then the victim would be locked into the culprit's whim, locked into victimhood, whatever his or her own attitude or intention' (see Tutu, 2004, p. 56). Compare this also with the above statement by Michael Lapsley.

19

For we cannot keep from speaking about what we have seen and heard

Coventry's double cathedral has become a symbol of reconciliation. Right at the beginning of this book, the question was raised as to why 14 November 1940 is still relevant today, and why it has a formative influence on the life and Christian witness of the Community of the Cross of Nails and is, so to speak, a part of its identity – and we will now explore this more closely.

Identity is formed through narrative structures. In the words of D. Ritschl:

> People are what they tell of themselves (or what is told to them) in their story, and what they make of this story ... When I am to say who I am the best thing is for me to tell my story. Each of us has his or her irreplaceable story, each person is his or her story.[247]

Our own personal unique stories are inescapably interwoven and inter-connected with the life stories of others. 'I am part of their story, as they are part of mine. The narrative of any one life is part of an inter-locking set of narratives.'[248] As we have seen, we often tell our own identity-reinforcing life stories at the expense of others. Yet even in this case, the stories remain linked with each other, be it only in the demar-cation of one from another. And thus, the attempt of the 'enemy image syndrome' to create a discrete identity that is completely self-sufficient

---

247 Ritschl, 1987, p. 19. The term 'story' is used as a (theological) technical expression for the never completely describable sum of all the individual recountable episodes/events in the life of a person or of a community. On the subject of narrative identity, see also C. Taylor, who thinks of life as an unfolding story: We 'grasp our lives in a narrative ... [M] aking sense of one's life as a story is ... not an optional extra; that our lives exist also in this space of questions, which only a coherent narrative can answer. In order to have a sense of who we are, we have to have a notion of how we have become, and of where we are going' (Taylor, 1992, p. 47). See also MacIntyre, 1985, pp. 211–19.

248 MacIntyre, 1985, p. 218.

and independent of the rival identity-groups, is unmasked as fiction or illusion.

What is true in general of our own identity, also applies to our Christian identity. We are part of a narrative religion. The Bible is the story-book of our forebears in faith. The people of Israel told stories when they wished to describe who God is and how they related to this God as a people. This religious tradition, this method of remembering and story-telling, is particularly evident in the way in which the memory of the Exodus, the Flight from Egypt, is kept alive – in the Pentateuch, parents are repeatedly instructed to remind their children of the Exodus as well the Commandments and laws which originated in those events (see Exodus 13.8; Deuteronomy 6.20–24). The commemoration of God's covenant with his chosen people on Mount Sinai is the central reference point for the community of faith:

> But take care and watch yourselves closely, so as neither to forget the things that your eyes have seen nor to let them slip from your mind all the days of your life; make them known to your children and your children's children – how you once stood before the Lord your God at Horeb (= Sinai), when the Lord said to me (= Moses), 'Assemble the people for me, and I will let them hear my words, so that they may learn to fear me as long as they live on the earth, and may teach their children to do so'.
>
> (Deuteronomy 4.9–10)

It is evident that the stories of the past are also relevant and meaningful for later generations. They establish and shape the Israeli community of faith. J. Assmann describes Israel, therefore, in terms of a 'memory-shaping community of remembrance', and the book of Deuteronomy as a 'paradigm of cultural mnemonics'.[249] It seems to me particularly important and indicative that the people of Israel, this community of remembrance, has not only handed down from generation to generation the memory of the high-points, the good and the successful events of their history. It is noticeable that the low-points, the defeats, the failures of the people, are also preserved and not consigned to oblivion. Psalm 106 is a striking example of this:

> Both we and our ancestors have sinned; we have committed iniquity, have done wickedly. Our ancestors, when they were in Egypt, did not consider your wonderful works; they did not remember the

---

249 Assmann, 1992, p. 202–12.

abundance of your steadfast love, but rebelled against the Most High at the Red Sea.

(Psalms 106.6–7)

The psalm continues with a long litany of the faults and the sinful errors of the chosen people. All this became a part of the Jewish Bible, and thus also a part of the official reading of what makes Israel what it is. The Holy Scripture thus makes it unmistakably clear that the identity of God's people can only be understood if it also includes the problem-laden stories as part of that identity. Christians live in this narrative tradition: the resurrected Christ explained to the two disciples on the road to Emmaus the biblical texts that related to him, 'beginning with Moses and all the prophets' (Luke 24.27). And the first Christians told stories when they wanted to describe who Jesus is. Peter and John, for example, refused to remain silent about Jesus before the High Council, saying:

'For we cannot keep from speaking about what we have seen and heard.'

(Acts 4.20)

This compulsion to reiterate the joyful message also led to the emergence of the four Apostles.[250]

The re-telling of these stories is also central to our faith today. Christians link the Evangelists' stories with their own personal stories. If you ask them, for instance, why they are working for reconciliation in the world, they still tell the story of salvation and deliverance that started with God's covenant with Israel and was brought to completion in the death and resurrection of Jesus Christ. Christian services and Christian prayers can also be described as an exercise in remembering. The celebration of the Last Supper, the Eucharist, is a memorial to Christ. At the last supper with his disciples, Jesus commanded them to 'do this in remembrance of me'. In the liturgical re-telling of this Last Supper, a historical person becomes – through the Spirit of God – present with his story in the here and now.

However, the concept of a *grand narrative* as an all-embracing all-descriptive explanation has been discredited lately by Jean-François

---

250 More precisely, the earliest Christians told 'many individual stories, again composed and selected in accordance with the guidance of a complete or meta-story which was difficult or perhaps even impossible to narrate. Nor is it a coincidence that the New Testament offers four such collections instead of a definitive one ... One cannot say, briefly and concisely, who Jesus is.' (Ritschl, 1988, p. 20).

Lyotard and other post-modern philosophers. Even though the objections to it cannot lightly be dismissed,[251] Christian faith still cannot abandon its narrative structure and meta-story in the sense of a coherent theology. And perhaps the hook for our faith is not so much an absolutely legitimate overall meta-story as the many little stories that are to be told, as A. Houtepen rightly remarks:

> God is not a God of the Great Narrative ... but one who is involved in all the little stories of human beings which are woven together and which become what – in configurative language – we call salvation story.[252]

In telling these stories, calling them to mind and reflecting about them, we are grounding ourselves in the community of Christian faith. This story-telling includes not only the stories of our biblical forebears but also those of our direct antecedents in faith from the recent past, as well as our own personal stories. To summarize this process: living our faith means 'learning to renarrate the stories of our lives truthfully, in all particularity and in the context of God's forgiving and reconciling love'.[253]

Coventry's ongoing commitment to reconciliation is an example of this 'crafting of our own particular stories into the larger context of God's story'.[254] For one thing, the double cathedral tells the story of God's salvation for mankind. The ruins of the old cathedral destroyed in 1940 tell of Christ's suffering, whilst the Tablets of the Word and the works of art in the new cathedral tell of resurrection and a new beginning. The story of our salvation is told through the architecture, and passed on from generation to generation; the very stones seem to speak to people. And for another thing, the story of God's reconciliation with mankind is repeated and passed on through the Community of the Cross of Nails. Those who work in the International Centre for Reconciliation in Coventry, and those Christians who are involved in the individual Cross of Nails Centres, have seen for themselves, time

---

251 In the opinion of M. Volf, Lyotard's critique is an important reminder for us Christians, to 'ask the right kind of question, which is not how to achieve the final reconciliation, but what resources we need to live in peace in the absence of the final reconciliation' (Volf, 1996, p. 109). According to Volf, we certainly must engage in the struggle against oppression, but any of our attempts to come to the final reconciliation will end up perpetuating oppression, since final reconciliation 'is not the work of human beings but of the triune God' (ibid, p. 109–10).

252 Houtepen, 2002, p. 154.

253 Jones, 1995, p. 168.

254 Jones, 1995, p. 168.

and again, the processes that are set in motion when they tell others the story of why they first became involved in working for reconciliation. By listening to Coventry's unique story of reconciliation, people are drawn under the spell of God's forgiving and reconciling love and start to become involved themselves in working for reconciliation. The Coventry story – kept alive in the memory by the Community of the Cross of Nails and symbolized by the Cross of Nails itself – can act as a catalyst both for individuals and for groups, to co-operate in making 'a kinder, simpler, a more Christ-Child-like sort of world' as Provost Howard put it in his Christmas address in 1940. It is through retained memories of this kind – good, but also painful memories – that the reconciliation work of the Community of the Cross of Nails is authorized and motivated.

However, what about the expression 'forgive and forget'? Shouldn't the injustice of the past simply be forgotten at some point, in order to give the healing process a better chance? The biblical message refuses to take this road. Amnesty, as part of the process of reconciliation, must not be confused with amnesia. Forgiveness must not lead to betrayal of the victim's past. In the words of Desmond Tutu:

> Forgiving and being reconciled are not about pretending that things are other than they are. It is not patting one another on the back and turning a blind eye to the wrong. True reconciliation exposes the awfulness, the abuse, the pain, the degradation, the truth.[255]

Remembering – including the pain – is part of the healing. Therefore, the past is not just brushed aside, but the memories are used to build a new community that learns from the errors and injustice of the past.[256] However, in this process the question of justice must not fall by the wayside. Regarding the concept of 'restorative justice', we have already seen that the needs of the various participants and their corresponding duties must be identified and addressed.[257] This includes amongst other things the question of compensation, the restoration of the dignity of those affected, and also the rehabilitation of the perpetrators. The Rainsbrook Secure Training Centre tries to make this concept the constant criterion of their actions, by asking to what extent damage that has been inflicted can be made good again, and what causative

---

255 Tutu, 2000, p. 270.
256 Volf, 1996, pp. 131–40, goes so far as to speak of the necessity of a 'certain kind of forgetting', so as to be able to remember in the right way.
257 See Chapter 8.3, pp. 88–90.

factors must be removed in order that the aggressor can break free for good from the spiral of violence. And when their land was handed back to the community of Protea, it was clear that the new South Africa was trying to face up to the truth of the injustice that had been done, and to restore justice as far as possible in the form of compensation and by giving back the land. The ceremony of handing back the land to the Protea Village Action Community can be viewed as the public acknowledgement of the injustice that had been done. Those who had been affected received restitution, their dignity was restored to them.

The reconciliation process can thus lead to a new kind of memory, to which the current Archbishop of Canterbury Rowan Williams draws attention:

If forgiveness is liberation, it is also a recovery of the past in hope, a return of memory, in which what is potentially threatening, destructive, despair-inducing, in the past is transfigured into the ground of hope.[258]

The goal is transformation, and the search for better relationships,[259] as we have already seen at the end of the previous chapter.

Suggestions for further reading

A useful discussion of Lyotard's critical work on narrative concepts is given in Kearney, 2003, pp. 179–90, which, whilst admitting the necessity for 'telling stories', sees that there is also the danger of an isolationist retreat into privacy and philosophical autism.

All theologies of reconciliation share the conviction that forgiveness does not just mean forgetting: see De Gruchy, 2002, p. 178; Stevens, 2004, pp. 46–7; Müller-Fahrenholz, 1996, pp. 40–1; Schreiter, 2002, pp. 66–8; and Jones, 1995, p. 237. Regarding the relationship between truth and peace, and the role of justice in acts of reconciliation, see Volf, 1996, pp. 193–231; and with a different focus, see also De Gruchy, 2002, pp. 180–213. Concerning secular reconciliation processes and their relationship to the provision of justice, see Rigby, 2001.

---

258 Williams, 1982, p. 32.
259 See Müller-Fahrenholz, 1996, pp. 31–43.

20

Endure everything with patience, while joyfully giving thanks to the Father

Between Britain and Germany, reconciliation has been accomplished: there are countless school exchanges, German students like to spend a term abroad in an English university, there are numerous partnerships between Anglican dioceses and German regional churches, and it is not at all unusual anymore to see a Bavarian Lutheran working in Coventry Cathedral and presiding at the Litany of Reconciliation at noon on Friday.

Many conflicts, however, are still awaiting resolution. Although God has already reconciled the world with himself (see again 2 Corinthians 5.19), there is still violence and enmity. We need only reflect on the Middle East to recognize that the desire for reconciliation calls for unending patience. We have seen that Coventry Cathedral's International Centre for Reconciliation (ICR) has been working for reconciliation in Israel/Palestine for many years – and yet, the ICR team had to live with the knowledge that despite their many years of involvement there has been little apparent change. This example shows clearly that the desire for reconciliation always requires long-term commitment. The first chapter of the Epistle to the Colossians, already mentioned, refers to this necessity – the letter's author begs and prays that God will strengthen the Christians who are reconciled in Christ:

> ... with all the strength that comes from his glorious power, and may you be prepared to endure everything with patience, while joyfully giving thanks to the Father ...
>
> (Colossians 1.11–12)

Sometimes, however, patience and longsuffering are mistaken for weakness. W. Dietrich considers this objection, but finds it to be completely invalid:

Patience is thought to be ennobled into a Christian virtue, characterized by passivity, calm acceptance of pain and injustice, and submission to fate. [In the German language, in particular, the similarity between the words for 'patience' (Ge*duld*) and 'tolerance' (*Duld*samkeit) also encourages this way of thinking] ... [However, patience is] far more of an active process, which holds firm to its goal through all eventualities, yet without the use of force.[260]

Two insights from Martin Luther's Theology of the Cross may help us to find this patience. In his Heidelberg Disputation, Luther encourages Christians not to seek for God in ambiguous worldly events, but in the crucified Christ. A true theologian is one 'who comprehends the visible and manifest things of God, seen through suffering and the cross'.[261]

Applying all this to a theology of reconciliation, I believe it means that Christians should not look on resignedly at the conflicts in the world and brood over a God who seems to have hidden himself away (*deus absconditus*), but that they should take the reality of the suffering in this world seriously and look upon it as a possible place in which God's presence can be seen. This happens in the knowledge that Christ, 'the image of the invisible God' (Colossians 1.15), has gone ahead before us on the painful path all the way to the cross. He who was crucified with three nails made it possible for us to believe in God as the Almighty in vulnerable form.

At the same time, Luther's Theology of the Cross can be viewed as meaning that patience and longsuffering must never be confused with tolerant acceptance of the situation in the world, but that sins and grievances must be addressed – a theme that we have considered several times in this book. Christian reconciliation is rooted firmly in the world, it is not escapism. A good theologian of reconciliation is always a theologian of the cross at the same time, as Luther set it down in tablets of stone: 'A theologian of glory calls evil good and good evil. A theologian of the cross calls the thing what it actually is.'[262] A theology of reconciliation has the patience to name grievances as what they are, whether in the Middle East, in parts of Africa, or in other places that are waiting for reconciliation.

In the end, this patience finds its strength in the hope of the kingdom of God, as can perhaps be illustrated by quoting another Bible story:

---

260 Dietrich and Mayordomo, 2005, p. 137.
261 Thesis 20: WA 1, 353.8-354.36. Translation: Grimm and Lehmann, 1957, p. 40.
262 Thesis 21: WA 1, 353.8-354.36. Translation: Grimm and Lehmann, 1957, p. 40.

Then Jesus told them a parable about their need to pray always and not to lose heart. He said, 'In a certain city there was a judge who neither feared God nor had respect for people. In that city there was a widow who kept coming to him and saying, "Grant me justice against my opponent." For a while he refused; but later he said to himself, "Though I have no fear of God and no respect for anyone, yet because this widow keeps bothering me, I will grant her justice, so that she may not wear me out by continually coming." And the Lord said, 'Listen to what the unjust judge says. And will not God grant justice to his chosen ones who cry to him day and night? Will he delay long in helping them? I tell you, he will quickly grant justice to them. And yet, when the Son of Man comes, will he find faith on earth?'

(Luke 18.1–8)

There sits the judge. The widow has just left him – her shrill voice, which has plagued him incessantly over the last few days, is still ringing in his ears. It has been impossible to get rid of her – time and again she has appeared at his door, always pleading her grievance. However, her piercing cries, and his concern that she might actually assault him in the end, have finally moved him to look at her case and to see that the woman gets what she deserves. But it was not out of charity, or in respect of God's commandments. No – it was just for the sake of a quiet life. And this is not the first such case that he has dealt with in this way. He may be an important person; but he is not respected. He lives up to his reputation as arrogant and unjust; a despot, who judges sometimes one way, sometimes another, according to which way is best for him.

This is the kind of judge that Jesus portrays to his audience. They all recognize this kind of man, and can picture the story vividly to themselves. Certainly there will be many of them who have been annoyed by just such a judge, and who are enjoying the way in which this one is now being made to look small in the parable. Such thoughts are still in the minds of his audience, as Jesus raises his voice once more: 'Listen to what the unjust judge says.' His listeners are surprised – their reaction must have been 'What on earth has a man like that to say to us that is worth hearing?' And then Jesus goes even further: 'Listen to this judge, for from his conduct you can learn something about God.' That can scarcely have fitted the picture that these people have just formed of the judge. Can a scoundrel like him be of any use in explaining something about God? After the first moment of shock, however, perhaps they are able to understand the fine distinction – for Jesus is not simply equating God with the judge, instead his argument runs like this: 'If this judge ... then how much more so God. If this judge – godless and despising men – could soften his heart, out of pure self-interest, and give the widow her due, how much more may you depend upon it that God will grant you justice.'

And now we have reached the heart of the matter. This daring comparison makes it surprisingly clear that there is one thing that we can rely on – God will see that justice is done. If God is infinitely more good, more righteous and more powerful than mortal man, then it is abundantly clear – God will see that justice is done. Of course, there are times when we all come to the end of our patience and ask ourselves, how can life be so unjust? And if there is a God, why does he do nothing? However, our text leaves no doubt about that. It tells us that God will see that justice is done, without question; and the world back then was no better than it is today. If we want to get to grips with the meaning of this, then we must also ask ourselves, what is the sense in saying 'God will see that justice is done' when it relates to that same reality that we so often perceive as unjust and hopeless? What exactly does justice mean in this world?

Every now and again, there are fortunate turns in history, when injustice and oppression are suddenly overcome – and South Africa is just such a case. Even as late as the mid 1980s, hardly anyone would have believed that the Apartheid which had been in place since 1948 would come to an end within ten years – yet in 1994 the country held free elections, and the once-persecuted opposition leader Nelson Mandela, who had been imprisoned for decades, became president. Of course, this change came too late for some of the victims; but at least the injustice was now called plainly by name, and was dealt with through a Truth Commission. Ninety-seven-year-old Frances van Gussling lived just long enough to see her family's land, which had been unjustly seized, ceremonially handed back to the Protea Community.[263] In one or two places, the ICR had the privilege to accompany the arduous process of South African reconciliation – the declaration of independence was merely the beginning, and the process will go on for decades. Coventry's 'stories' of other victims and aggressors who have already dealt with and come through one such process by means of truthfulness and respect, and with forgiveness and an awareness of their own guilt yet without forcing everyone do the same, can serve as a model and

263 See Chapter 12.1, p. 132.

an encouragement for the work of the Cross of Nails Centres in South Africa.

However, there are many other conflicts in which this stage has not been reached. So then it is necessary to carry on doggedly trying, so that at some point in time the opposing parties can allow each other justice and forgiveness – without 'calling evil good and good evil'. For example, take the case of September 11 2001 in New York – many of the victims are still suffering to this day, because they pine for those who have died; because their trauma still haunts them; and because the aggressor still remains so abstract and invisible that they simply do not know who to turn their hate against, who they should forgive or with whom they need to be reconciled. Wounds such as these may never heal, even after the gaping hole at Ground Zero is filled in again and a new skyscraper rears up majestically in its place. Where will the work of reconciliation start there?

And yet reconciliation is essential there – more so than almost anywhere else in the world – and the reconciliation must be as profound as that of Coventry. For it is just as difficult to draw the lines of demarcation between victim and aggressor here as between the citizens of Dresden and those of Coventry. Moreover, the foregoing and subsequent events are just as complex; for the symbolic significance of the attack is strengthened by the fact that the towers of the World Trade Center also represented a global economy from which the industrialized countries are virtually the only ones who profit, even though it is based mainly on the raw materials of the poorer countries. Such symbol of our wealth, in the eyes of those poorer countries, becomes a symbol of exploitation backed up by military strength; and by the wealthier nations, the attack on New York was seen as the excuse for waging war, which by now has led to the killing and injuring of a hundred times more victims than did the attack on the World Trade Center itself.

But are we justified in this? Simply because we are 'the good guys'? Why were we unable to convince the Muslim world of the humanitarianism of our set of values? Do we think that it is possible to do this if we ourselves abandon our own principles in our fight for freedom? Why is it that the hypocritical and hateful polemics of Islamic fundamentalists are so terribly plausible to a large sector of the population? And who can pretend that they do not profit from the circumstances suffered by those who hate us? How long will it be before we realize that the most effective weapon against terrorism is justice?

This whole topic shows just how cruelly hate and aggression can be stirred up on both sides, and how easy it is today to dress up old enemy images in new clothing. How hard it is, on the other hand, when we try to do justice to all the victims on both sides, and to point out all the guilt on both sides! Anyone in the western world today who calls attention, amid the fight against terrorism, to our own faults and failings, is fighting a losing battle and will be accused of siding with the terrorists. And it must be just as difficult in Islamic countries to stand up for the victims of terrorism and insist on correcting their own 'image of the enemy'.

However, the Coventry message fits this situation. It is not enough to say 'Father, forgive them!' in a merciful but morally self-righteous way. Saying 'Father, forgive', on the other hand, includes the recognition of our own culpability as well. In this prayer we hear the despair over our own suffering – but at the same time the despair over our own shortcomings. It is a cry for justice – but also the obligation to seek for it with all our strength. When it comes to terrorism and the fight against it, this distinction is important to every one of us.

Such a demand is enough to make anyone dizzy, and no one can hold it against the victims if they are unable to grant forgiveness to their oppressors, because they have not shown any repentance. Even if they have, it still is a courageous and more than difficult step. However, Provost Howard was convinced that reconciliation at less than this level would be of no use in the long run because, although it certainly cushions against evil forces and structures, it does not break through them or overcome them; and it was this conviction that gave him the iron will to attempt this work, against all reason and in the face of mocking, and to go on doggedly and undeterred, even when it seemed both to those who were involved and to the onlookers that the work was pointless or even wrongheaded.

Doing it imperfectly, as mankind is bound to do such work, we cannot hope to make everything absolutely right again; but it does at least give us a foretaste of what it might be like when one day God himself comes and makes all well. And this brings us back to our parable:

> For that same Jesus who talked about God's justice in such provocative terms, is to go to his own death shortly afterwards through the world's injustice. Though innocent, he will be crucified, a political failure and despised by society. In the eyes of the world, this is as desolate as all the

other innocent deaths in this world. However, it is our firm belief that the Cross was not the end – we live in the belief that this failure conceals a serene victory, which works below the surface to alter injustice and conquer the hearts of men despite the powers of this world. This is how God provides justice today – as a foretaste and as a hope. For we still believe, two thousand years after the death of Jesus, that with his coming the kingdom of God was begun, and it is our hope that one day God will finally establish his kingdom and achieve justice in full. We await the Day of Judgement, on which God will overcome all human strife, bring all injustice to light and expose all wrongs.

We live in this conviction, in this belief, and in this hope and expectation. And this is what gives us the strength to work on, filled with 'patience and endurance', so that here in the present at least a hint of God's future justice can be seen, and soft traces of his work of reconciliation can be recognized. The widow in the parable can serve as an example: we should be impatient and outraged, forthright and outspoken in exposing injustice. We must be challenging and energetic, tough and enduring, and support the cause. With God's help, these present initiatives will create tiny examples of his justice.

Many of the issues are ones that we will be unable to solve. But the belief that God provides justice also means that it is not in our power to right all the wrongs of this world – only God can do that. And whenever we come up against our own limitations, we must cry out loudly and impatiently 'Father, forgive!', and together we must pray that God will fulfil his promise and make us whole again. It is precisely this unremitting prayer that the gospel commends to us, until the Lord comes again; to keep in mind that there is still much in the world that is not right, to awaken in us the longing for that all-embracing justice that can only come from God, and to live in the certainty that in the end God will bring about complete reconciliation with our foes. This belief and this hope are symbolized by the Cross of Christ – and also by Coventry Cathedral, and by one hundred and sixty Cross of Nails Centres all over the world. It is our task – as we are reminded by the parable of the widow – to ensure that the Son of Man finds this faith in us when he comes again.

Suggestions for further reading

For Luther and the distinction between the hidden God and the revealed God, see Ebeling, 1972, pp. 226–41.

21

We have not ceased praying for you

The Christian community is called upon to pray without ceasing. Like the parable of the pleading widow, the first chapter of the Epistle to the Colossians, which has already been quoted several times, also refers to this central basic ground of faith:

> For this reason ... we have not ceased praying for you and asking that you may be filled with the knowledge of God's will in all spiritual wisdom and understanding. (Colossians 1.9)

Much could be said about prayer; and indeed, much has been said. However, to conclude our six-fold consideration of the topic of reconciliation, it is sufficient to highlight three aspects: we pray to God and before God; we pray for one another; and we pray with one another.

Prayer in the loving glance of God. Fulbert Steffensky has this to say about personal prayer:

> Prayer is the utmost height of passivity – a renunciation of self-love and self-regard. It is a passivity that offers no resistance to that loving glance that sees us as fine and rich. In prayer, I know that I am neither self-made nor self-justified. I am 'receiving the loving glance'. In prayer we no longer offer any apology for ourselves – no justification, no excuse, no argument, no tangible strengths. Acceptance of God's grace, acceptance of his loving look, is not a matter of theological understanding but simply of prayer. Perhaps we are only able to tolerate ourselves and accept ourselves, because in prayer we are swept away in that loving look. Perhaps we can only be at peace, strong and sure of ourselves, when we are not obliged to be just ourselves – when we know that we are as we are deemed to be: 'When you look at me, I become beautiful.'[264]

---

264 Steffensky, 2002, pp. 16–17.

This passage evokes two ideas that we have already considered. In prayer we recognize that we cannot justify ourselves, but that we have all sinned and fallen short of the glory in which God originally created us (Romans 3.23); and in prayer we also recognize that everything comes from God. By his grace he accepts us. This attitude of praying finds what is perhaps its deepest expression in the cry 'Kyrie eleison' (Lord, have mercy) which forms part of the eucharistic service. Here, in these two words uttered before God, all our powerlessness, shortcomings and need for help are laid bare. In the same way, for the Community of the Cross of Nails this is all summed up in the words 'Father, forgive'; at the beginning of every act of reconciliation between people is the plea that God might forgive us sinners and break down our preoccupation with ourselves and our 'enemy images'.

Prayer for one another: 'Praying for other people presupposes that we are touched by their plight. Sympathy moves us to intercede for them.[265] Praying for others comes out of a real interest in and sympathy for what the others have gone through. Jesus prayed for his disciples (see for instance the prayer in John 17), and we have already seen that St Paul and his pupils prayed for their communities. So it is only logical that the author of the First Epistle to Timothy urged his readers to follow his example:

> First of all, then, I urge that supplications, prayers, intercessions, and thanksgivings should be made for everyone.
>
> (1 Timothy 2.1)

Applying this once again to our theme, reconciliation is embedded in a community of like-minded individuals who intercede for one another. The Community of the Cross of Nails attempts to be just such a community of prayer, that lives in unceasing prayer for peace and reconciliation in the world, and in prayer that includes concern for the setbacks of others and pleasure in their success.[266] This element of reconciliation was reinforced by the Second International Conference of the Community of the Cross of Nails in 2004, which was attended by more than a hundred delegates from seventeen countries, who spoke of

---

265 Röhlin, 2006, p. 74.

266 Intercession does not just include those who are of like mind, however; The First Epistle of Timothy instructs us to pray for all mankind. As far as the writer was concerned, this included not only the Christian brothers and sisters, of whom one might expect that they would also pray for each other, but also those (heathens) who wield the authority in the world, as the next verse shows (see 1 Timothy 2.2).

their conflicts, their desire for reconciliation, their successes and their failures, in countless lectures and workshops. Since the conference, those who took part will certainly have given much more thought in their intercessions to the needs of the other Cross of Nails Centres.

Prayer with one another: Prayer is a deeply personal act, but at the same time we are part of a community of those who believe and pray. The act of praying together finds expression in church services, in which those who pray can see that they are not alone, and can feel safe and secure in a community of prayer. This community of prayer is even greater than the sum of those who are gathered together at that moment, it includes the living history of prayer of the preceding generations. The whole church of God is praying – and because it prays in the name of Jesus, he also confirms that prayer in his spirit.

And at this point, two examples from the Community of the Cross of Nails will clarify what has been said. Just as in Coventry every Friday, Christians gather to pray in the ruins of the old cathedral, so people are meeting in many Cross of Nails Centres all around the world to pray the Litany of Reconciliation together and to plead for peace in the world. And communal prayer was of course also the recurring theme in the Cross of Nails Conference in 2004 – the delegates met every day for morning and afternoon prayer, led each time by representatives from different centres or regions. I remember in particular the evening prayer on the penultimate day of the conference: a huge map of the world lay spread out below the Cross of Nails, and all those who were there were invited to pray for the healing of the fragmented world. They came forward, uttered their prayer for a region in crisis (either their own region back home or some other one), then lit a candle and placed it on the corresponding point on the map. A South African woman prayed for the children in her country, a Czech brought before God Europe's unemployed, and the representatives of the Cross of Nails centres in the Middle East lit a candle for peace in their region; and the rest of the congregation affirmed each prayer in turn. The prayers for one another and with another flowed together in the loving glance of God.

Suggestions for further reading

Röhlin, 2006, offers an introduction to the topic of 'prayer'.

22

In conclusion: Be kind to one another, tender-hearted, forgiving one another, as God in Christ has forgiven you

Before me on my desk stands a little copy of that statue by Josefina da Vasconcellos that moves so many of those who visit the ruins of Coventry's old cathedral (see the photograph at the beginning of Part Three). The full-size version of this statue was presented to the cathedral in 1995, to mark the fiftieth anniversary of the end of the Second World War.[267] In the Peace Garden in Hiroshima, in front of the Versöhnungskapelle (Chapel of Reconciliation) in Berlin (on the direct line of the former Berlin Wall), and outside Northern Ireland's parliament building at Stormont, there now stand further copies of the statue by da Vasconcellos. What the eye encounters in all these places are the figures of two people, male and female, in a close embrace. Both have fallen to their knees – bending far forward, they lean upon each other – it is the only way in which they can bridge the gap that has grown up between them; and now they link their two kneeling bodies, to form a bridge. They prop their hands on one another, to find a hold. Comforting, protecting, one of the man's hands lies on the woman's head. Both heads are pressed close together, her forehead resting on his shoulder.

How long must it have been, how much patience and how many prayers were needed, before they were both ready to open their arms and reach out towards the other? It is impossible to embrace with your arms folded in front of you.[268] But at any rate, the two have now put the allocation of

---

267 Da Vasconcellos originally created the statue in 1977 with the name 'Reunion', as a contract commission for the University of Bradford, where it was installed in the university's School of Peace Studies. Following restoration work, the piece was renamed 'Reconciliation' for the artist's ninetieth birthday in 1994.

268 See Volf, 1996, pp. 140–7, who describes and interprets the 'drama of the embrace' in detail.

guilt, mistrust, and denial of sympathy far behind them. They are meeting here on a level playing field – neither of them bows down to the other, or has to look up to the other. Not in a proud and upright bearing, but on bended knee, they accept each other, and the wonder of reconciliation is fulfilled. Have they already acknowledged their sins and hesitantly uttered words of regret? Has the search for truth and justice already begun? As I picture it to myself, the pain and the suffering are still there, the evil memories are still vivid – and yet their comforting and embracing hands are able to open the doors to healing. A bridge to reconciliation has been built; the embracing arms hint at a strong and enduring link – yet still the gulf is not fully bridged, and the knees of the couple are still widely separated; the process of reconciliation is not yet complete. However, the embrace gives a strong foretaste of that which is to come, and of how one day it might be.

It has been necessary to limit these considerations on a theology of reconciliation to the basics. But these thoughts remain basic guidelines because reconciliation can only be experienced on the spot, whether it be in South Africa, in Dublin or in a British prison. There is no abstract formula or general-purpose blueprint for how to achieve reconciliation. It became clear in Part Two that the worldwide Community of the Cross of Nails is bound to be a very varied and colourful community. Each parish, each initiative, each institution that is a part of the Community, lives out its own particular story, tells this story to others, tries to provide specific answers to the specific requirements of its own situation and thus to allow reconciliation. This means that there are wider gaps to bridge in some places than in others. In some cases the parties involved are quickly able to reach out their hands, in other cases more patience is needed before the parties are ready to embrace each other in reconciliation.

In short, reconciliation must be worked out to suit the situation, against the background of the memories in that place – the violent ones as well as the good ones. And so each centre brings into the Community its own individual 'story' of reconciliation, and its own particular abilities, and adds a new dimension to it. Amidst all this variety, and in different ways in each situation, the Cross of Nails Centres seek for that reconciling embrace that is expressed in the sculpture by da Vasconcellos. And above all, they know that they are unified in those words from the Epistle to the Ephesians that bring to a close the Coventry Litany of Reconciliation:

Be kind to one another, tender-hearted, forgiving one another, as God in Christ has forgiven you.

(Ephesians 4.32)

Bibliography

Allen, John, *Rabble-Rouser for Peace: The Authorised Biography of Desmond Tutu*, Riser, 2007.

Amanze, James. A., *History of the Ecumenical Movement in Africa*, Gaborone, 1999.

Amt für Presse- und Öffentlickeitsarbeit der Landeshauptstadt Dresden, *13 Februar, 60,. Jahrestag der Zerstörung Dresdens* [13 February: 60th anniversary of the destruction of Dresden], Dresden 2004.

Appleby, R. Scott, *The Ambivalence of the Sacred: Religion, Violence and Reconciliation*, Rowman & Littlefield, 2000.

Arthur, Paul, *Special Relationship: Britain, Ireland and the Northern Ireland Problem*, Blackstaff Press Ltd, 2000.

Assmann, Jan, *Das kulturelle Gedächtnis: Schrift, Erinnerung und politische Identität in frühen Hochkulturen* [Cultural memory: Text, memory and political identity in early civilizations], Munich 1992.

Barth, Karl, *Church Dogmatics*, Volume IV: The Doctrine of Reconciliation, § 57–59, London / New York 2009.

BBC West Midlands, Extract from radio broadcast with John Gaunt on 30 October 2004, 9.00am–12.00am.

Becker, Elisabeth, Versöhnungsdienst: Dresden 1965 Eine Rückschau [Service of Reconciliation: Dresden 1965 in retrospect] (typewritten manuscript in the archives of Evangelisch-Lutherische Diakonissenanstalt, Dresden; no date).

Bringt, Friedemann and Fritz, Stephan et al., Dresden, 13: Februar – Ein Rahmen für das Erinnern, Aufruf vom 22, September 2004 [Dresden, 13 February – a framework for recollection, Appeal on 22 September 2004] (available as of December 2007 at www.dresden.de/de/02/110/03/01/c_010.php; English version: www.dresden.de/en/02/07/03/c_01_remembrance.php).

Burch, Sam, 'Cornerstone Community: Reconciliation Ministry in West Belfast', in *Christian Social Action*, October 1988, pp. 20–23.

Clapsis, Emmanuel, 'Ambivalenz, Subjektivität und spirituelles Leben Für eine: Kultur des Friedens durch Achtung von Andersartigkeit' [Ambivalence, subjectivity and spiritual life. For a culture of peace by respecting otherness], in *Ökumenische Rundschau* 55 (2006), pp. 183–200.

Community of the Cross of Nails in Northern America, *The Manual: Revised 2006* (available as of December 2007 at www.ccn-northamerica.org).

Cornerstone Contact, March 2007 issue (Magazine of the Cornerstone Community).

Coventry Cathedral, The Order for the Service of Remembrance and Dedication at 11am on Sunday, 10 November 1940. Attended by the Mayor and Corporation (Order of service in the archives of Coventry Cathedral).

Coventry Cathedral, Consecration of the Cathedral Church of Saint Michael Coventry on Friday 25 May and Saturday 26 May 1962 (Order of service in the archives of Coventry Cathedral).

Coventry Cathedral, The Commissioning of the Dresden Working Party during The Communion on Sunday 14 March 1965 at 10.30am (Order of service in the archives of Coventry Cathedral).

Coventry Evening Telegraph, edition dated 1 July 1965.

Davenport, Rodney and Saunders, Christopher, South Africa: A Modern History, 5th edition, London 2000.

De Gruchy, John W., Reconciliation. Restoring Justice, London 2002.

De Klerk, F.W., The Last Trek: A New Beginning, The Autobiography, London 1999.

Deininger, Claus, e-mail to the author dated 20 July 2007.

Der Sonntag, edition dated 26 September 1965.

Diamond, James, e-mail to the author dated 24 July 2007.

Dietrich, Walter and Mayordomo, Moisés, Gewalt und Gewaltüberwindung in der Bibel [Violence and the overcoming of violence in the Bible], Zurich 2005.

Dresdener Neueste Nachrichten, Special edition 'Dresden Frauenkirche' dated October 2005.

Dubow, Saul, Scientific Racism in Modern South Africa, Cambridge 1995.

Ebeling, Gerhard, Luther. An Introduction to his Thought, London/Glasgow 1972.

Episcopal Church in the USA, Episcopal Overview. Fact 2005 (available as of December 2007 at www.episcopalchurch.org/documents/Episcopal_Overview_FACT_2005.pdf).

Evangelische Kirche in Deutschland, Christen und Juden III: Schritte der Erneuerung im Verhältnis zum Judentum [Christians and Jews III: Steps to restore relationships with Judaism], Gütersloh 2000.

Falk, Johanna, e-mail to the author dated 23 April 2007.

Falola, Toyin, Violence in Nigeria: The Crisis of Religious Politics and Secular Ideologies, Rochester 1998.

Fitzduff, Mari, A Typology of Community Relations Work and Contextual Necessities, Belfast 1991 (reprint with no page numbers).

Frank, Jerome D., Sanity and Survival: Psychological Aspects of War and Peace, London 1967.

Frauenkirche Dresden, Ökumenischer Festgottesdienst, 30 Oktober, 18.00 Uhr (Order of service for the ceremony of consecration of the Frauenkirche on 30 October 2005; bilingual brochure).

Friedrich, Jörg, Der Brand: Deutschland im Bombenkrieg 1940–1945 [The Fire. Germany in the Blitz], 7th edition, Munich 2002.

Fröhlich, Elke (ed.), Die Tagebücher von Joseph Goebbels: Sämtliche Fragmente, Teil 1: Aufzeichnungen von 1924–1941, Bd. 4 [The diaries of Joseph Goebbels. Part 1, entries for 1924–1941, Vol.4], Munich 1987.

From Protea to Coventry, August 2000 (a collection of personal accounts, no page numbers; from the records of the International Centre for Reconciliation, Coventry Cathedral).

Grimm, Harold and Lehmann, Helmut (eds), *Luther's Work, volume 31: Career of the Reformer I*, Philadelphia 1957.

Gröpler, Helmut, *Die Engel hielten den Atem an: Das Nagelkreuz von Coventry* [The angels held their breath. The Coventry Cross of Nails], 2nd edition, Berlin 1994.

Hardwick, Susan, e-mail to the author dated 23 April 2007.

Hardwick, Susan, e-mail to the author dated 16 October 2007.

Hasselhorn, Jost, e-mail to the author dated 24 July 2007.

Haufe, Edith Sr., letter to the author dated 15 May 2007.

Herz, Dietmar, *Gaza und Westbank: Geschichte, Politik, Kultur* [Gaza and the West Bank: History, politics and culture], 5th edition, Munich 2003.

Heyroth, Jochen, e-mail to the author dated 10 May 2007.

Hinton, Deborah, e-mail to the author dated 10 April 2007.

Hoke, Stuart, *The Fire Sermon – Our Shelter from the Stormy Blast: Theology & Mission in the Wake of 9/11*, 24 February 2005, St Magnus the Martyr, London (author's MS kindly made available).

Houtepen, Anton, *God: An Open Question*, London / New York 2002.

Howard, Richard T., Notes on Visit to Kiel, 14–21 September 1947 (hand-written diary; Archives of Coventry Cathedral).

Howard, Richard T., an address by Provost R. T. Howard to Christians in Kiel (hand-written script for 18 September 1947; Archives of Coventry Cathedral).

Howard, Richard T., *Ruined und Rebuilt: The Story of Coventry Cathedral, 1939–1962*, Coventry 1962.

International Centre for Reconciliation, The Kaduna Peace Declaration of Religious Leaders, signed 22 August 2002 (Records of International Centre for Reconciliation, Coventry Cathedral).

International Centre for Reconciliation, Presentation of the Coventry Cross of Nails (guidelines dated 14 April 2003, records of the International Centre for Reconciliation, Coventry Cathedral).

Internationale Bildungs- und Begegnungsstätte (ed.), *Haus im Bau: 10 Jahre Internationale Bildungs- und Begegnungsstätte Minsk. 1994–2004* [House under construction: Ten years of the International Education and Conference Centre, Minsk, 1994–2004], Minsk / Dortmund 2004 (bilingual Russian – German).

Internationale Bildungs- und Begegnungsstätte (ed.), *1 September 2006: Umbenennung der IBB Minsk nach Johannes Rau. 1994–2007* [Renaming of the IBB Minsk after Johannes Rau], Minsk / Dortmund 2007 (bilingual Russian – German).

Jackson, Bill, 'Crossing the Barricade: The Beginnings of the Cornerstone Community' (5-page MS; undated).

Joest, Wilfried, *Dogmatik. Bd. 1: Die Wirklichkeit Gottes* [Dogmatics, Vol.1: The Reality of God], 3rd edition, Göttingen 1989.

Jones, L. Gregory, *Embodying Forgiveness: A Theological Analysis*, Grand Rapids 1995.

Jugendwerkstatt Bauhof (ed.), *Starke Mädchen and couragierte Frauen: Bilder, Gedanken, Gedichte und Skizzen* [Strong girls and courageous women: pictures, thoughts, poems and sketches], Halle 2005.

Jugendwerkstatt Bauhof, Homepage (available as of December 2007 at www.jw-bauhof.de).

Käsemann, Ernst, 'Erwägungen zum Stichwort,Versöhnungslehre im Neuen Testament' [Considerations on New Testament reconciliation teaching], in Erich Dinkler and Hartwig Thyen (eds), *Zeit und Geschichte: Dankesgabe an Rudolf Bultmann zum 80*, Geburtstag, Tübingen 1964, pp. 46–59.

Kattmann, Ulrich, 'Sind wir alle Neger? Biologische Rassenkonzepte sind wissenschaftlich nicht haltbar' [Are we all black? Biological concepts of race are not scientifically tenable], in *Geschichte lernen* 17 (93), 2003, pp. 4–6.

Kearney, Richard, *Strangers, Gods and Monsters: Interpreting Otherness*, London / New York 2003.

Kieler Nachrichten, edition dated 4 January 1947.

Kilroy, Anne Sr., e-mail to the author dated 24 January 2007.

Kilroy, Anne Sr., e-mail to the author dated 1 February 2007.

Konkel, Michael and Schuegraf, Oliver (eds), *Provokation Jerusalem: Eine Stadt im Schnittpunkt von Religion und Politik* [Provocation Jerusalem: A city at the crossroads of religion and politics], Münster 2000.

Krämer, Gudrun, *Geschichte Palästinas* [The history of Palestine], 3rd edition, Munich 2002.

Ladissow, Alexander, e-mail to the author dated 17 January 2007.

Lampen, John, *Building the Peace: Good Practice in Community Relations Work in Northern Ireland*, Belfast 1995 (also available as of December 2007 at www.community-relations.org.uk/filestore/documents/Building_the_Peace.pdf).

Landau, Yehezkel, *Healing the Holy Land: Interreligious Peacebuilding in Israel/ Palestine* 2003 (United States Institute of Peace, Peaceworks Series 51; available as of June 2012 at: www.usip.org/files/resources/pwks51.pdf).

Lapsley, Michael, 'Bearing the Pain on Our Bodies', in H. Russel Botman and Robin M. Petersen (eds.), *To Remember and to Heal*, Cape Town 1996, pp. 17–23.

Lausanne Consultation on Jewish Evangelism, The Willowbank Declaration on the Christian Gospel and the Jewish People, 1989 (available as of December 2007 at www.lcje.net/willowbank.html).

Lederach, John Paul, *Building Peace: Sustainable Reconciliation in Divided Societies*, 5th edition, Washington, D. C. 2002.

Lederach, John Paul, *The Moral Imagination: The Art and Soul of Building Peace*, Oxford / New York 2005.

Leitungskreis der Deutschen Nagelkreuzgemeinschaft, Brief an die Leiter/-innen der Nagelkreuz-Zentren/-Gemeinden n Deutschland vom Juni 1991 [letter to the leaders of the Cross of Nails Centres/Communities in Germany, dated June 1991] (records of the German Community of the Cross of Nails).

Leitungskreis der Deutschen Nagelkreuzgemeinschaft, Lebensregel verabschiedet am 23 Mai 1993 in Halle [Rules for living agreed on 23 May 1993 in Halle] (available as of December 2007 at www.nagelkreuzgemeinschaft.de/Informationen/Lebensregeln.html).

Leitungskreis der Deutschen Nagelkreuzgemeinschaft, Kriterien für die Befürwortung einer Bitte um Übergabe eines Nagelkreuzes, angenommen auf der Sitzung vom 10–13 Oktober 2003 in Kreisau [Criteria for assessing a request for the presentation of a Cross of Nails, agreed at the meeting 10–13 October 2003 in Kreisau] (records of the German Community of the Cross of Nails).

Liechty, Joseph and Clegg, Cecelia, *Moving Beyond Sectarianism: Religion, Conflict and Reconciliation in Northern Ireland*, Blackrock 2001.

MacIntyre, Alasdair, *After Virtue: A Study in Moral Theory*, 2nd edition, London 1985.

Magerman, Dirk, letter dated 10 August 2004 to the International Centre for Reconciliation (Records of the International Centre for Reconciliation, Coventry Cathedral).

Magermann, Dirk, e-mail to the author and others dated 31 January 2007.

Mandela, Nelson, *The Long Walk to Freedom*, London 1994.

McKenna, Fionnuala and Melaugh, Martin, Education in Northern Ireland (available as of December 2007 at www.cain.ulst.ac.uk/ni/educ.htm).

McKittrick, David and McVea, David, *Making Sense of the Troubles*, London 2001.

Montville, Joseph V., 'The Arrow and the Olive Branch: A Case for Track Two Diplomacy', in Vamik Volkan, Demetrios A. Julius and Joseph V. Montville (eds.), *The Psychodynamics of International Relationships, Part II: Tools of Unofficial Diplomacy*, Lexington 1991.

Müller-Fahrenholz, Geiko, *Vergebung macht frei: Vorschläge für eine Theologie der Versöhnung* [Forgiveness sets you free: Suggestions for a theology of reconciliation], Frankfurt 1996.

Munayer, Salim J. (ed.), *Seeking and Pursuing Peace: The Process, the Pain and the Product*, Jersualem 1998.

Munayer, Salim J. (ed.), *In the Footsteps of our Father Abraham*, Jerusalem 2002.

Munayer, Salim J., e-mail to the author dated 2 February 2007.

Musahala Newsletter, Summer 2007 edition (available from Musahala, Jerusalem).

Omond, Roger, *The Apartheid Handbook: A Guide to South Africa's Everyday Racial Policies*, Harmondsworth 1985.

Oppelt, Hans (ed.), *Würzburger Chronik vom denkwürdigen Jahre 1945* [Würzburg Chronicle for the memorable year 1945], Würzburg 1947.

Osaghae, Eghosa. E., *Crippled Giant: Nigeria since Independence*, London 1998.

Pakoe, Petrina, e-mail to the author dated 19 July 2007.

Perthes, Volker, *Geheime Gärten: Die neue arabische Welt* [Secret garden: The new Arabic world], Berlin 2002.

Racial Reconciliation Institute, *Racial Reconciliation: Cincinnati – Cathedral in the City, 2005* (DVD, available from Christ Church Cathedral, Cincinnati, Ohio).

Rebound, Homepage (available as of December 2007 at www.reboundecd.com).

Rigby, Andrew, *Justice and Reconciliation: After the Violence*, London 2001.

Ritschl, Dietrich, *The Logic of Theology: A Brief Account of the Relationship between Basic Concepts in Theology*, Philadelphia 1987.

Röhlin, Karl-Heinz, *Beten: Ein Training für Anfänger und Geübte* [Praying: Guidance both for beginners and those with some experience], Munich 2006.

Rolston, Bill, *Drawing Support: Murals in the North of Ireland*, Belfast 1992.

Rolston, Bill, *Contemporary Murals in Northern Ireland: Compiled by Bill Rolston, 1998* (available as of December 2007 at www.cain.ulst.ac.uk/bibdbs/murals/rolston.htm).

Rolston, Bill, 'Music and Politics in Ireland: The Case of Loyalism', in John P. Harrington and Elizabeth J. Mitchell (eds), *Politics and Performance in Contemporary Northern Ireland*, Amherst 1999, pp. 29–56.

Sabbah, Michel, Christmas Homily 2002 (available as of December 2007 at: www.lpj.org/Nonviolence/Patriarch/XH02eng.htm).

Sanderson, Krystyna, *Light at Ground Zero:. St Paul's Chapel after 9/11*, 2nd edition, Baltimore 2004.

Sampson, Cynthia, 'Religion and Peacebuilding', in I. William Zartman and J. Lewis Rasmussen (eds), *Peacemaking in International Conflict: Methods and Techniques*, Washington, D. C. 1997.

Schreiter, Robert, *The Ministry of Reconciliation: Spirituality and Strategies*, 4th edition, New York 2002.

Schuegraf, Oliver, 'Weltweit für Frieden und Versöhnung: Coventry's Beitrag zur Bewältigung von Konflikten' [For peace and reconciliation worldwide; Coventry's contribution towards overcoming conflicts], in *Nachrichten der Evangelisch-Lutherischen Kirche in Bayern* 59 (2004), pp. 80–4.

Schuegraf, Oliver, 'Telling God's Stories Again and Again – Reflections on Remembrance and Reconciliation', in *Modern Believing* 37, Issue 3 (2006), pp. 31–42.

Silverstein, Brett and Flamenbaum, Catherine, 'Biases in the Perception and Cognition of the Action of Enemies', in *Journal of Social Issues* 51(1989), pp. 52–72.

Sparks, Allister, *The Mind of South Africa: The Story of the Rise and Fall of Apartheid*, Johannesburg/Cape Town 2003.

Spence, Basil, *Phoenix at Coventry: The Building of a Cathedral*, London 1962.

Spillmann, Kurt R. and Spillmann, Kati, 'On Enemy Images and Conflict Escalation', in *International Social Science Journal* 127 (1991), pp. 57–76.

Steffensky, Fulbert, *Der alltägliche Charme des Glaubens* [The everyday attraction of faith], Würzburg 2002.

Stein, Janice Gross, 'Image, Identity and the Resolution of Conflict', in Chester A. Crocker, Fen O. Hampson and Pamela Aall (eds), *Turbulent Peace: The Challenge of Managing International Conflict*, Washington D. C. 2001, pp. 189–208.

Stevens, David, *The Land of Unlikeness: Explorations into Reconciliation*, Dublin 2004.

St Paul's Chapel, The Holy Eucharist. September 11, 2005, 9.30am (Order of service).

Suberu, Rotimi T., *Ethnic Minority Conflicts and Governance in Nigeria*, Ibadan 1996, reprint 1999.

Taylor, Charles, *Sources of the Self. The Making of Modern Identity*, Cambridge 1992.

The Forgiveness Project, The F-Word: Images of Forgiveness. Photography by B. Moody and interviews by M. Cantacuzina (exhibition catalogue, undated).

Thomas, John, *Coventry Cathedral* (The New Bell's Cathedral Guides), London / Sydney 1987.

Thomas, Merrilyn, *Communing with the Enemy: Covert Operations, Christianity and Cold War Politics in Britain and the GDR*, Oxford / Berne 2005.

Thomas Kambaya, Sylvester, All Saints Cathedral Church, Khartoum (Information pack for the 2nd International Conference of the Community of the Cross of Nails, July 2004; records of the International Centre for Reconciliation, Coventry Cathedral).

Thomas Kambaya, Sylvester, e-mail to the author and others dated 13 January 2007.

Thomas Kambaya, Sylvester, e-mail to the author and others dated 10 February 2007.

Tonge, Jonathan, *Northern Ireland: Conflict and Change*, London/New York 1998.

Transparency International, Corruption Perception Index 2007 (available as of December 2007 from: www.transparency.de/Corruption-Perceptions-Index-2.1077.0.html).

Treutmann, Holger, Vortrag über die Arbeit der Frauenkirche anlässlich der Mitgliederversammlung der deutschen Nagelkreuzgemeinschaft in Dresden am 28 Oktober 2007 [Lecture on the work of the Frauenkirche, on the occasion of a the AGM of the German Community of the Cross of Nails in Dresden on 28 October 2007].

Trinity Televison and New Media, *The Spirit of St Paul's*, 2002 (DVD, available from the Parish of Trinity Church in the City of New York).

Trinity Televison and New Media, *Revelations from Ground Zero. Spiritual Responses to 9/11*, 2003 (DVD, available from the Parish of Trinity Church in the City of New York).

Trinity Televison and New Media, *An Invitation to Reconciliation on 9.11.05* (Archive of the website of the Parish of Trinity Church in the City of New York: available as of August 2007 at www.trinitywallstreet.org).

Tsimhoni, Daphne, *Christian Communities in Jerusalem and the West Bank Since 1984: An Historical, Social and Political Study*, Westport/London 1993.

Tutu, Desmond, *No Future without Forgiveness*, New York 2000.

Tutu, Desmond, *God has a Dream: A Vision of Hope for Our Time.* London / Sydney / Auckland / Johannesburg 2004.

Valentine, John, *Settlement Ceremony: Land Claims for Protea Village.* 24 September 2006 (DVD of live recording by John Valentine, available from the Church of the Good Shepherd, Protea).

Verney, Stephen, *Fire in Coventry*, Atlanta, 2nd edition Georgia 1988.

Voices, the Magazine of Lagan College, Lagan College Celebrates 25 Years, Edition 2006.

Volf, Miroslav, *Exclusion and Embrace: A Theological Exploration of Identity, Otherness, and Reconciliation*, Nashville 1996.

Williams, Harold C. N., Coventry – a Symbol of Reconciliation, lecture by the Very Revd Harold C. N. Williams, Provost of Coventry Cathedral to the Anglo-German Society in Hanover on 7 February 1961 (bilingual; Archives of Coventry Cathedral).

Williams, Harold C. N., Commissioning of the Dresden Team in Coventry Cathedral – 14 March 1965 (typewritten sermon; Archives of Coventry Cathedral).

Williams, Harold C. N., Building a Community (unpublished memoirs of circa 1989, Archives of Coventry Cathedral).

Williams, Harold C. N., Order My Steps in Thy Way: The Community of the Cross of Nails (brochure dated 1982).

Williams, Rowan, *Interpreting the Easter Gospel*, New York 1982.

Wilson, Jenny, e-mail to the author dated 6 January 2007 (with two attached texts, written in March 2000 and May 2004).

Zehr, Howard, *The Little Book of Restorative Justice*, Intercourse, PA, 2002.

Acknowledgements of Photographs

The author and publisher acknowledge with thanks permission to use the following photographs. All other photographs are by Oliver Schuegraf.

p. 5   © Coventry Cathedral
p. 52   Roland Dietsch
p. 68   Juliane Mostertz © Stiftung Frauenkirche Dresden
p. 90   © Rebound ECD
p. 108   James Wheeldon
p. 123   © Musahala
p. 154   ICR © Coventry Cathedral
p. 160   ICR © Coventry Cathedral